JEREMY NEELY

FALLING DOWN

My Life Story as Seen Through
the Eyes of the Prodigal Son

ISBN: 978-0-578-56934-5

Dedication

To my dearest Kaci –

If only the ink on these pages could rewrite our history to erase the pain we have caused one another and magnify the great love we share. I cannot imagine ever being loved more purely by anyone other than you.

To my amazing daughters: Allison, Aubrey, Emma, and Ella –

I cannot imagine a life so full and rich without each of you in it. You each are so uniquely talented and lovely.

Acknowledgments

I would like to thank everyone involved in the process of making this book:

To my wife and girls for allowing me space and freedom to not only write but also to heal from old wounds.

To my mom and Aunt Marcia for tirelessly praying for me.

To Grandpa and Grandma Boss for being the Christlike example that made me want to look past the junk of Christianity and get to know the source of it.

To Floyd Smith for spending six years of his life showing a 'punk' that Jesus didn't come down to this earth without showing us how we should live. Without your investment, I don't know where my heart or my life would be.

To Jesse Smith for being an unwavering source of encouragement and support.

To the rest of my family, thank you for loving me when I was simply unlovable.

To Joe and Eric, thank you for being willing to listen to me, speaking honestly to me, and for kicking my rear end when I needed it.

To my editor, Alison Carson, for being a trusted source and handling such a nasty story with grace and mercy. Your heart and talent are a blessing beyond words.

To the anonymous donor who fronted the money to make this project possible, thank you for allowing the redemptive story of Jesus Christ to be told by me.

Thanks to everyone who has been a part in pointing me to Jesus. Although you haven't been mentioned personally, you are not forgotten.

Last, but certainly not least, my eternal thanks go to my Lord and Savior, Jesus. Thank You for answering when I knocked, for lovingly and patiently digging into the darkest part of my soul to shine Your light, for bringing peace to me and my family. Yours is the kingdom ... not mine.

Foreword

I am so happy that Jeremy listened to the voices in his life that encouraged him to write this testimony. While it is true that everyone has a story, not all stories are redemptive in nature. Jeremy's is, and because it is, God can use it to call others to redemption.

The experience of 'Falling Down' in life is common to us all. The details may vary, but the hurt, the emptiness, the anger, and the feelings of helplessness that accompany the falling are universal. That is why telling this story is so important. Everyone needs to hear that they can come home. Home to healing, restoration, and love, because God never stopped loving them in the first place.

> But in your hearts revere Christ as Lord. Always be prepared to give an answer to everyone who asks you to give the reason for the hope that you have. But do this with gentleness and respect. 1 Peter 3:15.

Jeremy and his amazing wife, Kaci, have been sharing parts of their story for years now as 'musicianaries' known as NEELY. Now that Jeremy has put it into print, it can be shared even more widely and in greater detail. Though parts of the story are not pretty, and I am sure they were painful to tell, Jeremy has done a remarkable job of doing so with 'gentleness and respect.' Gentleness and respect toward the readers and toward his wife and family. Thank you to Kaci and the family for supporting Jeremy in the writing of this book!

I am already thanking God for the lives He will impact as Jeremy's story is shared through this book!

Blessings,

Randy Cordell

Lead Pastor, Lakeshore Christian Church, Tennessee

Endorsements

If you love stories about how God works, you are going to love this book. In *Falling Down*, you come face to face with the reality of sin's brokenness but, even more powerfully, you get to see God's grace on display. This is a gritty story that will overwhelm you with God's faithfulness. I gladly recommend it to you.

Micah Fries
Pastor, Brainerd Baptist Church, TN

A priceless window straight into the soul of a recording artist sold out to God, a 'pirate for Jesus Christ' willing to put everything on the line to plunder souls from the enemy's camp – even in defiance of the Christian music industry's unwritten rules. Jeremy Neely pulls no punches in this brutally transparent behind-the-scenes account. Pick up this book, and you'll root for him on every step of his journey through rejection, addiction, anger, and depression to wholeness and healing.

Linda Thompson
Award-winning author of *The Plum Blooms in Winter*

Jeremy Neely is one heck of a storyteller. Having heard his adventures and experienced some adventures with him, *Falling Down* is like sitting on your front porch with an iced beverage and hearing a modern-day prodigal story. I've known Jeremy and his family for a while, but this book just emphasized what a journey they have had. The promise of mercy and grace to anyone who wanders is at the forefront of this tale. Give this a read if you need a good kick in the pants or a hug from someone who's been there.

Chris Ward

Pastor, Missionary, Recovering Prodigal

Falling Down is a remarkable, exciting, and tender story, that Jeremy dramatically recounts, of how the incredible and unyielding grace of God was shown to an angry young man who became a follower of Jesus. As Jeremy says, "Writing songs is a process," and so is life with Christ. At times, I found myself holding my breath in silent confirmation that God's ways are indeed mysterious, and at other moments, I chuckled along recalling God's faithfulness even in the darkest days. Easy to read, faith-building, and convicting. A super read.

Simon Lawrenson

Calvary Chapel, Southampton, UK

If you want a book about someone normal, keep looking. If you want to learn how the Creator God of the universe can use individuals who are totally not normal, like Jeremy and Kaci Neely, then look no further. Their style of music and ministry tends to rub some religious people up the wrong way, but I love it! And I see the Lord Jesus Christ blessing it.

Ron Dozler

Senior Pastor, Calvary Chapel, Myrtle Beach, SC

This book is for anyone in pursuit of a better life. *Falling Down* is a glimpse into the heart of a prodigal son who finds his way back to the place of redemptive grace, mercy, and love. Jeremy Neely is authentic, transparent, and delivers a potent message: No matter how bad you've messed up, God can still use you. You'll be drawn in from the start as Jeremy takes you on a journey consisting of ups and downs, laughter and tears. Jeremy illustrates how hard work, talent, and failure can blend together to create a story of redemption.

Sue Ann Cordell
Founder of Shineworthy Lifestyles™ and author of *Simplify: A Life Anchored in Purpose* and *Social Graces: A Practical Guide to Surviving the Holidays*

Falling Down reminds us we are all marred clay longing to be made again into what seems good to the Potter. It is an engaging account of Jeremy's journey upon the road of redemption and restoration. I am thankful he did not omit the potholes, pain, or speed bumps he encountered. In doing so, he reveals to us God's tenderness towards the broken and lost. *Falling Down* is a vivid testimony of two marred vessels made holy and useful to God, prepared for His work and His glory.

David Homchuck
Senior Pastor, Calvary Chapel Maine Highlands,
Dover-Foxcroft, ME

Contents

Prelude

Dark, distant, hollow eyes.

That was the startling image staring at me.

The only thing more startling about the emptiness in those hollow eyes was that I was staring at my reflection in the mirror.

Years of using drugs, consuming alcohol, and engaging in sexual relationships in an attempt to numb the tumultuous rage that boiled in my soul had done its damage.

I was no more than a shell of a man. A shadow of my former self.

How did it come to this? How did I grow up in a good home with a great family and find myself here?

More to the point, could I ever return home?

***

Shortly after moving to Nashville, TN, in early 2010, my wife, Kaci, and I began traveling the world doing acoustic storyteller concerts as our full-time career. Storytelling is a role that we fell into easily for our music is our testimony. Between songs, we tell a combination of our personal testimony and how that influenced the writing of the song. From beginning to end, it's a condensed life story that gives folks an intimate glimpse of our lives. Yet, it is only a snapshot.

God has been encouraging me to write a book since 2010, shortly after we started doing our acoustic storyteller tours. If you've never experienced 'the Lord telling you to do something,' well, it can be hard to explain, let alone understand. He uses so many different ways to 'speak' to us, and it totally defies coincidence. One of the many ways the Lord spoke to us was through people. Without fail, after a show, at least one person would say to either Kaci or myself, "I wish 'so and so' were here to hear your music and story."

For seven years, I pushed the project off. I would write a short story here and there from my past, but I never sat down and dedicated time to write my entire story. When you've never had any experience with a big project, such as writing a book, it feels overwhelming. It was easier to pour my time into other tasks that I could accomplish quickly. With hindsight being 20/20, I can honestly say that I was also avoiding facing some of my past.

Two individuals in our church, Lakeshore Christian Church, in Antioch, TN, gave me guidance and also offered to ghost-write this project for me. Still, to write a book seemed like a huge mountain that I couldn't climb, and I didn't make any attempts to start. Then I had a major medical incident in August 2017 while we were on tour in England that forced me to slow down our fast-paced lifestyle. During this time, the Lord gave me clarity about how to tackle this project by breaking it down into short stories. After all, I am a storyteller.

I will divulge up front that for a large part of my life, I laid blame on others for my actions and who I had become. But as the Lord worked in my life and began revealing my character flaws, I started to understand that *I* was the issue, not others. That still didn't prepare me for unpacking my past to the degree this project has required. While I am a 'the glass is half full' type of person and usually carry a smile on my face, I found that there were some pretty deep hurts that I still needed to deal with. This process has brought peace where I had never realized I needed it.

Growing up, I was a mouthy kid who always went toe-to-toe with my parents, pushing their buttons. Many times, I lashed out and acted out in public. My list of 'wants' were a mile long, and I constantly made them known. Never showing gratitude for what I had or received, I just moved on to the next 'want.' I was never content and never thankful. This created a distance between my dad and I when I was growing up that I always blamed on him until

I became a father and had to put up with a strong-willed, mouthy, disrespectful, and thankless child. The Lord works in mysterious ways, and He used my children to show me where the actual problem lay in my relationships growing up.

At the same time, my parents somehow managed to instill within me compassion for other people. Part of my emotional swings was due to my conscience eating me up after I had wronged or hurt someone. Really, I am a very tender-hearted person. All through life, I have worn my heart on my sleeve. And I have a huge heart for the underdog – a few times, I even got beaten to a pulp defending those who couldn't defend themselves. My daughters have a good laugh at me because a good television commercial can make me cry!

I've always thought of myself as a rather simple person, but to put my life down on paper makes me look extremely complex. Yet, I think that is just part of being a human being. We are all simple in the fact that we want to fit in, to laugh, to have a sense of worth, to love, and ultimately, to be loved. Complex in that our tastes and desires drive our emotions and thoughts with a seemingly endless buffet of possibilities to fulfill our every want. All in an effort to find a tribe. To fit in.

It is with this in mind that I tell not only my story but also the story of how the One who created each of us so lovingly intervened in my life and restored the broken remains of Jeremy Neely.

My hope is that you get a comprehensive look into my life. More than a glimpse or a snapshot. Not a sugar-coated tale putting me in a good light, but raw and real. I'm not going to paint myself in a good light like some great martyr; equally, I won't gloss over the ways I was horribly hurt and mistreated or the ways I hurt and mistreated others. I can't change what happened, and it hasn't been easy for me to recount some situations and write so openly about them. You may wonder why I bothered to revisit my past, and the reason is simply that I want people to see the redemptive and healing power of Jesus Christ.

I have said often, "I was raised an inch from the truth." Yet, I thought I could take life by the horns and live it my own way. After all, isn't that what is depicted in the media? By our peers? We can just go out and do whatever we want and be happy?

In the Gospel of Luke, a story is recorded that Jesus told about a young man who I can identify with in this regard:

"There was a man who had two sons. The younger one said to his father, 'Father, give me my share of the estate.' So he divided his property between them.

"Not long after that, the younger son got together all he had, set off for a distant country and there squandered his wealth in wild living. After he had spent everything, there was a severe famine in that whole country, and he began to be in need. So he went and hired himself out to a citizen of that country, who sent him to his fields to feed pigs. He longed to fill his stomach with the pods that the pigs were eating, but no one gave him anything.

"When he came to his senses, he said, 'How many of my father's hired servants have food to spare, and here I am starving to death! I will set out and go back to my father and say to him: Father, I have sinned against heaven and against you. I am no longer worthy to be called your son; make me like one of your hired servants.' So he got up and went to his father.

"But while he was still a long way off, his father saw him and was filled with compassion for him; he ran to his son, threw his arms around him and kissed him.

"The son said to him, 'Father, I have sinned against heaven and against you. I am no longer worthy to be called your son.'

"But the father said to his servants, 'Quick! Bring the best robe and put it on him. Put a ring on his finger and sandals on his feet. Bring the fattened calf and kill it. Let's have a feast and celebrate. For this son of mine was dead and is alive again; he was lost and is found.' So they began to celebrate.

"Meanwhile, the older son was in the field. When he came near the house, he heard music and dancing. So he called one of the servants and asked him what was going on. 'Your brother has come,' he replied, 'and your father has killed the fattened calf because he has him back safe and sound.'

> *"The older brother became angry and refused to go in. So his father went out and pleaded with him. But he answered his father, 'Look! All these years I've been slaving for you and never disobeyed your orders. Yet you never gave me even a young goat so I could celebrate with my friends. But when this son of yours who has squandered your property with prostitutes comes home, you kill the fattened calf for him!'*
>
> *"'My son,' the father said, 'you are always with me, and everything I have is yours. But we had to celebrate and be glad, because this brother of yours was dead and is alive again; he was lost and is found.'"*
>
> *Luke 15:11-32.*

While the details differ, that is my life story. I may not have come from a wealthy family that could pass me great riches as I defiantly walked my own path. However, I was very fortunate to have a great family, and I had a treasure laid before me worth more than anything in this world: to know love from birth, to be raised with the truth and knowledge of our Creator and His Son, and to see the tenets of how He designed us to live actually lived out by those around me. Honor and integrity were instilled in me. Yet, I walked away from it all.

To 'fall down' in life holds two very conflicting definitions, depending on the context and the current state of the heart. As I walked away from the way I was raised and into a life of sexual sin and addiction, I was 'falling down' into a darkness that all-too-many of us know. I squandered my 'inheritance' in a selfish act of hedonism, not once caring about how the consequences of my actions would impact others or carry into the future. I was 'living in the moment.'

Later, I experienced the complete opposite side of the coin of 'falling down' when, in my brokenness, I literally got on my knees before the Son of God and expressed that my way was folly and that I would trust that what He had originally intended for me was indeed good.

This is my song. My life story as seen through the eyes of the prodigal son:

I'm falling, falling down, don't know which way is up
Wallow in my sin, as pride raises up
Can't keep me down from this pedestal I'm on
Walking my own way while still claiming God's

I can see You, I can see Your beautiful face!
And I long to feel Your loving embrace
How beautiful it is to fall down

I'm falling, falling down, and I've been here before
I had to get my fix, just like before
Can't keep me out of this world I'm living in
Walk in my own strength convinced that it's His

I can see You, I can see Your beautiful face!
And I long to feel Your loving embrace
How beautiful it is to fall down

Though the darkness comes in all around me, I, I look to You
Though the stench of my life still surrounds me, I cry out to You

PART ONE

PRE-SCHOOL YEARS

The Beginning:
St. Joseph, MO

On February 19, 1975, I was born to two small-town, Northwest Missouri kids, John and Teresea Neely, in St. Joseph, MO.

My dad, John, grew up in Bolckow, MO. He was one of five children (one of whom mysteriously died as an infant) and was raised by his mother, Mary, who lived with her former father-in-law, Wilbur Neely. The Neely's were 'that family' in town. You know, the family that when the kids come over, you expect something to go missing, or if there's any mischief in town, it must have been them. I remember my dad telling me that in their household, you didn't leave money or anything valuable lying around or it would disappear.

My mom, Teresea, grew up in a totally different environment. She was raised on a hobby farm nestled between Bolckow and Rosendale overlooking the river bottom land. My grandfather, Lloyd Heckman, loved to farm. Grandpa Heckman was a welder in St. Joseph, but on nights and weekends, he would 'scratch dirt' on his farm. My grandpa was also a believer in Jesus Christ and was a teaching elder at a local church up until a stroke took his ability to function later in life. My mom was also one of five children. Most of my memories growing up are from this side of the family.

Some of my earliest memories include my parents taking me to my Grandpa Heckman's farm on the weekend. I remember cuddling on my grandpa's lap and watching Saturday morning cartoons. Specifically, Bugs Bunny, Scooby-Doo, and The Justice League. My grandmother would dab sausage gravy on her finger and feed it to me. Thus, my love for gravy, as well as my flawed ideology that gravy is a food group, was born.

My dad barely made it through high school. Not for lack of brains, because he can pretty much figure out how to do anything mechanically. As he got older, he and his older brother, Terry, wanted more in life than what they had. They 'married up' into respectable families and began the long journey of change. There was still a lot of that scrappy street kid in both of them, and I can even see it now, but I am also amazed at what they did.

Uncle Terry and his wife, Aunt Cindy, would be a consistent source of encouragement and mentorship throughout my life. My last memory of Uncle Terry, who died in a freak accident in 2013, is of him beaming with pride as he excitedly introduced me to all of his friends before Kaci and I played a well-attended show in downtown St. Joseph.

Growing up in the late 70s and early 80s, 'white trash' – those who tend not to take care of themselves or their property and are known for coarse language in public – wasn't nearly as prevalent as it is today. But I would have never known about it anyway, because the environment my parents and my family (on my mother's side, along with Uncle Terry and Aunt Cindy) raised me in wasn't too far removed from the fictitious community of Mayberry – a quintessentially perfect small town with upstanding citizens who work hard, keep their houses and yards clean, and who look out for each other.

Thus, my story begins in a small apartment in downtown St. Joseph, MO, just a few blocks east of the mighty Missouri River and a couple of blocks north of the Civic Arena, which holds significance in who I am today, but we will get to that later.

The neighborhood was on the decline even back in those days. Those old apartments were abandoned and torn down long ago. Around 2010, give or take a few years, a new movement to redevelop St. Joseph began to take hold, restoring the once-bustling gem that dotted the mighty Missouri River.

Obviously, I don't remember much of my very early years, but I do remember a couple of older people who lived in an old red brick apartment building (that is no longer there) who showered me with love.

While I didn't remember the details surrounding this, I also remember an old lady across the street who would wave at me. Recently, my mom filled in those details. There was a nursing home across the street, and this old lady daily sat and looked out of the window. Whenever we exited our building, she would smile and wave at us. Feeling heartbroken for this old lady, Mom took me across the street to visit her. Mom recalled that the woman could not speak but loved having company. Especially that of a child.

I also remember Mom taking me for walks amidst the old buildings of St. Joseph.

As I've grown, the memories of that time have faded and jumbled somewhat, but the warmth and love I felt during those early years have never left me nor faded.

Cosby: In My Heart,
I'm Always Going Home

I was three years old when Dad and Mom had had enough of city livin' and moved us 15 minutes east of St. Joseph to the small village of Cosby, MO.

Still to this day, whenever I round the bend on Highway O overlooking the Platte River valley, I recall the first time I laid my eyes upon it. I was in Uncle Lloydie's truck – his real name is Lloyd, I'm not sure where the 'ie' came from! I saw cornfields covering the valley leading to the river's edge, pastures with cattle lining the hillside, and trees coating the hills on the opposite side of the valley. I saw Highway O snaking its way downhill towards the river bridge and then vanishing as it curved up to the right and over the next hill and out of the valley.

The other thing I remember about that ride, and the many more that followed in Uncle Lloydie's red Chevy truck, was the music. As a matter of fact, that's really what I remember the most because it was the first time I *felt* music. I felt it trickle down into the deepest parts of me, and even at three years old, I was moved to the core of my being. I guess you could say that this was when my Creator planted the seed of the gift of music in my life.

Every time I saw the valley stretched out in front of us, I always knew that we were nearly home.

While our house was within the town limits of Cosby, we were surrounded by several acres of pasture, and throughout my childhood, we raised cattle, hogs, turkeys, chickens, a horse, and numerous dogs and cats. There was plenty of adventure to be had with old railroad tracks to the east of the house and a creek (we pronounce it 'crick' in 'Missoura') that ran along the rear of our back pasture.

The fence line has changed, there are no longer rows of apple trees, and many of the old barns and sheds have been removed, but the little old farmhouse, while having several additions added to it over the decades, still stands, and my parents still reside there.

Back then, the small town operated on a sort of self-policing system to keep us kids in line. If we got into trouble, we would get our butts beaten by whichever adult caught us and then sent home. By the time we got back, those folks had already called our moms, and we got our butts beaten again. For me, the worst part came next: waiting for Dad to come home from work. The waiting was worse than the spanking I'd get from him. But that's what made it a successful system – you didn't have to experience it very often to learn to be more constructive in your activities.

Then there was just lousy counsel and bad timing. One particular time, I was hanging out with some of the local town kids after school. There was an old abandoned house at the top of our drive, and one of the kids suggested we throw rocks at it. That quickly turned into breaking the windows out with rocks. We didn't get far into the process when Dad pulled into the drive. We were caught red-handed. I know I got my rear end whooped, but the most effective punishment was looking into the eyes of the couple who lived two doors down (who we affectionately referred to as Grandpa Kenneth and Grandma Katherine) and apologizing for my actions.

Another bright spot of growing up in small-town America in those days was that the church was the cornerstone of the community. It seemed like the church was an active part of everything that happened. Yes, I would eventually run away from the church and even deny the existence of God, but I never denied the value of the church being active in the community. I realize that doesn't make sense! I was angry, not stupid. I knew that the good social morals in American culture were rooted in Christianity.

The ideal of Mayberry would eventually have to crumble. I don't know precisely when this change took place. Long before my time. As we grew older and finished the 6th grade, we were shipped off to Savannah, MO, for middle school and high school. It only takes a couple of bad eggs to ruin the whole batch, and when you're dumped into a large group of kids, especially city kids, there's likely to be those bad eggs. Over time, because the school district dumped all the rural schools into Savannah, the smaller communities were impacted. This infection was happening long before I was ever forced to go to those institutions. All in all, I have a few good friends and memories from Savannah, but not many. We will get to those chapters later.

PART TWO
MUSICAL
FOUNDATIONS

Charlie Pride:
A Dream Is Born

I was four years old when my parents took me to my first concert, and it proved to be another defining musical moment. Looking back on my childhood, it's quite surprising that they took me, let alone bought me an album, because we were not well off.

We were in the standing-room-only section on the upper level of the Civic Arena in downtown St. Joseph. In the distance, the spotlight shone on a tiny little man ... well, he was tiny from my perspective at the back of the arena! And the music. Oh, I could *feel* the music like I did in Uncle Lloydie's truck. This time, the response of the crowd amplified that core rocking feeling. That 'tiny man' was none other than country music legend Charlie Pride, and the album that Dad and Mom bought me ... I wore that thing out!

To this day, music is as much of an emotional experience for me as it is technical. Yes, my perfectionist nature has allowed me to be quite successful in Nashville, where a solid sense of rhythm is a must, but I still *feel* the music. It flows out of me rhythmically and dynamically as I'm absorbed by it, and it becomes my mission to convey that emotional moment.

It all started that day when I heard Charlie Pride at the St. Joseph Civic Arena. At the ripe young age of four, I made a firm decision: "This is what I want to do with my life."

How does a dirt-poor, small-town kid with no chance of his parents affording a musical instrument or lessons find his way to Nashville, TN? Hang in there...

Uncle Lloydie: Feeding Me Music

Uncle Lloydie was one of my mom's younger brothers, and he was a huge musical influence in my life. His truck had a good stereo system, and he wasn't afraid to crank up the rock and roll.

I guess you could say that he was the 'cool uncle.' He was a bachelor who lived on the old family farm. It was always the running joke in our family that Uncle Lloydie lived off of Mountain Dew soft drinks and Ruffles potato chips. So much so that for as long as I can remember, those were his gifts every Christmas!

Uncle Lloydie fed me a steady stream of great music, primarily rock and roll. I will never forget the first cassette tape he gave me – it was the album *Synchronicity* by The Police. I still find myself singing the words, *"There's a little black spot on the sun today..."*

But it didn't matter what he gave me, I would wear it out. The beats, the guitars, the melodies, the emotion! I was like a sponge soaking it all in.

When folks mention the prevalent guitars and the thick rhythms in our songs, I smile and think of the musical foundation that Uncle Lloydie gave me via all those cassette tapes and rides in his truck. Def Leppard, AC/DC and Ted Nugent were some of the guitar-heavy music I would listen to with Lloydie.

It's also no wonder that I followed in his footsteps by living on a diet of Mountain Dew, Little Debbie snacks, and potato chips through high school and most of college. The older I got, and the more my metabolism hit the brakes, the less I could eat that way.

Dad's Eclectic Garage

As much as I know my way around a garage or home project, I'm also a great assistant. If I'm assisting you on a job, I will probably have a tool waiting for you to turn around and grab before you even knew you needed it.

That's because of my dad. If he was in the garage working on something, I was expected to be there working too.

Back then, I was heavy on the whiny, lippy, disrespectful side, and my dad was heavy on the impatient side. He didn't exactly have a father-figure growing up, so he was muddling through fatherhood the best he could. Put a disrespectful, strong-willed child into the mix, and it made for interesting times. So, through a lot of scolding and yelling, I learned how to be one heck of an assistant. It was one small way to keep the peace, and it also meant that the job was finished quicker, and I could get to wherever else I wanted to be a lot faster.

The other thing that I learned in Dad's garage came from the radio. I discovered that there was a lot of good music out there, and it wasn't confined to any one genre!

One day, Dad would have on a rock station, and we jammed to Led Zeppelin, Pink Floyd, and other rockers, and the next there would be a country station playing George Jones, Waylon Jennings, and the likes. But it didn't stop there. There were other stations: oldies stations, pop stations ... it was always different.

On any given day, I might have Buddy Holly, Elvis, Porter Wagoner, Hank Williams, Led Zeppelin, Journey, or an eclectic array of artists' music running through my head in that garage.

I don't ever remember my dad making any kind of statement that one form of music was better than the other. He just put on different stations. He didn't just listen; a lot of times he sang along.

You take that eclectic musical upbringing along with my rebel spirit and smash it together – that is where you get my non-genre credo. We aren't rock, we aren't country, we aren't gospel music... we are NEELY!

Whether my dad knew what he was doing or not, he fed the artist within me.

I feel alive and free when I am simply making art through my musical talents. It may come out as a bluesy, country, worshipful, or flat-out rock song. To me, genres (and demographics for that matter) make me feel claustrophobic, and they stifle my creativity. Yes, I have written and can write formulaic music that will sell, but I don't feel alive doing that.

This mindset, this credo, who I am as a singer-songwriter and human being, has its roots in that rickety old garage, with that ever-eclectic radio, at the end of our driveway in Cosby, MO.

PART THREE

ELEMENTARY
SCHOOL YEARS

Little Sister

In 1980, I got a surprise in the form of a reality check. My first glimpse in life that I was not the center of the universe came in October in the person of my sister: Teresea Anne.

Teresea Anne is the polar opposite of me in several ways – shy, softly-spoken, smart, respectful, and quiet. She didn't let me get away with anything, though. She stood her ground, and we regularly fought like cats and dogs.

By the same token, she has always supported me. She would say encouraging things to me when everyone else seemed to be bent of tearing me down. I'll never forget something she said to me one morning as I was getting ready for school. I was in the shower belting out some Hank Williams Jr. the way anyone likes to sing in the shower – loudly. When I came out, Teresea Anne said, "You're going to be a famous singer someday."

I know there are certain God-moments in life. Times when He uses someone to encourage a person in a way that will carry them through the darkest of times, to give them just enough hope to keep scratching, clawing, and fighting for the dream that He so carefully wove into them when He knit them together in their mother's womb.

This was one of those moments. I hung onto Teresea Anne's words through thick and thin.

It's likely that I also remember that moment for another reason: because it was one of the times when we were *not* fighting. Although I'm sure a good fight followed shortly after!

Small-Town Imagination

Before the days of cell phones, tablets, computers, gaming consoles, hundreds of TV channels, and media at your fingertips, was an age of imagination.

The economy in the 80s wasn't the greatest (from what I'm told), and none of my friends had the means to have lots of toys. While we didn't know we were poor, we did know not to waste food because it was hard fought for and not easily come by.

What did we do to pass our time without a myriad of toys and gadgets? We made stuff up!

I particularly remember our summer breaks.

Dead branches and sticks became rifles and pistols as we played old western or army adventures that would fill our summer days with action and adventure. We fashioned forts with whatever scraps and branches we could find, making our last stand against the onslaught of our imaginary, invading hoard. Shouts and screams flew as our imaginations entwined, and each of us would help weave the story to its completion. This went on for hours upon hours.

Hide and seek was definitely a staple in our gaming repertoire, but the funniest version of this tried and true classic was when the pasture was overgrown (just before Dad would mow and bale it). We crawled and tunneled our way through the grass for hours, evading capture. We got covered in chigger bites, but we didn't care. The hunters would find the highest ground possible and scan the pasture waiting for those hiding to make the mistake of moving too much grass. The rule was you had to stay moving. Otherwise, the game would drag on, and everyone would lose interest.

Another thing we enjoyed doing was riding our bikes all over town. This was not an easy feat considering the low gears of the bicycles we rode and the steep Missouri hills. It was always more fun to go down the hills than up them. After a while, we learned a powerful tool to help us get up the next hill: momentum.

In everything we did, fast pace was key. Back then, no one considered fastpitch softball to be 'a girls sport,' so that's what we played. We rode our bikes uptown to the ball field, which was on the east edge of town, but we called it 'uptown' because we had to climb two huge, steep hills to get to there. Then, we'd play pick-up games all afternoon.

Of course, to us, fastpitch softball was baseball. We would each call out the name of our favorite Kansas City Royals baseball player and pretend to be him while making a diving catch or smashing a ball over the center field fence (at that age, we couldn't get close to hitting a ball to the fence, let alone over the fence).

In those days, the ASA (American Softball Association) had boys' fastpitch leagues. Each town had its own teams broken into age brackets, which made springtime fun at school. With no school in Cosby, I went to Helena Elementary School in the neighboring town of Helena. Cosby had its fastpitch softball team, and Helena had its team, so at recess, we would split up by town and play pick-up games that would garner much nonsense talking and many laughs. It was intense, but it was always fun. Sportsmanship was always emphasized at home and at school.

I look back on those summer days in amazement. Not only could we entertain ourselves for hours on end, but none of us had air conditioning in our homes. In fact, our family didn't have air conditioning until I was a sophomore in high school. Even then, it was a tiny window unit that could barely keep the lower level of that old farmhouse cool during the day.

Years later, on a hot day at a promotional event where Kaci and I were signing autographs before a summer performance in a park, a lady stated, "I don't know if I'll allow my kids to come out, it's just too hot." I laughed and conveyed that not only did I grow up without air conditioning, but I would also play two to three ball games in a polyester uniform on days as hot as that one. The lady huffed in disgust and walked off. I thought, "People like her are what's wrong with youth today."

That's what life was like growing up. In the summer months, we would go out and play from the time the sun came up to the time the sun went down. During tournaments, we might play as many as three ball games in one day in the heat of the July sun in our old polyester team uniforms. Afterward, we would return to a house that had been baking in the heat and was cooled only by box fans in the windows. Yeah, it was hot, but that was life, and we just dealt with it. Still, those were the days!

The Well Went Dry

Before the days of Helena Elementary, my only playmate was my cousin Curtis. Even after I entered school and made friends in town, the adventures I had with Curt were legendary ... in our minds at least.

Curt and I would roam and explore, sometimes getting ourselves into trouble as we got side-tracked from our chores. One time, Uncle Steve (Curtis' father) ordered us to go and do the chores, which consisted of watering the cattle. I'm not sure how it came about, but we ended up down at the pond catching crayfish until we were called in for supper. After eating, we went exploring again until we were called back in ... we could tell by the tone of voice that we were in for it.

As it turned out, we had started our chores but never finished them. Meaning, we hadn't turned off the water at the cattle trough. Which ran the well dry. This meant no water in the house. Not only did that mean no baths, but it also meant no drinking water. Ultimately, for Curt and I, it meant big trouble with some pretty severe consequences! Needless to say, from that day on, I always double-checked the water after chores, no matter where I was doing them!

Grandpa's Strawberry Patch

Many of our exploits were either at Curt's family farm, the Campbell farm (the Campbell's were his paternal grandparents) or at my grandfather Heckman's farm. The Campbell farm was literally a stone's throw away from the Heckman's farm.

Once, Curt and I went moccasin hunting down by the small pond between the farms. After an unsuccessful hunt, we headed back to Grandpa Heckman's house, which took us through his strawberry patch.

Now, I've got to take a little rabbit trail here to say that I've never eaten such sweet-tasting strawberries as the ones that grew in my grandpa's strawberry patch. Certainly not from a grocery store! The closest I came was later in life when we began touring through the United Kingdom. The strawberries we bought in England and Wales were so sweet, and they took me back in time to Grandpa Heckman's strawberry patch.

On this occasion, Curt and I trudged through the patch and unwittingly stumbled across a hornet's nest. We heard an unworldly buzz but had no idea what the noise was or what it meant. Then the swarm descended on us and began to sting us. Howling, screaming, and crying, we ran with our arms flailing as the hornets continued their assault.

The only thing I remember after that was being caked in a mixture of baking soda and vinegar that was supposed to help take the pain away. Curt took the brunt of the attack. Before I ever heard the age-old adage that you just need to be faster than the other guy, I knew it to be true.

The Big Pink Rock

Between the drive and the road at Grandpa Heckman's farm is a huge, pink rock. My cousins and I would spend hours upon hours climbing all over that rock.

The imaginary purposes of that big pink rock were never-ending. It was the safety when playing tag or hide and seek. It was my lookout point for Curt as I could clearly see the Campbell farm just down the hill. It was a ship amid a raging sea. It was the Starship Enterprise and the Millennium Falcon. It was a wagon heading across the plains, and a deserted island surrounded by sharks ... that big pink rock was everything under the sun!

Driven by Star Wars, GI Joe and other TV shows, cartoons, movies, and books, our imaginations went wild! We didn't have cable TV and had no way of watching the GI Joe cartoons, and we probably only saw Star Wars once as trips to the movie theater were too expensive ... but we didn't need all of that, our imaginations ran wild!

If we were lucky, we might get an action figure for a birthday or Christmas gift, and the saga would continue as we fought evil all over the world or universe, depending on who we were that day.

As Curt and I grew older, our cast grew as well. Teresea Anne came along when I was five, and Curt was the big brother to Sandy, Amanda, and Melinda. Then our other cousins came along: Ryan, Bethany (or as my dad and I called her, "Bethy"), and Mark.

Any given Sunday afternoon, you'd find all of us kids on top of that rock playing to our heart's content, which gives a little bit of an insight into how big that rock is.

Children are always in a hurry to grow up. Now that I'm an adult, I look back and wish that I had cherished those moments with my cousins on that big pink rock.

Grandma Heckman

My Grandma Heckman passed away when I was seven years old, but that doesn't mean I don't have some good memories of her.

As I shared earlier, I remember her feeding me gravy as a toddler, giving me that good southern love of all things gravy. I also remember her making chili with whatever meat she had and one of those frozen chili bricks people buy from the grocery store. After she'd mixed that frozen brick with the meat, and right before she put it in the pan with some tomato juice, she would put some of that chili paste on a saltine cracker for Curt and I. Her memory lives on through chili and crackers, for I now love to mix crackers into my chili! My family makes fun of me, and I know I just lost all the 'chili purists' out there, but it takes me back to simpler times.

The animals on the farm were another story. I saw Grandma grab big black snakes by the tail and snap them like Indiana Jones would crack a whip, which would kill them. Then, she would hang the snake over the fence. She believed some old superstition about it raining within a couple of days after hanging a snake on the fence. On multiple occasions, I also saw her grab a chicken by its head, whirl it at her side like a jump rope then take it into the house to prepare it for dinner. You ain't ever had good chicken noodle soup until you've had farm-fresh chicken noodle soup!

It was a working farm, so I saw, and partook of, a lot of things that most city folk can't handle since they are used to their food coming from a grocery store. We had to castrate boar hogs and calves (making them steers), and butcher turkeys and chickens. It's just what we did to survive, but we did it as a whole family.

Grandma was in and out of the hospital a lot. I didn't ever visit her because I was quite a handful, and Mom wisely didn't take me. When she was healthy ... I remember her laugh, but I also remember that you didn't cross Grandma!

One time, in particular, I knew I was pushing her buttons. After all, pushing people's buttons was a gift of mine. I thought I was pretty quick and could outrun her. Not only did she run me down, but she got me by the ear. Then she whooped my behind with a big old wiffle ball bat that looked like Fred Flintstone's club. My grandma must have been a Jedi because she just reached out her hand, and that wiffle ball bat just jumped into her hand from across the yard! I know a lot of people get all up in arms over spanking. Shoot, I would have been out of control without it. I don't remember what I said or did, but I can guarantee you that I earned every lick I got. That day I learned two hard lessons that stuck with me: first, don't cross Grandma; second, there ain't no running if you do.

It was overcast on the day of her funeral. I didn't go. I'm not sure why, but in some ways, I'm glad I didn't. My last memories of Grandma are of her laying in a hospital gurney in the front room of their old house. I remember her eyes as she looked at me. Her eyes told me she loved me and was sorry to leave. While I don't like seeing her in that gurney in my mind's eye, I know I was loved dearly.

PART FOUR

MIDDLE SCHOOL YEARS

Fastpitch

My dad worked a lot. When he wasn't at work, he was usually working on a vehicle at home or some other project because 'money didn't grow on trees' and he could save his family a lot of hardship by taking care of it himself. If he couldn't do it, he basically traded his skillset with those of his friends who might be able to do the job. This is called 'the good ol' boy' system, another self-policing system that worked well in our small community. It meant that if someone screwed you over by taking and not giving ... it would be the last time they'd be helped. So, if Dad wasn't at work or working on a project at home, he was likely helping out one of his good friends.

Even with all of that on his plate, he still found time to either play catch with me or hit fly balls to me in the pasture. Don't forget, I was mouthy and strong-willed, so it's doubly amazing that my dad spent time with me like that. Actually, running me all over that pasture probably gave his ears a break from my constant lip or the list of wants I had!

I must've been about 5 or 6 when Dad took me to a department store in St. Joseph (we didn't have Wal-Mart back then!) to buy my first baseball glove. When we got home, we oiled it, put a ball in the pocket, and tied it up. That process was repeated for days to break it in.

One thing Dad never did was take it easy on me. He had a kind of a pass-fail system. "Boy, that ball will hurt a lot worse if you don't get your glove on it." After a while, when you are actively playing catch with an adult, playing with your peers is a piece of cake.

From the time they announced summer fastpitch league sign-ups in my 1st Grade class at Helena Elementary School, I was hooked. I dutifully played for the Cosby team until a certain team came along when I was in middle school: Keller Construction.

Keller Construction was a hand-picked traveling team (before the days where every child got a trophy and was on a traveling team). Back in those days, if you got hand-picked to be on Keller Construction, it was like being drafted.

Dad had a good friend in Helena who worked with him in St. Joseph by the name of Skip. Skip's son, also named Jeremy, was one heck of a pitcher. Keller Construction snatched Jeremy up in a heartbeat. I don't know if it was an unspoken competition between Dad and Skip, or if Dad was sick of hearing about how good the Keller Construction team was, but when I got the call to try out ... not a chance. Dad and Mom would not let me, and there was no moving them.

By the time they saw the advantages and allowed me to join the team, I was in middle school, and the team was no longer sponsored by Keller Construction but by Walton Ford. Which was OK with me, because our team uniforms were freaking AWESOME! Not only did we have custom uniforms complete with well-placed Ford logos, but we also had amazing custom-made warm-up jackets with our names embroidered on them.

The hard part for my parents was that we practiced more than once a week in Savannah. Back then, folks didn't drive all over the place. That cost money, so this was a huge sacrifice for our family.

Then there were the games. When I was on the Cosby team, we play around a dozen games over the summer break. But the Walton Ford team was not only playing against teams in our own age bracket but also teams in higher age brackets. For instance, when I was in the 14 and under team, we played in the 14 and under league, the 16 and under league, the 18 and under league, and any men's teams that were willing. We were beasts!

This is where my love for travel began. Every year, we played in the Ringneck Tournament in Sioux Falls, SD, plus any other regional tournaments our coach could find as well as state and national tournaments (it was almost a given that we would win the state tournament and go to the national championship tournament every year).

I also played on our church's softball team, which usually caused problems because there were a few older folks who couldn't handle a young teenager being able to outplay them. I would always fume when they'd stick me in right field, but I would still make plays they could never dream of making. Every once in a while, they would throw me a bone and put me in at shortstop, and I'd make a diving catch or turn a double play, which would land me right back in right field. Seen and not heard was easier on their egos.

I learned valuable lessons from playing on the Walton Ford team, coached by Robert Davis. First, don't ever apologize for being good at something – if you're good, be good, and keep striving to be better. Second, be humble – don't rub people's noses in it if you're better than them, always be a good sport. Third, be brutally honest when you're not good at something. My time on Walton Ford's fastpitch team gave me these valuable lessons, but it also hurt me in ways.

Those hurts came in the form of my teammates. They were guys I went to school with, but I never got to let my hair down and be me. They had played together for years, even won a national championship together. I was an outsider. In a matter of seconds, I could go from 'hero to zero.' I could make a diving catch and be congratulated by my teammates, only to get back to the dugout to have them stare past me when I spoke to them … like I was invisible or didn't exist. And if I did feel like I was making any headway towards a friendship, all bets were off when we got back to school. I might as well have been a leper. And oh, don't even mention the mistake...

Before I get to the story of my mistake, I need to set it up. The distance between bases in fastpitch softball is much shorter than in regular baseball. I can't remember who we were playing, but I know it was a tournament. I was a versatile athlete, and I could play any position except pitcher and catcher. As far as pitching, I could throw the ball hard and fast, but when a batter got in the box, I had zero control. Catching … well, two reasons I was not a good catcher: first, I had horrible eyesight and had 'coke-bottle glasses' (I was legally blind without them); second, I could hardly stay in a crouched position. Still, to this day, I can't crouch down for very long before my knees start screaming at me. At this time, Coach Davis had me playing 3rd base, and I was 'pulled in' or positioned a third of the distance toward home plate because of the threat of a bunt (remember, the distance is much shorter than baseball). The batter crouched to bunt, I sprinted to the plate, he pulled back and got around on the ball, sending a line drive down my throat before I could react. To this day, I still have problems breathing through my nose because of a deviated septum. The other side effect: my nerve and confidence at 3rd base were shot.

Fast forward a couple of years. We were playing our older counterparts (Walton had two teams: an older team and our team, the younger guys). On this occasion, we were beating the older guys, and with the smell of a great upset looming, they were bringing it hard and fast. There were two guys on base. Again, Coach Davis had me at 3rd base, and I was pulled in because of the threat of a bunt. I had fielded plenty of balls that night and was back in it, or so I thought. I can still hear the hiss of the ball as it came at me. I never saw it, though. In a half attempt, I made a weak stab toward the ball, but in a full attempt, I jumped away from it. Which surprises me because I honestly don't remember seeing the ball, I just heard the hiss as it came towards me and went past me, all the way down the 3rd baseline, bringing all those runners on base around to score.

The interesting thing to me, in hindsight, is that I don't remember any other player on our team ever receiving such beratement, even when they committed an error in a critical national championship game. That beratement followed me through the summer season and into the school year.

To make matters worse, that mistake embarrassed my dad. To ensure that it wouldn't happen again, he took me 'uptown' in Cosby to the baseball field, placed me up against the fence of the backdrop behind home plate, while he stood just in front of the pitcher's mound and drilled line drives at me as hard as he could hit them ... until I quit jumping out of the way.

At this point, the hurts in my life were piling up. I said 'screw you' in the only way I could to my teammates by walking away from the team. It wasn't much of a statement because they didn't care anyway.

Leaving the team didn't mean the end of fastpitch for me; I continued to play throughout my school years. And being an athlete, I was already playing other sports throughout the year: summer was fastpitch, fall was football, winter was basketball, and spring was track and field. Ultimately, I encountered the same types of people in the football team as I did at Walton Ford, which only compounded the hurt I was feeling.

Shortly after leaving the Walton Ford team, I was out playing a pick-up game with the guys from the old Helena and Cosby teams, just having fun. An old guy was watching us play, and he approached me, asking me to be on the Helena team (Cosby no longer had teams by this time because no new families had moved into the area).

"No pressure," he told me, "I just want to see y'all have fun like you were today."

I accepted his offer, and for the first time in a long time, I had a blast playing ball again.

As a matter of fact, I went out with my boots on that season.

It was a tournament in Savannah, of all places. We were losing. I didn't care because we were having fun, but we were still making some pretty impressive plays from time to time. I don't remember who we were playing or any of the details of the game. I just remember getting up to the plate and the pitcher grunting with all he had.

There was a reason for that grunt, too. Throughout my fastpitch career, I was known to be able to do one thing with startling consistency: I could get to first base. That usually happened because I was a hitter, and it put pressure on the opposing pitcher and forced them to lose their nerve a bit. So, I learned to be a patient batter, and one way or another, I got on base whether it be by a hit or by walking. If you were the opposing team, though, you didn't want me on base because I was not only a super-smart, well-coached base runner, but I was also fast – I could round the bases and score if I could get a hit in the gap. My strengths meant that I could pick the other team apart and force errors.

Back to the game. The pitcher wound up, pushed off the mound and grunted with all he had. I stepped into my swing and took that pitch for a ride. I didn't even look up, I just made a beeline down the 1st baseline. I easily crossed home plate before the ball was back to the infield. I was back in the dugout when I heard the umpire holler, "Young man, come back out here."

In my mind, I did a quick inventory. I didn't throw my bat, I didn't talk trash (I was quite good at that, too), I touched all the bases … crap, what did I do wrong?

I'll always remember what happened next.

The umpire had the bat and the ball in his hands, looking at both. Then he looked up at me and said, "In all my years of being involved with ball games, I've never seen anything like this." He then held up the ball and bat and continued, "Young man, you hit the ball so hard that you tore the leather cover!"

Sure enough, the ball was torn, and not on the seam. It had torn right in the middle of the leather surrounded by a smudge of colors directly from the barrel of my bat. The umpire then announced it to the crowd on both sides of the field, presented me with that game ball, and I walked back to the dugout to applause.

Shortly after I got a call to go back to the Walton Ford team, which I respectfully declined.

I went out with my boots on.

Two Outcasts

The landscape of education changed a lot between the preceding generations and mine. For instance, Cosby used to have its own school with classes from kindergarten through to grade twelve.

I'm not sure when it happened, but the schools were consolidated. Cosby's school was closed down, and the kids were bussed over to Helena for kindergarten through to 6th grade. Still, for me, those were the good old days. My class at Helena was approximately 20 students, and everything seemed perfect.

That's not to say there weren't problems. As I've pointed out, I was a rebellious, mouthy, little smart alec with an attitude. I spent my fair share of time in the principal's office, and those were the days when the principal had a wooden paddle and was not afraid to use it!

Just like at home, I earned every lick I got with that old wooden paddle at Helena Elementary School!

I have fond memories of Ms. Newell, Mrs. Hensel, Mrs. Byrd (though I'm pretty sure I caused her to have a nervous breakdown), Mr. Ochse, and one of my favorite teachers, Ms. Mead, who I have since forgiven for getting married and becoming Mrs. Curran. Just joking. All of us 6th-grade boys had a crush on Ms. Mead back in the day.

Then the darkness.

After the 6th grade, the powers that be shipped us off to Savannah. I'm not going to mince words here. Savannah is a typical small-medium town of around 5,000 that's rife with cliques. You're either allowed into the clique, or you're one of the lesser.

I don't know who in their right mind came up with this idea and actually thought it was good. They took small-town schools from all over the district and dumped them into one giant mess in Savannah. It was a recipe for disaster.

And this happened at the worst possible moment for any kid ever: the beginning of middle school.

Overnight, I went from a class of approximately 20 students who all grew up together and was tossed into a teenage, hormonal, middle school mess and into a class of nearly 200 students all trying to figure out who they are and all wanting to just fit in.

Even now, I will go out of my way to drive around Savannah, MO. Yep, it was that bad.

Real friends were hard to come by, but over time, I made friends that I would fight for any time of the day. Those folks are the few saving graces who got me through those dark days. I'm so thankful for those few kind and loving souls who pulled me in and gave me a sense of being and acceptance! One of those saving graces is still a great friend to this day: Eric Sivertson.

Eric's dad was a pipe fitter who moved his family to wherever the work was. At that moment in time, work had taken them from South Carolina to Northwest Missouri. The work was actually in Kansas City, but Eric's dad didn't want to raise his family in a big city, so they settled for Savannah.

Since Eric didn't grow up in Savannah, he was in the same 'outcast' boat as me. He's got a heart the size of Texas, but he's as tough as nails. Eric's 'give a crapper' was already broken at that young age, and he couldn't care less that he didn't fit in. To him, that was their problem. He saw me floundering, just trying to fit in, and he threw me a lifeline. We were fast friends and hung out a lot.

Nowadays, we laugh at how dumb we were. When I could talk my parents into letting me stay with the Sivertson's, Eric and I would walk around Savannah, going nowhere in particular in the freezing cold, wearing nothing but shorts and t-shirts. What were we thinking? What were we trying to prove? Only the Lord knows.

The cool thing about being with Eric was that we didn't go out and cause trouble – we didn't vandalize or any of that junk. Most of the time, we just walked around town, talking and dreaming, or we played pick-up games of basketball or played catch (he taught me how to throw a curveball). Granted, we would both end up getting into some mischief through our adolescence, but for the most part, ours was a true friendship that ended up enduring the years.

To this day, Eric is a sounding board for me. I know I can run anything by him, and he will give me an honest opinion. We both know that we can blurt out anything with complete confidence that those words will go no further and our friendship will still endure.

"You Want Me to Play What?"

Two of the things that I loved and excelled at, music and art, were never a priority in our curriculum at elementary school, and as I've said, our family did not have the resources for private lessons. At Helena Elementary School, there was not a music teacher on staff; the only music instructor we had bounced from school to school on different days of the week. Even with that, I'm not sure we even had a weekly music class. It seemed more like a time out for teachers than actual musical instruction for us students. I was always in trouble in music class because I was bored out of my mind!

In the 80s, the saxophone became popular in pop music. I remember seeing Clarence Clemons playing the sax with the E Street Band, and I was sold – that's what I wanted to play!

Before entering middle school and being dumped into the Savannah cesspool, we had the opportunity to meet with the band director and 'choose' our instruments. This was a big deal for several reasons. First and foremost, this would be expensive! It didn't matter whether Dad and Mom rented or purchased an instrument, it really wasn't in the budget. This was going to be another sacrifice for our family. Second, this was my opportunity to learn to play music and tap into the force moving inside of me that I so desperately wanted to get out.

Unfortunately, the meeting didn't go well.

It's absurd how some moments in time are burned into your memory. It's not always the most amazing moments that we remember with vivid detail. Some of those memories are nothing but the deepest disappointment one can bear.

This was one of those days.

As I recall, I wasn't even asked what instrument I would learn. Immediately, I was told I would play the tuba.

Uhm, no.

I already had a list in my mind: Of course, the saxophone was my first choice, but my second was the trumpet because Uncle Lloydie played it, and since he was one of my heroes, I wanted to follow in his footsteps if I couldn't play the sax. Beyond those two options, I would have loved to have been on the drumline. My last choice was the clarinet. My mom played the clarinet back in her band days, so I was intrigued by the instrument.

The band director informed me that he only needed four or five sax players, and he had all he needed. Later, I would find out that he added almost double that number for that year's incoming 7th graders.

Then I was told my lips were too fat for playing the trumpet! If you look at some of the great trumpet players alongside any of our press photos, you'll see that he was feeding me a line of crap there as well.

As far as the drumline was concerned, I was too small. Meaning, not strong enough. If you had seen some of the other little skinny, beanpole kids he allowed in, your anger would be rising right now at what he was doing to me ... he was crushing my dream!

He didn't even address the clarinet. He merely waved it off like he was swatting away a fly.

"Your options are the tuba or the trombone."

What the heck was I supposed to do? It felt like my chest was being crushed, just like my dreams. Words cannot express the depths of terror and disappointment I felt that day as my dreams were railroaded right down the toilet.

Out of options, and with great trepidation, trying to salvage my dream of being a musician, I chose the trombone.

There are a lot of factors that contributed to my failure in playing the trombone, but here are the two main ones: first, I didn't even remotely want to play this instrument; second, when the switch from Helena to Savannah happened, the bus no longer picked me up at the end of our drive, which was still a good 200 meters long, but over a quarter of a mile away. All of which meant I had to walk that distance with a backpack full of textbooks, my football shoulder pads and helmet, plus that stinking trombone! If that wasn't bad enough, then I had to find a seat on the bus with all that riding around and on top of me. Then once I got to school, and we were usually late, I had to run to the band room to drop off my trombone, then frantically try to make it to my locker to deposit my football gear and excess books.

Why did I have to carry my football gear? Ah, well in another teenage-crushing decision, the powers that be in Savannah make a sudden decision that it would no longer have a 7th-grade football team. So, Tyler Kelley's dad stepped in and negotiated the use of the school equipment, and he coached the 7th-grade boys for a Saturday morning league in St. Joseph. I guess that's where the good-will ended because the school wouldn't allow us to utilize the lockers.

Dad and Mom were pretty supportive and tried to encourage me the best they could, but they had to know I got a bad deal. In the end, I made it a full quarter (around ten weeks), and then I quit. Mom was super supportive and made phone calls to the school, trying to get them to switch me to another instrument, and when that failed, she worked to ensure the instrument would be returned without putting a financial strain on the family.

Due to this ordeal and the way I was treated by students on a daily basis, I made the decision to keep my musical dream hidden from everyone at Savannah, trusting no one, not even my closest friends. This was the one thing I would not allow Savannah to crush!

Decades later, when Facebook became big, you should have seen all the friend requests come in with comments and messages saying, "We never knew..." That's because I kept my dream safe, making sure that no one would have the opportunity to crush me completely.

Nuts

I f trying to fit in and the marathon walks to the bus stop with all my books, football gear, and instrument wasn't enough, just tack a bully on top of it all. I don't remember the kid's name, and I barely remember what he looked like, but I remember the frustration of the situation.

I was in 7th grade. He was a junior in high school (11th grade) who had been held back a year. At some point, he decided he didn't like me and was going to make my life a living hell. No matter where I sat on the bus, he forced his way into a seat near me.

He would proceed to beat me. Every single day.

There was no way to hide the bruises. They were all over my back and chest. My parents encouraged me to handle it correctly by reporting it to my homeroom teacher and working up the chain.

I don't know if this is a reaction limited to males or not, but I hated this course of action. As you might remember, our bus was usually late, and this meant I was often late to homeroom. Now, not only did I have to run all over campus dropping off my instrument and football gear, but I also had to go up, in front of the whole class, try to hold it together, and announce that I was getting beaten mercilessly every morning with a bus full of witnesses (yes, even the bus driver) that chose not to do anything. It sucked big time!

I took a few more weeks of beatings before I finally, overloaded with shame, went to my homeroom teacher.

As expected, she immediately rushed to grab another teacher. They both looked me over and gasped at the bruising. There was no conferring, other than to find a fellow teacher to cover homeroom so that my teacher could take me to the principal's office. Thankfully, she waited with me the whole time.

The principal, just like the teachers, was aghast at the bruising and the story of how they came to be. My parents were called in, the bus company was called in, and I'm sure the bully's parents were called in as well. All in all, the process did jack squat.

The driver and everyone on board the bus continued to turn a blind eye while I continued to take a beating. More calls were made as my parents tried to get someone to do something.

Finally, enough was enough.

We were at the dinner table one night. I don't recall how the subject came up, but Dad and Mom told me, "You've tried it the right way. Now do what you have to do to stop this."

The next morning, the only seat I could find was next to the bully. Because of all the phone calls and meetings with parents, he was only getting meaner, and I'm sure he set it up that morning so that the only place available for me was with him.

Before the bus even started to move, every name and dirty word in the book was hurled at me, and he started shoving me. I turned my back to him, and he began to punch my back. Then he put his back against the bus window and began kicking me.

Snap!

I have always had a huge, tender heart that shattered into a million pieces if I thought I had done someone harm. However, if you push me past my limits ... well, as my friend Marty Lyle would say, "I go cold fries."

'Cold fries' is a term Marty came up with. It basically meant a person snapped and was so angry that they became irrational. The term was birthed from Marty's observation of seemingly kind, normal people who went completely 'ape crap' (another of our terms) when they had to wait for their food at a fast-food restaurant only to receive cold fries.

I've seen little old ladies lose their religion over cold fries. It's a real-life condition!

Back to the story, the bully got one kick into my back that knocked me across the aisle of the bus. I forced myself back into my seat and saw a second coming out of the corner of my eye. Dodging to the side, I missed the full force, but his shoe raked across my back and arm. I put my feet on the edge of the seat across the aisle and thrust backward as hard as I could, ramming the back of my head into his face. I then turned around and promptly gave him a quick jab in the face.

There's a reason David used a slingshot against Goliath and didn't engage in hand-to-hand combat. I should have listened better in Sunday School.

While I did cause some damage, I was a chubby little 7th grader against a junior in high school who should have been prepping for college. Thus, I really only threw gas on the fire.

His violence escalated as he punched and kneed me in my face and body. I was still fighting, but I was also working my way in closer so he couldn't get the full force behind his blows. Eventually, it turned into a grappling match, and he wrestled me around to the bus seat and got on top of me.

The bus driver didn't say a thing, let alone attempt to break up the fight. I knew I was overpowered and done for.

In the melee of the wrestling and throwing me down on the bus seat, when the kid jumped on top of me, he somehow straddled my head. I don't know how it happened or which way he was facing – it's been decades, and honestly, it was all a blur because I was just trying to survive.

And that survival instinct kicked in.

One thing I do remember is that Dad and Mom's words flashed in my mind, "Do whatever it takes."

So, I did whatever it took.

Like a flash of lightning, without even thinking, I grabbed whatever I could in a bear hug, and I bit down on whatever was in front of me with the intent of taking it off. What happened to be directly in front of me was the kid's crotch. His blue jeans were probably the only thing that saved him from becoming a eunuch because I bit his nuts as hard as humanly possible.

He screamed like a little girl and jumped off of me like I was a red-hot bed of coals.

By that time, the bus had just started moving, and we still had an hour to go before we got to school, and he screamed and sobbed the whole way. I was never bugged again. And surprisingly, no one ever made fun of me for biting that kid's nuts.

France

In elementary school, we did a three-week foreign exchange program with a school near Versailles, France. As a student, your family could send you over and host a child or simply just host a child. My parents opted to just host a child. While I didn't think so at the time, it was the right call, and it opened the door for much better adventures later.

As the time drew near for our French student to arrive, word went out that the translator who was coming with the French team did not have a place to stay. Knowing there would be a language barrier with our student, my parents contacted the school and agreed to host the translator.

Thus, our family met Enid, our now long-time friend. She was born and raised in England, but in her university years, she moved to Paris, met a young Frenchman named Jacques, and they subsequently married. Enid became fluent in French, which gave her opportunities such as this one as a translator.

Our family and Enid fell in love with each other during her three-week stay, and she offered our family the opportunity to come and stay with her and Jacques in France. This was something she often wrote about in our correspondence after her departure.

Back in those days, the average Joe in America never thought of the concept of email. Most people in rural Missouri never even thought of the idea of having a computer in their home. All of our correspondence was done via postal services, and it took weeks for a letter to cross the Atlantic.

Dad and Mom always saved money for our vacations, which were never anything lavish, but they were fun and adventurous anyway. Following Enid's stay, Dad and Mom decided to cancel any upcoming vacations and save their money for a family trip to visit Enid and Jacques.

The summer between my 7th and 8th-grade years, our family took off for a three-week holiday in France, of which I still have the fondest of memories. Jacques and Enid have two children. Their oldest daughter was away working for a family in England for the summer, and I didn't meet her until decades later. However, their son and I became as thick as thieves. Both of us dreamed of flying military jets and poured over books and magazines on the topic. We also found some fireworks in the marketplace and tried to blow up some shrubberies, only to be disappointed by the weak pop they created.

One memory I have, which we all still laugh about, is from Paris. Jacques is a fun-loving prankster, and after a day of seeing the sites of Paris, he told us he wanted to take us on one more scenic drive through Paris before we retired to their home. Much to my mother's horror and my dad's laughter, Jacques took us on a path through the red-light district. I remember all the doors of those little rooms tightly packed side by side. The memory I have that still sticks out more than anything else from that trip: the one-legged prostitute. For whatever reason, in my middle school mind, I found that utterly hilarious and laughed until I cried.

Several scenarios played out on the trip that were unhealthy for a young man right in the midst of puberty. The beaches were the worst. There, the non-Continental women stood out like a sore thumb because they were the only ones with tops on.

Another instance that scarred me on several levels was an incident at a services, or as we know them in America, a rest stop. I needed to use the lavatory, and when I entered, the place was completely empty. What I found was a series of holes in the floor with footprints on each side, showing you where to place your feet. Not rocket science, so I started the process of relieving myself.

Right in mid-stream, a woman walked in. If that wasn't bad enough, she came to the hole right next to me, dropped her drawers, grabbed the handles on the wall, and popped a squat. Granted, there were other factors in my life that fed into it, but these scenarios became foundational to what I call the perversion of my sex drive. In this case, I use the word 'perversion' in the strict sense of not keeping my eyes, mind, or body pure for my future wife.

We experienced so much more than that while in France. Jacques and Enid planned their holiday around ours, and we made a huge circle around the country. We even took a day trip to Switzerland, where I bought myself a genuine Swiss Army knife.

The waters of the Mediterranean were so warm and so much fun to play in. This was my first experience in any body of water other than a pond, lake, or river. I guess it kind of spoiled me and gave me a false sense of what the ocean is really like. We spent a few days around Cannes, and I loved any chance we had to go to the beach.

As we worked our way up north, we did more things inland. Then we finally made it to a part of France known as Brittany to stay with some of Jacques and Enid's friends. The promise of going to the beach again had me excited. I just didn't quite understand the difference between the Mediterranean and the North Atlantic. That day, I got a crash course.

On the Med, it didn't matter if it was sunny or overcast. Either way, the water was warm. It turned out that sunny or overcast really didn't matter too much in the North Atlantic surf either. It's just cold, either way.

This day was overcast. I remember it well because it was shocking. In hindsight, I should have known something was up because the kids were the only ones gearing up for a swim. The adults were thinking, "There's no way I'm getting in that frigid water!" You don't think of those things as a kid, though.

I was in a dead sprint towards the water, the current had just pulled the surf out, and a fresh wave was cresting. That was the way I loved it in the Med. Timed just right, you could run right into the wave (a smaller one, of course), and it just washed over you and tumbled you over a bit.

Never have I felt anything so stinking cold in my life! As I plunged into that wave, I swear my next move was to leap on top of the water and run out of that ocean as quick as a flash of lighting. My day at the beach was done!

That was a mistake I would never make again!

Later, we visited the teacher who came with the exchange group. Her home was right at the mouth of the River Seine on the Atlantic coast. We went to the fish market and got fresh seafood, but we also took some nets down to the Seine and caught some fresh shrimp for dinner. I was prepared for the cold water this time and didn't mind wading in the water. It was one of the neatest experiences of my life.

While in northern France, we also visited the Normandy coast. Though kids might get tired of museums and visiting sites, that wasn't the case for me this day. I knew what had happened from school history lessons, but to see it, to see the cemetery at Omaha Beach, was another thing. I was in awe as I listened to the stories of what those brave men did for people they had never met. Hearing the French speak so highly of the Americans who gave the ultimate sacrifice so they could be free has to be one of the single most powerful moments of my life.

That trip deepened my love of travel. It also taught me that just because another culture does something differently, it doesn't make it wrong. Our family is still in contact with Jacque and Enid. During our 2016 European tour, Kaci, myself, and our second daughter, Aubrey, stayed almost a week with Jacque and Enid. As of this writing, we have made plans for them to come and stay with us in Nashville.

Jacques is still as much of a prankster as ever.

PART FIVE

HIGH SCHOOL YEARS

Good Ol' Boys

Once we hit our freshman year and moved to high school, Eric's class schedule clashed with mine, which took us in different directions. I began finding my place within a group of guys who would become lifelong friends: Marty Lyle, Dustin Smith, Mike Nigh, Derek Owen, and Tyler Kelley.

It's actually confusing to try to explain the 'moral code' we created, adopted, and followed like it was a law. Mostly because it was chalked full of inconsistency and hypocrisy. It was based on honor, integrity, and hard work. Yet, when it came to things like stealing, smashing pumpkins, procuring alcohol, and the sexual objectification of women … all bets were off.

An example of this was when we would head out into the country and circle up on an old dirt road to commence drinking. We had the creed, 'If you drink, you don't drive.' And if anyone did drive while drunk, they were shunned from the group. It was a simple understanding in all things mischievous that we did: if we were messing around on an old country road and hurt ourselves, that was one thing, but we, as individuals and a whole, would not put innocent lives in danger.

On the rare occasion that any of us get together these days, the old tales come rolling out. Laughter erupts as we relive those old days. Some of our exploits have probably entered the realm of legend. Who knows fact from fiction in the details after all these years? We just know that we had a blast.

One such legendary moment involved a failed evening of pumpkin smashing, a porta potty (or 'portable toilets' as the Brits call them), and some quick thinking on Marty's part.

Around Halloween, we had a tradition of pumpkin smashing. Looking back, it was a pretty horrid thing to do to folks – sometimes we'd smash them on the person's property, and other times, we would steal them and smash them elsewhere. At the time, we looked forward to pumpkin smashing season with as much, or more, fervor as we looked forward to deer or bird season opening.

This night was a bust. We were all dejected and heading our separate ways. I don't know who was in whose vehicle, but I do remember Marty Lyle and Derek Owen were in Marty's flatbed Ford truck.

Now to truly understand how this night went down, you have to understand these two characters and their families. Marty was the bombastic, quick-witted, strong-as-an-ox, son of successful rancher and businessman Joe Lyle. In all of our eyes, Joe might as well have been the governor. Actually, that's what we called him. Not to his face, of course, because when we were around adults, we addressed them as 'sir' or 'ma'am,' which stems from Missouri's southern roots. It seems odd, I know, but we were on the edge of the south, and we held to those values. All in all, we thought Joe Lyle walked on water, ate bullets, and crapped ice cream. They say the apple doesn't fall too far from the tree, and sure enough, Marty was and is his father's son through and through.

Derek was pure gold. While all of us wore the 'all-American boy' facade, Derek lived it (minus his love for pumpkin season). Derek was a great athlete and was as full of pranks as the day is long. He came from a good family who were dedicated believers of Jesus Christ. Not only did they claim it, but they also lived it. Not in a preachy way, but in a way that attracted people to it. I remember a few times when life seemed overwhelming that I found myself confiding in Mr. Owen. The example they set was one of many that stuck with me through the years.

Back to the evening in question. With the stinging taste of defeat from a bad night of pumpkin smashing season on their tongues, Marty, in the spur of the moment, whipped alongside a construction project and declared, "We're gonna borrow a crapper." Of course, 'crapper' wasn't the word he used, but I'll leave the expletives out.

Even though Derek was a great and willing prankster, I'm sure there were plenty of objections that went on in that old flatbed Ford that night. However, Marty was a persuasive force, and they quickly formulated a plan to get that crapper on the flatbed.

Once the porta potty was secured, they were on their way, and this is where the legend began.

As they cruised down an old asphalt road, they passed a vehicle that turned out to be the sheriff's truck. The sheriff hit his lights and got right behind the flatbed. Marty didn't even think of trying to outrun the sheriff, and his mind worked out another scheme. You see, he was a smart cookie, and being a teenager with his own cattle business who bought and sold tens of thousands of dollars' worth of cattle in a single transaction, he had bags of confidence too.

Derek, on the other hand, was shaking like a dog crapping a peach seed. To hear Marty's side of the story, as soon as the lights of that patrol vehicle lit up, Derek was begging the Lord, out loud, to deliver them. But with the confidence of a young entrepreneur, Marty engaged the officer. Because we all got the story from these two the next day, I can't tell you how that exchange went. There are only three people on this planet who know for certain, and I'm sure you'd get four or five different versions from them.

All in all, we do know that the officer claimed that someone had reported a stolen porta potty. We also know that Marty spun a yarn about finding the said porta potty along the highway, and being the good Samaritans they were, he and Derek had stopped and loaded up the porta potty to bring it down to the sheriff's office to be returned to the rightful owner.

At the end of the conversation, the porta potty was returned, and Marty and Derek walked free. They declined any kind of reward (which I doubt amounted to much, if anything, for an old porta crapper, but who knows?!).

Another legendary moment was the night we were going to TP Dana Miller's home (TP = toilet paper, and TP-ing her house meant covering it with as much loo roll as possible).

Dana and I worked together at a local fast-food restaurant and continuously played pranks on each other. She was not only sneaky, but also a very witty and formidable foe, and she had seriously one-upped me on one particular occasion, and I was going to get retribution.

I gathered the boys, Marty, Derek, Mike and Dustin (I don't recall Tyler being with us), and we laid out the plan in the confines of Mike's front room. We were going to TP her house. I know, not very creative, but she had me on my heels, and it was the best I could come up with.

Somehow, in the grand scheme of things, I became the driver. The driver? This was my gig, my battle, and yet I was going to be at the curb keeping the car ready? Whatever! I needed to get one on the scoreboard. I knew none of my guys would ever give up on an operation, so I got on with it.

It was well after midnight. We were completely blacked out: clothes, shoes, face paint. With the lights off, I drove up the block from the south as there was a good breeze from the north. Honestly, I don't know what that had to do with anything, but in our infinite wisdom, we wanted to come in from the 'downwind' angle. Like that would give us the higher ground, somehow!

Just as the boys were ready to commence, we heard a calm voice from an open window, "You boys really don't want to do that."

Crap! How in the world did Dana's dad know?!?! We didn't have a contingency for an emergency retreat.

The boys bolted for the car. As they were piling in, they shouted, "GO, GO, GO!"

So, I began going!

In the chaos, Dustin hadn't made it into the car, and his foot somehow found its way under the rear wheel. He limped for months after the dust settled on that heart-breaking defeat.

As the years have gone by, and the legend has grown in all of our minds, we swear that we felt the car go over something like a speed bump. We recall with hilarity the agonizing groan of our brother in arms taking one for the team and seeing Dustin hobbling after us like a wounded soldier from a war movie while Marty was shouting, "Man down, man down!"

What really haunts us ... how in the world did Dana get the upper hand?!

Mustang and Chuck

The older I become, the faster time seems to go. It wasn't always that way. I think time operates the opposite way prior to an individual turning 16 – at least, it did growing up in rural America in the late 1980s. Time dragged on for-ev-er! Nowadays, we finish with July 4th celebrations, and it seems like Christmas is on our doorstep just two days later. When I was a kid, that might as well have been an eternity.

The countdown to freedom was what dragged on. In this case, freedom was driving. As a young American teenager, I remember having 'the driving dream.' Yes, a large segment of our populous would have 'the dream' on a regular basis. To own your own car, to be able to just drive, to be free!

But the closer I got to 16, the more I realized that Dad and Mom didn't have the money to buy me a car. I would have to buy my own!

In those days, we didn't have all these lawn-mowing services with high-tech, fancy devices. It was just local teenage boys with push mowers. And that wasn't exactly a gravy train, either. It was $15 to push mow an acre lot! Granted, this was also back when the minimum wage was $3.35 an hour, but still, by the time we spent 6 – 8 hours pushing a mower uphill (and it had to be perfect), it worked out to be a lot less per hour.

From the end of my 7th-grade year, I worked multiple jobs: I helped a couple who ran a snack business out of their garage, I mowed two yards 'uptown', and I put up hay for farmers.

Now, as a side note: those two years were, as Charles Dickens wrote, the best of times and the worst of times.

I had become somewhat chubby, to say the least. I don't remember how short I was, but I had definitely not hit my vertical growth spurt yet. Horizontally, I was more than healthy! My waist size during my 7th and 8th-grade years was slightly bigger than my current waist size as an adult. Pudge, pure pudge!

So, a combination of a growth spurt and putting up hay for farmers took me from a chubby teenager to a skinny fit-looking young man.

Back to the work itself. Putting up hay was no picnic! Small bales of hay, weighing between 60 – 100 pounds per bale, sometimes numbered in the thousands across the fresh-cut pastures. Most of the wagons that rode behind the tractor were between waist to chest high, and the bales would have to be stacked at least six high, if not more. Plus, they all needed to be out of the field yesterday!

As back-breaking as that part of the job was, the absolute worst part was unloading the wagons and stacking the bales in the barn.

The barn. Yeah, it always looks like a romantic place in TV shows and movies, but in the humid July heat of Missouri, it was nothing short of hell. The stagnant air full of hay dust could nearly choke you if you didn't wear a handkerchief around your face. Even then, you couldn't escape the 'hay boogers.' Yep, 'hay boogers.' Nasty thick black mucus that coats the nostrils and sinuses. I'd be blowing them out for days, and I always hoped one didn't make its way south to hang out for the public to see! What really got me was my clothing. The very clothes that saved my butt out in the hot sun became an insulating blanket in the stagnant building that was nothing more than an oven radiating the sun's heat.

Really, my attire was a blessing and a curse. To keep myself from burning to a crisp as well as protecting my skin from the constant poking of the straw, I would wear boots, jeans, a thick long-sleeve shirt, a handkerchief around my neck, and a hat. Out in the sun with a breeze, that's amazing, believe it or not. In an oven-like barn ... not so amazing. Most of the time, my clothes were soaked through as if I had just run down to the pond and dived in off the dock. All joking aside, it's still the best attire to keep your body cool and hydrated in that setting ... it just doesn't feel like it at the time.

Two summers of that work kick-started my metabolism, eventually taking me down to 3% body fat and paving the way for my daily lunch diet of two Little Debbie nutty bars and a can of Mountain Dew all through high school. Without gaining an ounce, I might add.

And three summers of work put me in a position to purchase my first car. A 1967 Mustang Coupe.

Now, don't get any ideas here. The car wasn't one that was restored and in mint condition, but it certainly wasn't a pile of junk, either. That old car ran like the wind with her 289 short stroke, and she sounded like a big American muscle car. She definitely had some swagger.

She didn't have any paint, just primer, but at least it was all the same color. She still looked tough with her oversized rear mag wheels sticking out of the side, giving her a slight downward tilt. I ran her hard, but I also took care of her like a baby, which was costly.

Enter my friend Joe Gazarek, and his step-dad Chuck.

Chuck owned a gas station and garage on Highway 71, which went through Savannah, and he helped Joe rebuild an old Chevelle. My friends and I seemed to consistently find our way over to Joe's house for backyard pick-up games of basketball. After I got my Mustang, while hanging out at one of these games, Chuck offered to let me use a bay at the garage to change the oil. After a while, he saw that I had a knack for car maintenance. I worked hard, and I put stuff back where I got it from (that probably got Chuck's attention the most), so he offered me a job. I did everything from oil changes, to brakes, to exhaust work, to washing and detailing cars for a local dealership that Chuck had an agreement with, and I pumped gas.

There were days when Joe and I were the only ones there. Two 16-year-olds, cars in the air with others waiting to be worked on, running a station. The few short years I worked at Chuck's are likely what gave me the foundational business acumen that has allowed me to have a small business in the music industry. Although Chuck was cranky, he was always willing to show us 'why' we did something wrong, the ramifications of it, how to make it better, and how it impacted the bottom line. He also taught me a lesson I still utilize today in the business of music: income streams. He did not solely rely on one source, whether it be fuel sales, the garage, or the car washing/detailing. In Savannah, none of those individually would support his family. All three together, though, made for a viable and comfortable living for his family. Income streams ... don't leave a stone unturned.

There was one job that Chuck and I had scheduled to do on my Mustang that we kept putting off, and it later came back to haunt me: changing the tie rod ends.

Little did we know that the tie rod ends on old Mustangs are notorious for breaking. In case you don't know what tie rods are: tie rods attach to the wheel of the vehicle and to the steering column. Not only do they provide steerage for a vehicle, but tie rods also provide stability for the vehicle overall.

Late one Friday night, after a football game, I was heading home. By the time I had finished the game, cleaned up, packed up, and headed out the door, not only was it late, but I was also tired. I specifically remember that this was one of those nights where I was really watching my speed. As I came to a hill corner combo at the old Heller farm, I heard a loud ping-pop sound, followed by screeching tires. The world went blurry for a few seconds before a loud crash and a sudden stop.

All I know is that the Lord was with me that night, protecting me. That hill rose sharply before curving to the north, and most drivers begin to accelerate before the corner, as I did that night, to keep their acceleration up and around the corner. From the tire marks left behind, the folks who helped Dad drag the vehicle out of the ditch and back home suspect the car spun at least one, if not two, 360-degree turns before slamming head-on into the ditch, which rose like a solid wall of earth. In essence, I ran head-on into a solid wall of earth at approximately 50 – 55 miles per hour.

Yet, I walked away from that accident. My face mangled the chrome and wood steering wheel, but I only required half a dozen stitches over my left eye. Other than the stitches, I had a concussion, and there are a few things that are still cloudy about the days following the accident.

I do remember the shock on the face of Mike High (an acquaintance of mine who was a grade above me in school) when he found me. I was bleeding like a stuck pig. My face was a blood mask, and the front of my shirt and jeans were soaked in blood as well. If Mike's reaction was shock, you can imagine the reaction of my parents.

Needless to say, that was the end of the Mustang. Running head-on into that wall of earth not only completely collapsed the engine compartment, but it also bent the frame.

Heatstroke

At the time of the accident, I was playing on the varsity football team. Due to my concussion, I couldn't even suit up for practice. The doctor didn't want even the slightest temptation as he did not want my head rattling in the least bit. In hindsight, this was a good call as the coach at Savannah probably would have had me running drills with no regard to my health or safety.

A couple of weeks later, when I was cleared, I was told that I would be suiting up for a junior varsity football game in Falls City, Nebraska. That didn't hurt my feelings any. My girlfriend would be there, and playing a JV game would be easy.

Junior varsity games, in those days, were played during the week and generally had an earlier start time so we could play during the daylight.

This day was hot, humid, and we were wearing completely black uniforms.

After two weeks on the sideline, my coach was itching to get me game-ready. The problem was he didn't use much common sense.

He had me playing halfback on offense, cornerback on defense, outside contain on kickoffs, return man on punt, and kick return ... I basically never left the field.

The last thing I remember of the game is jogging down the sideline towards my coach saying, "Coach, I don't feel so..."

The next thing I remember is waking up in the locker room with Dan Stevens, my long-time friend, mentor, and the cheerleading coach, hovering over me, barking orders at people. Dan had run to my aid when I collapsed on the sideline and had taken me to the locker room where he had folks get my helmet, jersey, and shoulder pads off so that I could cool down.

For the next couple of weeks, I was made to feel like I was inferior, a weakling, and that I had no place on that coach's team.

Long Branch Christian Church

A couple of miles north of Avenue City, MO, on Missouri State Highway D, you can take a right on County Road 311 and head east. Right before you get to the Long Branch Creek, there is a little white country church called Long Branch Christian Church.

I have no idea when I first attended Long Branch, but I don't recall a time as a kid when I didn't. It just seems that it was always a part of my life.

My mom seemed to be a part of anything that happened there. If it was Vacation Bible School, she was heading up the crafts. If it was Sunday School, she was teaching a class. There were revivals, Christmas plays, fundraising dinners, you name it ... there was not much life outside of the church, and I was OK with that because the families that made up this old church were just good folks and fun to be around. The church was one big family.

Every Sunday, I sat in the front row with my friend Jeff Farr. Well, almost every Sunday. His mom played the piano (or organ), so she had to sit in the front, and she made Jeff sit there so he wouldn't get into trouble. Pretty wise move. Except she allowed me to sit with them, which resulted in varying degrees of trouble, depending on the Sunday.

It ranged from mild 'sermonets' on the way home in the car – a second round of preaching from my parents! ... to Dad and Mom being so flabbergasted and embarrassed they couldn't even speak ... to nearly driving the pastor to stop a service – he looked like he wanted to rain down fire and brimstone on us. We were both mischievous by ourselves, but put us together, oh my!

Jeff's mom, Mrs. Farr, is a beautiful and patient woman who did a darn good job of keeping tight reigns on us. She was an inspiration to me as a self-taught musician. I'm sure she had some kind of formal training as a kid, but I distinctly recall her rough beginnings when she stepping up to fill the role as pianist/organist. Over time, she developed into a very accomplished musician who could read music as fluently as she could read English.

Her example gave me hope, and still to this day, it challenges me to keep pushing forward, even though I'm seemingly 'behind the curve' with my musical training. She never threw up her hands and said, "I can't." She just dug in and did it. As a younger child, I had begged Dad and Mom to let Mrs. Farr give me piano lessons. I didn't understand that pianos and lessons were expensive. Dad already worked his butt off just to make ends meet and lived with the ever-present fear of being laid off. Yet, over the years, Mrs. Farr showed me by her example that people don't necessarily need lessons, just drive, dedication, patience, and a lot of hard work.

In hindsight, Dad and Mom would have given me every opportunity to be the best musician I could possibly be. Back then, my list of wants and desires changed with the wind, and they had no idea of knowing how serious I was about music. Along with that, there was the economic climate in rural Missouri in the 80s and 90s, and the only way out was a college education. That's the mindset that was pushed on us at any rate.

Unfortunately, everything great about being part of a church was marred and destroyed by what happened when I was in high school: the folk at Long Branch began fighting between themselves. Accusations flew at the pastor and his family, and they eventually left. The wheels eventually came off, lines were drawn, and the church became a shell of what it used to be.

People who invested heavily in my life, whom I looked up to, no longer spoke to one another. It was like a great divorce. I was shattered. I couldn't understand why some folks avoided me and my family, or why others disappeared from my life. I was lost.

The hurt was indescribable.

The disintegration of my church family only compounded the hurt I was already dealing with from my time in Savannah Middle and High Schools.

We Are Not Immortal

Memories freeze in time in the mind's eye. Some amazing; some horrific.

While I had experienced the sting of death of loved ones in the past, it was nothing like experiencing the death of a peer.

By the time I was rolling into my junior year, I was a total wreck, wearing a mask of happiness, trying to hide the pain within. Yeah, there were good days, and I had some fun, but after being kicked around so much, it was hard to see joy through the pain.

That's why I do need to point out that there were some other good souls I encountered in high school. Regrettably, because I was frantically trying to fill the black hole inside of me with anything and everything to feel whole, I didn't hang out with these folks regularly – like three incredible and completely inseparable young ladies who befriended me in some theater projects I was involved in. I have no idea why I didn't hang out with them more. That was certainly my fault.

There were two other friends that I interacted with daily, who, like my band of brothers and the other good folks I mentioned, simply accepted me: Jeremy and Brandon.

The afternoon of March 13, 1992, is etched in my mind like no other.

I had just finished track practice, and my girlfriend was waiting for me so we could go and rent some movies. As I headed to my car, I saw Joe Gazarek, Derek Owen, and some other guys by the tennis courts, and I went over to chat with them.

Jeremy and Brandon pulled up to ask Derek if he wanted to go camping with them. Derek said he wasn't interested. I don't remember the exact details – whether someone picked Derek up, he drove himself home, or someone else drove him home – but whatever the situation was, he did not get in that car, and it saved his life.

Brandon had a blue IROC Z28 Camaro, and it was an amazing car. Horsing around like guys do, Brandon threw a little gravel and shot out of the school parking lot. I talked a little longer with the guys, then my girlfriend and I drove over to the movie rental store and picked out a couple of movies. As we walked out of the store to get into my car, we heard sirens. I had a bad feeling about the sirens and stood there for a moment listening to them. I shook it off, got in the car, and we drove down to Cosby for dinner and a movie with my family.

I can't tell you what we were watching. The phone rang. One of my parents went to answer it, then returned to tell me I had an urgent phone call.

It was Mike Nigh. The words that were coming over the phone didn't seem real. I had been laying on the floor watching the movie, but now I was pacing the room, rapidly firing questions at Mike, my voice breaking, and I began crying over and over, "No! No! No!"

As we later found out, those sirens were first responders rushing to the scene of an accident where a blue IROC Z28 Camaro had lost control, skidded sideways down an old asphalt road, and T-boned an old tank of a car driven by some poor old lady. The Camaro ended up shaped like a C around the front end of her car. The side impact was so bad that the driver's door was pushed near the passenger door, with not much room between the two.

The old lady survived, but Jeremy and Brandon were gone.

These were good, softly-spoken, smart young men who treated everyone with the dignity and respect they deserved. I knew them well enough to know that they didn't exactly like everyone they came in contact with, but they sure didn't treat those people badly.

Because of how I've just described Jeremy and Brandon, there was not one single person in Savannah High School who was not wrestling with the thought, "Why them, and not me?"

One mistake on a winding, rural Missouri road, and two good people paid the ultimate price.

Their tragic and sudden deaths happened around the time that Long Branch Christian Church was falling apart, and on top of that, I'd taken an emotional beating for five years. I can honestly say that throughout my childhood, I experienced the presence of God and that I knew what He had designed me for and called me to do.

But this?

This was too much.

I was out!

If Christians fighting and good people dying was what the whole Jesus thing was about, then I wanted nothing to do with it. That thought process was birthed out of anger, stoked by the old dogma that 'God did it.' And like the prodigal son, I chose to walk away. I turned my back on God and God's people, rejecting the spiritual inheritance that would have kept me safe from the further hurts I inflicted upon myself. And thus, my journey of falling into darkness began.

The Death of Innocence

I made a great decision early on in high school: I joined the gymnastics team. I knew that I was starting the sport way too late in life to ever be successful, but I needed the kind of strength, flexibility, and agility that the sport of gymnastics would develop in me.

There were absolutely all kinds of name-calling surrounding this decision. Thankfully, I wasn't the lone guy. Quite frankly, I was already being treated like crap, so it was just part of the course. It still hurt, though.

The competitions were rather painful as well. There were no other schools in our area that had gymnastics teams – I'm not sure there were any others in the state! So, we generally had to compete against other gyms, and because most of those kids started when they were knee-high, we were competing against kids several years younger than us. I hate losing, but this wasn't just losing ... it was embarrassing.

I will admit the other draw to the gymnastics team was the girls. Ultimately, I ended up dating one of those girls in high school, which I regret for both of us. To this day, I discourage my daughters from the dating game at that age and encourage them to focus more on creating lasting friendships with young men. Our first daughter, Allison, bucked this system, which actually helped with all three of her siblings. They have seen the folly in the constant need to be 'taken.' The good news is that Allison made it out way better than Kaci and I did, and she ended up marrying her best friend.

The young lady I dated in high school was actually a pretty nice girl. As I said, she was a member of the gymnastics team, but she was also an All-American cheerleader. Through those high school years, we both missed out on a lot because we were constantly together. For instance, we missed hanging out with some people who might have been a lot closer, maybe even life-long friends, which is one of my deepest regrets. By the same token, spending time with her probably saved me from doing even more stupid stuff that I would have done with the guys.

She was raised in a Mormon family. While they weren't exactly regular attendees, there were tenets of her faith that were important to her, such as purity. Had I respected that, had we both respected that, we both would have likely saved ourselves a lot of trouble. There are a lot of reasons why we should never have dated, and many of those arguably depend on whether you are a person of faith or not (surely your argument will be tainted depending on what side of that faith you fall on as well). Regardless of any of those reasons, the biggest reason we should not have dated, besides that she was not right for me, was that her mother was the meanest, angriest person I've ever been around, and to top it off, she hated my guts. That should have been all the warning I needed.

Ah, but I wouldn't listen to reason.

She was a year younger than me in school, and when we met, she was dating Jeremy Scarbrough, a guy on my softball team. Now, Jeremy has risen to the level of a brother, and I know that if crap really hit the fan and he needed to saddle up to come and help me, he would be there in a heartbeat ... and I for him. But back in those days, there was no love lost between us. I'm not even sure either of us knew why. And once I'd wiggled into the picture and stole his girl from him ... yeah, it got worse, and then I knew the reason he didn't like me.

My girlfriend and her friends introduced me to the sport of cheerleading as well as Dan Stevens, or Mr. Dan as we called him then.

Mr. Dan was an anomaly in that he was the high school cheer coach. Not a lot of men signed up for that post back then. However, he was more than highly qualified for the job as he was a former yell leader at Northwest Missouri State University. He was in the sport back before they restricted pyramids and stunts to only two and a half people high. Before that restriction ... I don't want to think about it. The sport is dangerous enough as it is.

Mr. Dan taught at-risk students, so I never had him for any classes (believe it or not, I was a good student), but I can tell you he was one of those old-school, hard-as-nails teachers. Tough, but very fair. People respected him. He sized me up pretty quickly and somehow knew I needed an adult male to confide in. To this day, I still have his ear and use it regularly.

You may laugh, but in my senior year, I quit all other sports and became one of the first male cheerleaders at Savannah High School. I got to spend time with my girlfriend (not to mention a bunch of other beautiful ladies) – check. I got to work out – check. I had colleges interested in me, and they were offering paid scholarships – check.

Laugh all you want. I did the math, and I won!

Marty Lyle and Dustin Smith both joined the cheerleading squad as well, for the same reasons.

Two dangerous things were going down at this time. First, from somewhere, this credo reached the ears of our group: "If you don't have sex before you're 16, you aren't a man." Second, my girlfriend and I now had even more common interests and were spending even more time together. The mixture of peer pressure and temptation proved fatal.

After a year and a half of dating, with pressure from me as well as pressure from our peers, she relented, and the relationship turned sexual.

That is yet another deep regret I have in life.

It was also the beginning of the end of our relationship.

I don't know many young men who hold back the details of their sexual exploits, especially not in the locker room. Ashamedly, I was no different. To make matters worse, the guy who later married the girl I was bragging about had a locker right next to mine. They had a couple of kids before they divorced. While I don't know any of the details because I've spent most of the rest of my life avoiding Savannah like the plague, I do know the hurt and the anger of living in the shadows of other men. I know first-hand what that does to a man (and though I can't speak on behalf of the female population, the same principle of living in the shadows of ex-sexual partners applies to women as well). The guy who married my first girlfriend, well, he had a front-row seat to listen to some jerk brag about his exploits with his future wife. This is one of the most shameful things I carry in life.

We were together for around eighteen months to two years after that point. I was a year ahead of her in school and had made the Northwest Missouri State University cheer squad. Northwest wasn't a huge university, but it was big enough to create a perfect storm for a hurt, angry young man. It was also one of the top party schools in the nation. One of the casualties of that year ended up being my high school girlfriend. Deep inside, I knew our sexual relationship was wrong, and it was wreaking havoc on me. Then some things happened during the breakup, which made it even worse.

All this kept heaping more pain, upon pain, upon pain.

While I'd been drinking socially with my mates for some time, it had gradually become something I relied upon to numb the pain. For a while, anyway. And then I added drugs into the mix. Both became an addiction.

Throughout my years of being an addict, there were some people along the way whom I couldn't fool, but for the most part, I was a high-functioning addict and received the same comments those peers from back in the day made about my musical dreams, "I never knew." Even those closest to me never knew.

"You'll Be Lucky to Work at McDonald's"

There were two career counselors at Savannah High School. I have no idea how they split their responsibilities. If I remember correctly, one focused on freshman and sophomores while the other focused on juniors and seniors. Mr. Schneider was a laid back and encouraging fella. The other ... well, I must have been a magnet for people wanting to crush me. She actually told me I'd be lucky to get a job at McDonald's and that I shouldn't even bother filling out scholarship applications for college.

Mr. Schneider, however, encouraged me to follow the 'Academic Diploma' program and to fill out every application that might remotely relate to me. He went above and beyond to help me fill out and submit scholarship applications. He also put together an academic plan for me to follow. I thought to myself, "I'm going to do this for him, to make him proud."

Some of the courses I took were amazing, and I still reap the benefits from them today. For instance, an old battle-ax of a teacher who actually taught my parents in high school, Mrs. Zaph, taught me the structures used by great authors over the centuries and how they used metaphoric and symbolic cues in their character creations. I never would have read some of the great works of literature, nor would I have been able to comprehend them, if it were not for Mrs. Zaph and that class. I have retained a love for reading, in part, because of her.

There were a lot of smart cookies in my classes. Most of them were genuinely good people, much like the others I regret not spending more time with. I must admit that I'd started to become the type of person I despised ... only hanging out with those good people when it suited or benefited me. In more recent years, I've found some of them on social media, and I have apologized. Others, I haven't found, but I pray that one day I will be able to apologize to them as well.

When we graduated, I wasn't close to the top of my class, but I was still around the top 10%-ish. Funny how those things mattered at the time. Now, I couldn't care less about my marks, and I can't even recall where I stood in my graduating class!

What I do remember is that my parents got me contact lenses for my graduation. Before this, contact lenses were out of the question because none would fit the shape of my eyes, but by this stage, new lenses were available. It took a while to get the correction and fit perfect, and they were expensive since disposable lenses had not yet been invented, but at least it meant I could kiss goodbye to those dreadful coke-bottle glasses for special occasions and for sports.

PART SIX
UNIVERSITY YEARS

Northwest Missouri State University

One thing that I can proudly say is that my parents only contributed $50 to my university fees. I earned my degree via athletic and scholastic scholarships, as well as good old-fashioned hard work.

I was awarded several scholarships. Between my scholastic scholarships and what I received as an athletic student, I received between $2,000 and $2,500 a semester over and above my fees. Back in the early 90s, that was a nice chunk of change! Instead of saving or utilizing it for anything good, it became party money.

So, financially, I was sorted. Academically, however, was a completely different story...

In high school, I wanted to become a doctor, so I initially majored in medicine. I was good at math and science, but I didn't love the subjects, and I certainly wasn't passionate about them. What I did like was the money and prestige that becoming a doctor would bring. Therefore, it's not a big surprise that this dream fizzled out fairly quickly.

Right from the start, my advisor discouraged me from taking the medical route. She flat out told me, "You might as well switch your major today. You are too white and too male to ever get into med school." She stared at me like I should be intimidated by this, but seeing that I wasn't going to change my major that day, she shrugged and moved on to what I guess she thought was a more important issue: "Here's the number and address of the student clinic. 1 out of every 3 students ends up with an STD. If anything weird starts happening with your genitalia, call them immediately."

Wow. OK. Interesting orientation.

College was an interesting place, and the student body was large enough to warrant huge lecture halls with hundreds of students in a single class. I quickly discovered that I was just a number and that the lecturers were indifferent to whether the students went to class or not. So, I just didn't go. I mean, I made it through high school near the top without any effort. Why should this be any different? Talk about a flawed mindset!

I learned a few other things about college. First, the politics were different from those I had encountered at high school. Second, I didn't have to walk around like a whipped puppy anymore, wondering if I was going to be accepted or rejected at any given moment. Despite recognizing this, I was still like a dog that had been kicked over and over, and I was very cautious about getting close to anyone because I expected further kicks. Yet, there was a little more freedom to breathe. Third, I had an unlimited supply of folks from whom I could obtain alcohol and drugs – there was always someone looking to get high.

I was known to be crazy, in a fun and memorable way. Drugs and alcohol not only helped to numb the pain, but they also lowered my inhibitions and gave me the license to be crazier than normal. As my friends will tell you, I didn't have to be under the influence to come unhinged, but the drugs and alcohol more or less took away any inhibition while giving me the excuse to do what I likely would have done in the first place. Slowly, I did more and more stupid things that impacted me emotionally and drove me deeper into alcohol and drugs.

By the end of my first semester, I had already changed my major. I went into it half-heartedly in the first place, and that pep talk with my advisor didn't help, but all in all the nail in the coffin was the fact that I couldn't breeze through it. At that time, if it wasn't easy, I didn't want to do it.

The cheer squad was good. One of the biggest blessings during this time was that I met my life-long friend, the best man at my wedding, and the first person to discover my musical secret: Larry Lawson.

It turned out that Larry and I had played football against one another in high school. He was a heck of an athlete and a fierce competitor, but after a broken ankle, he knew he would have to find another avenue to get an athletic scholarship for college. Like me, Larry came from a working-class family, and his only ticket to college was a scholarship. Our parents couldn't, and wouldn't, foot the bill for us. We became fast friends, and at the end of the first semester, I moved from my dorm room on the outskirts of campus to live with Larry in his dorm, which was right in the heart of campus.

One particular weekend, I was, or I thought I was, the only person left on the floor. This meant I had the community shower all to myself. It was an old building, and the shower room was concrete with tiled walls – the acoustics were pretty awesome. Everyone was gone, so I decided to take advantage and sing to my heart's content.

I don't know how far I got into the song *A Whole New World* from the movie *Aladdin*, but I just about screamed like a little girl and peed myself when I heard someone behind me say, "What the f***, dude! You're f***ing amazing!" After I finished my shower and got back to the room, Larry continued to encourage me, "Dude, I've never heard anyone sing like that before." Little did I know this would be the starting point of my music career and that the Lord would use Larry to encourage me to follow my dream for years to come.

The competitive nature in Larry and I drove us to be the best at everything we did. Cheerleading was no different. We both applied and became staff members for the National Cheerleaders Association (NCA) and ended up teaching summer camps together all over America. To be on staff for the NCA was basically the top of the game.

Going into Northwest, I had the advantage of three years of gymnastics and one year of cheerleading in high school. Larry went in completely green. He spent hour after hour trying to learn a 'roundoff,' the move that turns your body into position while building momentum, preparing you to thrust backward into back handsprings and/or backflips. Within only two years, Larry would be doing multiple back handsprings across the floor, ending in a full-twisting backflip. Some gymnasts work their whole lives and never achieve that skill level. He did it in two years. So, it's no surprise that he became an NCA staff member after only a couple of months of being a cheerleader.

Our coach at Northwest Missouri State University was amazing. Outside of cheerleading, he loved lifting weights, sports, and drinking beer. He was a former yell leader at Northwest Missouri State University and probably one of the most intense and competitive guys I've come across.

Coach took our job of heckling the opposing team very seriously; in his mind, that is what our megaphones were made for. There were a few basketball games where Larry, Lyle, a fellow yell leader named Bradshaw, and I almost had some opposing players take a swing at us. The referees had to step in between the players and us on multiple occasions. There were limitations, of course, lines we knew not to cross. We used our mouths but gave no physical indication that we wanted to start a fight. That was the deal. Just feet from the line, we could provoke a fight using our words as long as we didn't make any menacing moves towards the players. It was pure mind games. Before the game, our coach would brief us on which player he wanted us to take out of the game. And we were darned good at it!

Let's get real, though. As a competitor and an athlete, the real reason I was in this sport was for a shot at a National Championship. The same is true for most elite male cheerleaders. They aren't in it for the side-line and half-time junk. We are there for the girls and the glory, plain and simple.

The National Championship for mixed cheer squads was intense. The preparation was horrendous. The routine was a rapid-fire progression of tumbling passes, stunts, and pyramids, all happening in such a tight, synchronized fashion that if just one person was off by a fraction of a beat, it all fell apart. Often, when the routine was initially formulated, the majority of the squad members couldn't perform most of the elements. So, our days were broken up to incorporate weight training, individual gymnastics training, individual stunt practice with a partner, regular team practice, and then national routine practice. Oh yeah, and we still had to maintain our classwork in there somehow.

After months and months of doing this routine over and over on a daily basis, there came a breaking point. At one moment, we believed we couldn't do the routine one more flipping time without going insane and then, BOOM, the next moment, we had crossed over into a crazy euphoric zone where every tumbling pass and stunt worked, and it just became pure fun.

The Championship was where my years of playing fastpitch softball really paid off. All those years of competing taught me to take fear, nervousness, and anxiety, and channel them into intensity. My first and last trip with Northwest Missouri State University to the NCA National Championship tournament, held in Dallas, TX, gained us 3rd place amongst Division II universities.

For whatever reason, after that first year, our coach decided we would no longer compete in the National Championship. It was a tough pill to swallow. Many of the guys on the squad were so deep into their majors that they couldn't simply change schools in pursuit of that National Championship dream. That didn't apply to us young guns.

Due to the lack of competition, Larry moved to Barton County Community College in Great Bend, Kansas, in the fall of 1994. He almost convinced me to go with him. So much so that as we drove through Kansas that summer teaching cheerleading camps for the NCA, we stopped at a DMV, and I got my Kansas driver's license using Larry's new address in Great Bend as my primary residence.

By the end of my first year in college, I had lost one of my academic scholarships. I still had some cash left over each semester from the remaining scholarships, but I needed extra income. So, I got a job working night shifts at a local fast-food restaurant.

Being a college town, the night shifts entailed dealing with the onslaught of the drunken bar crowd as they finished their evening, or more appropriately, their morning of drinking. Thankfully, the lobby was closed, so it was just the drive-through open, but there was usually only a skeleton crew of three people working, trying to keep up with those who had the munchies.

That job introduced me to people who further pulled me down the drain through their gambling and drug shenanigans.

Kearney, Nebraska

During the summer of 1994, I traveled all over America, most of the time with Larry, teaching cheerleading camps for the NCA. Larry and I would roll down the highway between camps singing along to our favorite songs. Now that Larry knew my secret, I just belted it out. Unless I was alone in the car or with Larry, I continued to keep my singing to myself.

That was about to change.

If Larry was scheming anything, I never knew it. We rolled into the University of Nebraska Kearney, in Kearney, Nebraska, and met up with the staff as usual. The staff always came in a day or two in advance so that we could get to know each other and practice the routines together. While we used the same routines from camp to camp, we needed to be comfortable working with the new people we met in each place, especially since every guy and gal had little idiosyncrasies in their movements that could potentially throw off a stunt or a pyramid.

One such instance happened during our orientation at this university.

'Basket tosses' are one of those wow factor stunts for the crowd. In this stunt, three or four guys lock arms, load a girl on top of their hands, and throw her high into the air to do an assortment of tricks.

Some basket toss teams are efficient and can really launch a girl. I've seen guys send a girl up high enough in a basketball arena that she nearly touched the bottom of the big scoreboard in the middle of the court.

There are all kinds of dangers that can happen, however. The guys can get slightly out of sync, sending the girl to one side or the other, leaving them to frantically recover and move as one to get under her so she can be caught safely. Things can also go wrong if the team of guys wrongly assume that the girl is used to being tossed really high and move into full-power tosses too quickly.

This was the case in Kearney. Larry and I were darned good at what we did. Because we were nearly inseparable, we had worked together so much that our timing was near perfect.

But, since we were working at a professional level and had been around some of the best in the business, we got a little cocky and forgot to get acquainted with the new teammate we would be tossing. We loaded her in the basket (our interlocked hands), and in a fluid motion launched her into the air. She wasn't expecting it and had never been that high before. She completely unraveled.

The best thing a flier can do in this instance is to regain control and pull their body parts in. What they don't want to do is flail ... unfortunately, this girl didn't know that!

On her way down, her flailing elbow caught me right on top of the head. Thankfully, it didn't break her arm. For me, it was the last thing I remembered for a while. Evidently, I kept going, although Larry knew something wasn't right and kept an eye on me. Later, the entire staff went to a local diner, and apparently, I had trouble keeping my balance, and my eyes were wandering and going in and out of focus. That's when Larry was pushed over the edge. Immediately, he got me to his vehicle and took me straight to the hospital.

Fortunately, it was only a concussion, and I only missed the first day of camp. The other staff members picked up my slack but introduced me so the campers knew who I was and could expect my return.

The next day, I rolled right into my duties. It was a good week, and everything went well.

Then, on the afternoon of the award presentations, Larry nodded to the head staff member, gave me a sly look, stepped in front of the 300+ cheerleaders and coaches and said, "You're in for a treat today because one of our staff members is a gifted vocalist, and he is going to sing you a song."

Then he introduced me!

I heard him say, "Let's give Jeremy a big round of applause."

No one told me this was going to happen!

I was smiling on the outside but scared to death on the inside. As Larry passed me, I asked him frantically, "What the heck am I supposed to do now?"

He shrugged and said nonchalantly, "Sing *Don't Take the Girl*. You rock that song."

Completely acapella, never having sung before a group of people in my entire life, I stood there in front of the large crowd and sang Tim McGraw's *Don't Take the Girl*.

Everyone began swaying, singing along, and crying. When I finished, they erupted in screams and applause.

That's part of being on NCA staff, though. To those girls, we were almost god-like. My singing could have been horrible, and they'd still have screamed.

Yet, the seed that was planted all those years ago had finally been watered. I loved it. It reinforced what I'd always known – this was what I was made to do.

Larry would have me do this again and again during the next couple of summers. I owe him a lot for all of the encouragement he gave me through the years.

College Sport Magazine

At the end of the summer of 1994, the summer camps were coming to an end, and I was beginning to transition back to life at Northwest Missouri State University when my mom called to tell me that I had a letter from the NCA at home.

I didn't think much of it because I'd been receiving more correspondence than usual from the NCA following my concussion since they wanted to stay on top of it. I brushed it off as just another one of those letters and told Mom just to open it and let me know if it was anything important. Minutes later, she called back, beyond herself with excitement.

Before we get too far, I should probably preface this story with something that I didn't mention previously. In rural Missouri, there were only a handful of select sports that young men were involved in: football, basketball, wrestling, track, and baseball. Other sports were either for 'sissies' or, like soccer, 'were communist sports.'

My dad had always been proud of me for my achievements in fastpitch softball and was also proud when I later played football, basketball, and track. He tolerated the whole gymnastics thing because it would help my strength, flexibility, and agility in those 'real sports.' Plus, gymnastics didn't get much press, so he wasn't subject to the expected flak from his friends at work, which made it all the more tolerable.

When I walked away from all the other sports and went into cheerleading ... well, I'm not quite sure he was really down with that.

Mom, on the other hand, supported me through almost anything. If Dad made any sideways remarks, she usually shut him down.

On this occasion, I think my dad was finally impressed. Nothing he'd go and brag to the guys at work about, but I took it as a victory.

Back to the phone call and the letter. Mom proceeded to tell me that the NCA had sent me a letter to announce that I had been nominated as one of College Sport Magazine's top male cheerleaders.

Then came the hitch. Just like with any other sport, they were not merely selecting the athletes for their prowess in their respective sports but also their academic ability.

Uh-oh.

While I was still excited, I knew the nomination was as far as it was going to go. My party life was on the rise, but my academic life was on the decline. I knew it was only a matter of time before a representative of the magazine would contact the school and find out the truth. There was still enough of a GPA (grade point average) to keep me on a scholarship, but it didn't take a rocket scientist to figure out the trends. I was sinking and sinking fast.

TKE

Heading into the fall semester of 1994, I decided to do something I thought I would never do. I pledged to a fraternity, Tau Kappa Epsilon, which was usually abbreviated TKE or, as folks would say, 'Teke.'

There are really three distinct types of people when it comes to fraternities: those who want to be part of one, those who are opposed to them, and those who just don't care.

During my first year, for whatever reason, I decided that I was opposed to them. I saw them as a bunch of rich boys buying their friends. Then, Derek Owen (one of my high school buddies) pledged to TKE. The majority of my circle of friends from Savannah ended up at Northwest Missouri State University: Marty Lyle, Dustin Smith, Mike Nigh, and Derek Owen. When Derek joined TKE, we gave him all kinds of crap. Over time, we found out that TKE was a pretty legit group of individuals, and in the fall of '94, Marty and I followed suit. Mike and Dustin figured they weren't cut out for college and decided not to enroll for another year, so they didn't pledge with us.

There was another guy who pledged to TKE and also became part of the cheer team at Northwest: my mortal enemy from high school ... Jeremy Scarbrough.

The pledge process was a blast! It was designed to bring a pledge class together while weeding out guys who were not compatible. It's not to say that the incompatible guys were bad. Many of them were really down-to-earth, cool dudes. However, when it got tough, they just didn't click and mesh with the rest of the guys. They were never made to feel unwelcome; they just eventually trailed off and left.

Being part of the TKE fraternity is something I will always cherish, and I gained some amazing brothers (we became so close that we called each other 'brothers'), one of whom was Jeremy Scarbrough. I don't remember when or how, but we both just broke and helped pick one another up. Ironically, picking one another up was a concept we were taught by our coach on the fastpitch softball team in high school, but there, we only tolerated each other to get the win. Here, it was different. We both saw that the other was a darned good person, and we realized that whatever we were harboring as 'hatred' was sheer stupidity. This was a deep lesson on forgiveness and redemption, which I didn't fully grasp until much later in life.

Another bonus in joining TKE was that my high school mentor and cheer coach, Dan Stevens, was TKE alumni. Because of the teacher-student boundaries of high school, there were limits to how much Dan could invest and mentor. But now that I was in college, he was able to pour more into my life. Dan was always good at 'putting a shot across my bow' without coming right out and saying, "I know what you're up to. Get your crap together." We had a few of those talks during my first two years of college. I'm quite certain that Dan was one of the few who saw through my mask and knew that I was spiraling into addictions. He never dropped out of my life, though. If anything, he became more present. Others would see my weaknesses and leave me high and dry, but Dan never did. Even now, as I put my life down on paper, I find myself taking breaks to exchange text messages with him.

TKE had a house, which was not only a place where several brothers lived, but it was also the place where would we would all hang out, have meetings, and of course, throw huge parties. While we partied and played hard, some guys in the TKE house were 'salt and light,' and the Lord used their lives as a glimmer of light in the darkness as He drew me back to Himself. Two brothers from Nebraska, Matt and Scott Norlen, and Jeff Wilson would hold Bible studies in Jeff's room in the TKE house. They invited me on several times. There were times I really wanted to go, but the hurt and a million excuses held me back. I've never forgotten their example, though. They would have fun without crossing the line. They also had my respect as they never pushed the subject of God or made me feel inferior.

Where those guys would never cross the line, I, on the other hand, would see the line, sprint towards it, and fling myself as far across it as I could!

One of my female cousins later married a young man who joined TKE at Northwest Missouri State University more than a decade after I had left. He told me that, even after all those years, the exploits of Neely still lived on. I'm not entirely proud of that. Although some of it was just sheer fun and well-thought-out pranks.

In retrospect, I can see that I was loved and accepted, but I couldn't see it at the time. My 'legendary exploits' were merely me fighting to gain the acceptance I already had. Because of the constant rejection through middle and high school, plus my church family dissolving, and my high school relationship blowing up, I had a deep sense of being unlovable, and my self-worth was extremely low.

If someone wants to look hard enough, they'll always find a druggie, no matter where they are. Even in the TKE brotherhood, we had a few. Interestingly enough, most of the TKE guys didn't like the whole drug thing, and they actively discouraged it. But there were a few who pushed the limits ... and I found them. Drugs and alcohol were still the only things that numbed my pain.

Had I followed the leadership of that TKE chapter, I would have likely found my way home. Lord knows, He put great people along my path time and time again who could and would have helped me. But like the prodigal son, I thought I knew better, and I shrugged off anything good in order to feed my desires. I was a self-centered brat, and without verbalizing it, my life credo was: 'my kingdom come, my will be done.' Yet, that caused everything in my life to crumble around me.

Larry's Intervention

After the fall semester of 1994, I had the opportunity to move into the TKE house. It was pretty uncommon for a newbie to be able to move into the house, but there was an opening, and I was very well-liked. So, they voted on it, and I was allowed to move in.

This made my parents super happy, especially my mom, for I'd been sharing an old trailer on the outskirts of Maryville, MO. While it looked like a shanty drug den, the other two guys living there were actually really good students and had pretty strict rules, which included no smoking and no drugs in the trailer. I'm sure they were happy to see me go! Unfortunately, my downward spiral tarnished the relationships I had with them.

Drugs weren't tolerated at the TKE house, either. But now, I was closer to campus and therefore closer to my network of 'friends' from whom I would bum drugs. As part of my charade, I hardly ever bought drugs myself. Over time, I learned that if I played people right, I didn't need to buy an ounce, and by jumping from person to person, I was hardly ever called out as a leech. Plus, it covered my tracks, which was another reason no one knew about my habit. Yes, I was a mooch, but I was also a chicken. I saw people around me either get busted for possession or get caught buying from an undercover cop. Duh, there was no way I was buying or carrying!

Despite the rules, there were plenty of guys in the TKE house who were of legal drinking age, and because I was fun to party with, they would always make a 'beer run.' Which is a misnomer because my drink of choice was Captain Morgan's rum and coke. In the spring of 1995, I drank enough Captain Morgan to line the whole perimeter of my room with empty bottles. To put this into perspective, my room was actually meant for two people and had two beds, a sofa, an easy chair, and it still had space for a small refrigerator and a TV/entertainment center.

At the end of the spring semester, the university notified me that I would be placed on 'academic probation.' It came as no surprise to me. My GPA had slipped to a low of 1.21, which is a D ... or as I tell people, 'one step shy of stupid.'

All in all, it meant that I lost my remaining academic scholarships and my athletic scholarship. And the latter meant that my participation in the cheer squad was over.

I felt lost.

Again, I put on my mask so that no one could see the hurt, agony, and despair as I was spiraling out of control.

That summer break (from mid-May onwards), Larry Lawson and I traveled all over America teaching NCA camps again. We'd kept in touch after he moved to Barton County Community College since we'd become such great friends. I didn't breathe a word about my situation, but Larry wasn't fooled; he knew something was wrong.

By July 1995, I had reached the point of no return, and I couldn't hide my junk anymore. My coach at Northwest was calling me, excited for the prospects of the coming season, and I didn't have the balls to tell him that I was failing and wouldn't be able to be part of the team.

Have you ever been in that place where all your darkest secrets are about to spill out and be revealed? The fear, the panic ... it was overwhelming!

Finally, at the end of July, I broke and called the only person I knew I could: Larry. I spilled my guts out, telling him absolutely everything – every little detail leading up to and ending with the academic probation.

There was silence on the other end of the line for what seemed like an eternity. Then I heard a sigh, and he said, "I'll be there in a couple of hours."

True to his word, Larry pulled up to the TKE house roughly three hours later. His little Geo Metro car was packed to the hilt since he had been about to leave home to go back to Barton County Community College when I called him.

He burst into my room and said in a tone that I knew was serious, "Pack your s**t! You're coming with me!"

There was no way my refrigerator or any of its contents were going into that packed Geo Metro, and something inside me told me I was never coming back. So, I grabbed all my keepsakes and clothing, loaded it into Larry's car and plonked myself in the passenger seat.

Larry got in and shot off like a bat out of Hades. After a while of silence, he sighed and said, "Man, I love you like a brother. I don't know how this happened, but I've got you."

Little did I know that Larry had already made a phone call on my behalf to his cheer coach at Barton County Community College. Because I had made a name for myself in the sport, it was an easy sell. Right there on the phone, she told Larry that there were no more scholarship spots on the team, but she had just created a spot for me. Furthermore, she would ensure I had a work-study job on campus. The scholarship would cover books and tuition, and the work-study job, which was nothing more than me being in the weight room, would pay for my rent and food. In less than 20 minutes, Larry had got me a full scholarship to go to school at Barton County Community College.

For a while, we made small talk, not really addressing 'the elephant in the car.' As we passed through Topeka, KS, I had an idea of where we were going but had to ask to make sure. That's when Larry laid out all of the details of that phone call. My friend was going to place me under his watchful eye.

Barton County, Kansas

Once Larry left for Barton County Community College, his name was mud with our coach at Northwest. As a matter of fact, it was best not to even mention his name or major crap would hit the fan. Like I've said, our coach was an intense competitor!

I don't even want to think about what my name became in that circle once I left. And, honestly, there would have been good reasons for any bad feelings that were felt towards me. I was a coward. Larry didn't know this, but I didn't tell my coach at Northwest that I was leaving. I had talked to him on the phone just hours before I made the call to Larry, and I was such a chicken. I talked it up like we were going to have a heck of a year and we would win the whole shebang! A couple of hours later, I was packing all my essentials in a Geo Metro and running away from my problems. Never told a soul. Just left.

It was the last week of July, and we pulled up to Larry's apartment in Great Bend. There are only windy days in that part of the world, and the only variation in weather is hot or cold. Yeah, that's an exaggeration, but not by much. The place gets a few nice days here and there when there's little to no wind, but that's it. On this particular day, it was over 100 degrees as the sun was beginning to set with a stiff wind out of the west. I remember feeling dirt or sand pelt my skin as I stepped out of the car into what felt like a blast furnace.

"Great Bend, Kansas. It isn't hell, but you can sure see it from here," was the first thought that crossed my mind. I remember it clearly because that saying cracked me up pretty good, and I've made that same joke to others for decades now.

Being in Great Bend was a blessing and a curse.

It was a blessing because I finally felt wanted on several fronts. First and foremost, Larry went out of his way to rescue me from my issues. I've had good friends in life, but only a handful have been true friends on that level. Second, the coach at Barton went out of her way to get me on her squad. It's one thing to get accolades and such, but to have someone move heaven and earth to create a full scholarship position for you ... that's huge. I'm not sure what favors she had to cash in, but I made sure that I would not let her down. Third, my teammates accepted me with no ifs or buts, and I had not felt accepted like that since my days at Helena Elementary School. I was finally amongst people who genuinely cared for me. I felt safe among them, and I could be myself. So much so that I trusted them with the knowledge of my musical dream – something that I hadn't dared to share previously. They were incredibly supportive, and from that foundation, I began singing at various gigs, though not very frequently. All in all, I felt like my world was coming back together.

One of the biggest blessings during my year in Great Bend was the Huslig family. Their son Blaine had made the Barton County cheer squad that fall. Blaine was so much fun to be around. We became fast friends, and he was constantly at our apartment. His parents, solid Christians, were very active in Blaine's life and the lives of his friends. Soon, I became an honorary member of the Huslig family. I'm pretty vocal about people who profess to be believers in Jesus but do nothing more than piss others off and make them want nothing to do with their faith. Yet, there were several throughout my life, like the Huslig family, who were honest believers in Jesus and drew people in. I found myself, at times, being a part of their church and even engaging in spiritual conversations with Blaine's dad.

They never pushed me to go to church. I asked them if I could go. They never pushed me to talk about Jesus or other aspects of the Christian faith. I approached them about those topics. This became ingrained in my mind, and decades later, shaped how I would posture my music and the ministry that springs out of it.

Now for the not-so-good stuff about being in Great Bend. On the partying front, I literally jumped out of the frying pan and into the fryer. Between the last week of July and the first week of school, the cheer squad alone drank between 21 – 27 kegs of beer (1 keg is 124 pints). Many of my new teammates were city kids from the Kansas City and Topeka area who were avid drug users, so much so that they grew their own weed in home-made incubators.

I also started to understand the shackles of addiction. As the turmoil in me began to subside and I felt alive again, I found that I couldn't just stop drinking and using. I no longer *needed* either substance to numb the emotional pain. Now, I *had* to have a drink and use drugs because my body had become dependent on them.

Without the thousands of dollars that I'd previously had each semester from academic scholarships, I didn't have money for partying. Often, I had to make decisions like, "Do I eat, or do I drink and use?" The physical withdraws of abstaining absolutely sucked, but I cowboyed up and took them at times. Other times, I caved and found myself with only enough money to eat the bare minimum to function.

As the year progressed, my drinking did slowly revert to social drinking, and my drug use decreased. This was only possible because I was surrounded by good friends who truly cared about me. It wasn't easy, though. It was my first experience of detoxing, and the symptoms were unforgiving. There were times when my body ached so bad that death seemed like a sweet escape.

One menu item that sustained me during the times I caved into the pain and used my money to buy drink or drugs instead of food was a two-egg, mayonnaise, cheese, and barbecue sauce omelet with rice. Rice and eggs were inexpensive, a block of cheese could last me a couple of weeks, and mayonnaise and barbecue sauce packets could be grabbed by the handful at fast-food restaurants.

Not exactly healthy eating, but my body was burning calories like crazy due to our daily cheerleading schedule. It was nuts! Those people were serious about becoming a national powerhouse, and the schedule was proof of that!

My college day usually began around 7:00am at the library on campus. I admit that I tried to fall back into the old mindset I had at Northwest, the mindset that considered classes to be optional, but at Barton, people cared about me. Not just the cheer team, but the staff. My advisor caught on to my games early on and pulled me in and had a 'come to Jesus' moment with me. I honestly don't remember missing a class after that, unless I was deathly sick, and even then, I called her to let her know I was sick and made arrangements to make up those missed lectures.

Between 8:00am and 11:00am, I crammed in all the classes that would fit. After that, we only had 2:00pm – 4:00pm as an optional slot for classes, so if it could be avoided, students generally didn't use that time.

From 11:00am until anywhere from 7:00pm to 10:00pm, I was either in gymnastics training, weight training, open gym (which consisted of practicing stunts and refining gymnastic passes), or in actual squad practice with the coach, followed by more weight training, and then practice for the National Championship routine.

I got paid for work-study during my weight training sessions. Years later, coaching jobs were lost because of this kind of practice, though not in the cheerleading department because cheerleading is not considered an officially sanctioned NCAA sport. It affected other coaches because they were doing the same thing with their athletic students. In my situation, coaches were giving us money to live on by saying we 'clocked in' for work-study hours, while in reality, all we were doing was lifting weights. In the meantime, the other Regular Joe students who had been given work-study jobs in the gym actually worked. It was known from the top down that this was happening.

That's one of the big reasons Barton attracted some of the gifted athletes it did. Big-named coaches would send amazing athletes who were dumber than a box of rocks to Barton simply to 'get their GPA' in line with NCAA standards while playing at a very competitive level. Shoot, we had a point guard who was there because his coach from Michigan needed him to get his GPA up. I've never seen someone play ball like him. The following year, I saw him play for

Michigan for one semester, then he was gone – academic probation that he never came back from.

Barton also attracted Olympians who were on the track and field teams. We even had a guy on the basketball team who was shipped over from Africa. He had the starring role in a movie with Kevin Bacon called *The Air Up There* but needed some coaching before he would be considered for professional basketball.

My teammates were just as good. One of the gals on the squad had trained with the coach of Olympian gymnast Shannon Miller. Several of our guys were stand-out high school football players. One guy was a state-qualifying swimmer in high school. Then there was the guy we loved having in our corner – Herb. That year, Herb was the runner up in the Kansas state Tough Man competition. As it worked out, all of his fights in the competition were consecutive. If it had worked out another way, allowing him some rest time between fights, it's highly likely that he would have won the title. Needless to say, we were all arrogant, and no one ever talked trash without getting hurt.

Great Bend used to be an oil town. There was a lot of money passing around, and that's why and how they got top athletes – those old wealthy boys liked their 'live entertainment' and paid for it. However, it meant that athletes came with big egos and different backgrounds, and it resulted in many incidents being swept under the rug or never reported. For instance, Barton County Community College was riddled with date rape.

Kaci

arry and I lived in an apartment within a complex of two-story apartments. It had an enclosed courtyard at the back, and on the other side of the courtyard was another row of apartments. Larry's girlfriend lived across the courtyard and a couple of apartments down from us with a roommate. During my first fall semester, I was at that apartment quite a bit with Larry, his girlfriend, her roommate, and a girl by the name of Kaci from another apartment complex close to ours. We all became good friends who liked to hang out. This was a saving grace to Kaci because my first impression of her wasn't that great.

Before our friendships ever developed, one of the first things I had to do when I got to Great Bend, besides registering for classes and getting my books, was to learn a 'combo routine' for the incoming freshman orientation. The reason they called it a combo routine was because the routine included individuals from both the cheerleading and dance squads. I hated junk like this because all incoming students were required to come and watch, and since male cheerleaders were considered to be unmanly, many of the guys hurled insults at us and tried to start fights. One upswing was a cute blonde on the dance squad – Kaci. I showed off and goofed around quite a bit trying to impress her, but she acted like she wanted nothing to do with me. So, my first impression of Kaci wasn't nice at all as I thought she was a stuck-up snot (to put it nicely). Little did I know that she had just been through one of the worst things a young lady could ever face. In the meantime, I moved on and set my eyes on other girls.

One thing you should know about co-ed cheerleading: very few boundaries exist between the guys and gals. The stunts are hands-on, and sometimes our male hands were required to be in the intimate areas of females to stabilize a stunt or to keep a girl from crashing to the floor when a stunt falls apart ... in those situations, we grabbed her however and wherever we could. The result was some kind of desensitized intimacy that broke down physical boundaries, and it ultimately led to promiscuity. At Barton, I was fresh meat in a pool of people in an isolated, small community college. I didn't have to move on and set my eyes on other girls ... they came to me.

At first, Kaci's presence at Larry's girlfriend's apartment was hit and miss, but over time, she began to frequent more and more. We were a bunch of friends who loved to talk and laugh. These memories have formed the basis of how I have directed my daughters to search for their husbands: become friends first and let the chips fall where they may beyond that.

Two or three times, it seemed as if Kaci and I were getting close, like there was interest beyond friendship, but then she would distance herself for weeks. Slowly, she would start to come around again, and then the cycle would start over. Due to the verbal, emotional, and sexual abuse she had been subjected to, Kaci didn't think a guy like me could ever like a woman like her. Anyone who meets Kaci and hears her story is immediately filled with intense anger that anyone could ever hurt such a sweet person.

Just before our Christmas break, Larry and his girlfriend were going to go to the 'Winter Village' in Great Bend. I don't recall if that's what it was really called, but it was a full-sized winter village that looked like one of those little decorations people buy of Christmas villages. Larry's girlfriend said to me, "You should come with us." I replied something along the lines of not wanting to be the third wheel. She persisted with more of a hint, "No, you should come and take ... a friend." As she said this, she was nodding her head to the side in the direction of Kaci. Later, I found that she had the inside scoop, and I, being a typical male, was missing the cues. I remember turning to look at Kaci, and my heart started racing.

What the heck? I'd hung out with Kaci for months. She was a close friend, so why was I all of a sudden feeling like I was going to pass out?

I took a few breaths, then walked over to Kaci and asked her if she would like to go with me.

I'll never forget the look in her eyes that night. Her piercing blue eyes locked onto mine and her pupils were pulsing. She was radiant. Oh, and she said, "Yes."

Because of the situation, I'm quite certain that my memory is over-romanticizing everything, but the place was perfect, and so was the evening. There were little cottages set up around a small pond. Lights strung all around. Hot cocoa and apple cider for sale. Then there was a little arch bridge that crossed the pond. When I say pond, it was actually a super small body of water. Christmas lights lined the bridge as well. Somewhere along the way, I took Kaci's hand in mine, and we strolled around the little makeshift Christmas village.

It was a cold night, but it was unusually still. We walked to the top of the bridge and took in the scenery surrounding us.

That's where we first kissed.

And when we did, everything just made sense. I didn't want to be without her by my side. This was the woman I would love for the rest of my life, and I wanted to marry her.

Like so many in life, I would forget that feeling and those emotions, but I praise God that He is the great redeemer, and before we were ready to seal the deal and kiss goodbye to our relationship, I would remember my love for her again.

We continued to talk as we strolled around the village. Later, we made it back to my apartment where Kaci made sure I had her parent's phone number and that she had mine. The next day she was going home for the Christmas break, and Larry and I were heading to Dallas to be 'spotters' on the mat at the NCA high school nationals. Kaci and I didn't want to leave one another. Not now. I kissed her a few more times, and I walked her home.

Then I got some sleep before Larry and I headed to Dallas. To clarify what Larry and I were doing in Dallas for the NCA: a 'spotter' is an individual, usually a guy, standing off to the side, careful not to interfere with the routine, who can swoop in if a stunt goes wrong and ensure the safety of those competing. Usually, a squad has their own spotters, but often, because of the nerves of competition, they don't react in time.

This event was televised nationally, so the pressure was high for the young ladies performing, but also for us. There have been several cases of death, paralysis as well as an unending number of broken bones from stunts gone wrong in this sport. Not on our watch, though!

There were some close calls during that competition. One, I will never forget.

Larry and I liked to talk to the teams we would be on the mat with; we aimed to help them relax a bit. The particular team in question had a few young ladies who were terrified, and none of our talking and joking could get them to calm down. This put Larry and me on high alert. Just as they had told us backstage, the team's routine was jam-packed full of elements. In some cases, that made it harder for us to cover the mat. In routines such as this one, we'd have to pay special attention to any pyramid or stunt so that we could creep and catch anyone, or at least break their fall before hitting the ground. These girls came to a part in their routine where they formed two smaller pyramids at the front corners of the mat while forming a big pyramid in the back center. Larry and I had hand signals to let each other know who would sprint to the front of the pyramid and who would cover the back. Larry signaled back, and just as he did, those ladies lost it.

The young lady on top of the pyramid was two and a half people high in the air. Let's say, for the sake of averages, those young ladies were all 5 feet tall … that would mean the girl at the top was 12+ feet in the air when it fell apart.

She didn't come straight down; she shot forward because she wasn't thinking and pushed off as the pyramid crumbled. I had only a split second to react, and I made a sprint towards the spot where she was falling. Now, I know this may sound too good to be true, but later that evening, I received a lot of congratulations and free drinks from my peers for that catch, and they would recall it in the same fashion ... as I made my break for the falling young lady, I realized I was not going to be able to get under her to catch her, let alone break her fall. In an act that I can only call desperation, I dove for her. Somehow, I caught her with my arm around her waist, tucked in my shoulder and rolled, deposited her on her feet, and then jogged off to the side of the mat, all in what seemed like a fluid motion.

Needless to say, that pyramid crumbling rattled the team, and the rest of their routine was shaky, and they didn't place. Which is a shame because that meant the save wasn't televised, at least not by the network cameras. And thus, I'll never know if it looked as cool as I thought it did or as all my buddies played it up to be.

Even during all the excitement, the drinking, and the ladies, my mind was solely on Kaci, and my conversation always seemed to direct back to her. This actually made Larry quite happy because, for the first time in a long time, he saw me happy.

Our Christmas break was cut short since all Barton County cheer and dance members had to begin working on their routines for the spring Collegiate Nationals. When Kaci returned to Great Bend, things seemed different. She was acting aloof. Something told me that something had happened. Deep down, I knew that she had cheated on me.

Don't ask me how I knew. I just did.

In her defense: there's one thing young ladies can't seem to grasp in the mindset of males, in general, but specifically the 'players' or those who verbally and/or physically push a woman into sex. In the guy's mind, the woman is a piece of meat, and once they have had sexual relations with her, they can come back and get whatever they want whenever they want it because 'she is theirs.' It's a very sick mindset. I have seen it played out over and over in my life. These jerks push a woman into doing something she doesn't want, then months, even years later, when she finds a guy who is treating her with respect, they come along expecting sex again. Unfortunately, these women find themselves feeling trapped in a situation where they are seemingly stuck, and the predator wins again.

Kaci had never told her friends that the guy they set her up with over the summer had date-raped her. So, when she went to a party with these friends and the predator was there, they were clueless. He knew the game, she thought she was safe, he waited for her to get drunk, and then pushed her further than she ever wanted to go … again.

At that point, all I was really concerned about was Kaci. I cared for her more than anyone I'd ever known, and I just invested as much of my time in her as I could. Slowly, the walls around her came back down, and we began hanging out again.

There was never a time when I said, "Hey, do you want to go steady?" or "Do you want to be my girlfriend?" or anything like that. Our relationship had started in the fall as friends and just built from there. And just as a side note, from the very start, Kaci encouraged me to pursue my dream.

Later that month, she went back home for the weekend to visit her family and to work. She was a waitress and earned good money. As is common in Kansas in January, a blizzard came through and shut down the roads, leaving Kaci stuck at her family's home between Salina and Bennington. This was back in the day when a cell phone looked more like a small piece of luggage, and a lot of people didn't have them. What people did was make a long-distance call on a landline phone, and it was somewhat expensive.

So, she called me. We talked for hours. That was one big phone bill, which her mom still brings up from time to time, and we all laugh about it.

As the days rolled by that January of 1996, Kaci began to see that I wasn't going anywhere and that I was interested in her as a friend, not for sex, and we became inseparable. Because of the hurts I had piled on myself from listening to the whole 'you have to have sex before you're 16 to be a man' junk, and because of the tender heart and conscience my parents instilled in me during my youth, I simply did not act like a player, and I refused to treat women like a piece of meat.

One of my pledge brothers, Harvey, came to visit me for my birthday in February of 1996. He couldn't believe how far out into the middle of nowhere I had moved. "Good Lord, Neely! Did you move to the edge of the earth?" By this time, I had pretty much stopped using drugs, and drinking was only for social occasions. Harvey and I had some drinks and sat around and caught up. Later that night, Kaci came over, and we all went out to eat together. My pledge brother told me, "Kaci is the sweetest person I've ever met. Do not let go of her, no matter what!" I told Harvey that I thought she was the one. He agreed.

While Kaci and I claimed our Christian heritage and upbringing when it suited us, neither of us were 'saved.' If we had died at that moment, we both knew that we would have heard those horrible words, "I never knew you," when we looked into the eyes of our Creator. I say that to preface what happened next: that night, when I took Kaci home to her apartment, I stayed over, and I didn't leave her side after that.

We would go to school early in the morning to study together, do all of our classes, workouts, and practices before riding back to her apartment. I left my clothes and stuff at Larry's, but I don't think I spent one night there after my birthday.

Our schedules heated up as spring drew near. The dance and the cheer teams were heading to the nationals, and it was intense. The dance team looked pretty tight, but all eyes were on the cheer team. As a team, we were doing elements that only a few elite individuals here and there were doing. For instance, the new big stunt at the time that wowed the crowds was the guy popping his partner into the air with so much force that she did a backflip and landed with him catching her by her feet and leaving her standing in his hands. This stunt was called a 'rewind to hands.' Well, our whole squad did 'rewinds to lib,' meaning we tossed our girls in the air with so much force that she did a backflip and we caught her above our heads by just one foot, and the girl had her other foot raised up by her knee. We did this in a V formation with the first couple starting and the others following suit ... it was like a wave motion that went through the formation. Then, one by one, each girl would grab the bottom of their foot that was raised and stretch it out to the side. As if that was not enough, then we would pop our girls into the air again, where they would do a double spin before landing in our arms.

That was just one of the elements we had as a squad that really impressed people.

Our squad walked into the NCA Nationals in Daytona, FL, that spring of 1996 with a lot of confidence. It was justified, too – our team members had fantastic abilities, and we had trained hard. What we did not count on was the few young ladies on the squad who had never before competed at such a level.

Because Larry and I had been in the backstage area as spotters on several occasions, we recognized the look in their eyes, but there wasn't a thing in the world we could do but hope for the best. We went out on the floor with much anticipation. We started rocking our routine, and we were rolling. We nailed the hardest part of the routine, the ripple-up rewind to lib, and the girls all stretched their legs out on time. Then it unraveled. For whatever reason, when we popped the girls for the double-twisting dismount, two of the ladies flipped out. And just like the girls in the high school team, they didn't recover, which affected the rest of the routine.

We ended up with a 3rd place finish. That was a complete kick in the cookies for all of us competitors because we knew we were the best. The dance team totally rocked the competition, and they walked away with a 2nd place finish. For this, we all got together and partied. Of course, the ladies on the dance squad lovingly gave us crap about out-placing us. It was all in good fun. At the end of the day, we were proud of them for going out there and nailing it. Right before the celebration, as we were walking by some of those old-style candy machines, I took out a dime, inserted it into a machine, twisted the knob, and got my little bubble from the dispenser. Inside was a yellow toy ring with a smiley face on it. In my unorthodox style, I walked Kaci out on the pier, pulled out the smiley face ring and asked her to marry me. Thankfully, she loved my creative quirkiness and said, "Yes."

From that point on, we began planning our life together.

After we got back to Great Bend, one form of business was replaced with another. Now, instead of preparing for games or competitions, many of us were focusing on where to go next. Because Kaci and I had given our hearts to one another, we were looking at going to the same university. That spring, Kaci, Larry, and I all received our acceptance letters from the University of Kansas in Lawrence.

Larry and I were rock solid from all the weight training and gymnastics we did to prepare for the nationals, so we decided on a different course at KU, and we were going to try to walk onto the football team. In the meantime, we went to Lawrence at the weekends to look at apartments. During this time, as we continued to talk about our life together, Kaci and I determined that we should get married that July so we could live together without the fear of our families finding out we were doing so as an unmarried couple.

In mid-April, as we were heavy into apartment hunting as well as finishing school, Kaci came back to her apartment one morning with tears in her eyes. She could barely look at me and wouldn't talk to me. Fearing the worst, I convinced her to tell me what was on her mind.

"I took a pregnancy test this morning. I'm pregnant," Kaci told me as she began to cry, mostly out of fear that I would bolt.

My response shocked her, "That's awesome!"

I hugged her and comforted her, telling her how excited I was to be a father and to spend the rest of my life with her. But a new fear set in. Now we had to tell Kaci's parents.

While I knew that my parents would wish that we would have done it the right way, I also knew they would be excited and wouldn't give much push back. After all, while they didn't know the extent of my issues, they were not totally naïve, nor were they in the dark that I had troubles. For several years, my mom had braced herself to receive a call to say that I had gotten a girl pregnant. She was overjoyed that it was Kaci and that we were getting married.

It was more of a horrific shock to Kaci's family.

There are valid reasons why God says 'no' to premarital sex. I'd already experienced the inner turmoil it caused when I crossed the line with my high school girlfriend, and I'd suffered the emotional pain of our separation. Now, I had to face another fact: it didn't matter how our families reacted, at the core, our sin affected them as well as us. We dishonored our families, bringing shame upon them. You can debate this however you want, but even amongst families that don't want anything to do with God, parents still hope for the best for their children. Anything less than that results in them feeling like failures, and they believe that everyone looking in from the outside views them as such.

We made each other look foolish, too. I felt like I had let Kaci down and made her look like a slut. I also felt like I made myself look like an undisciplined player who couldn't keep himself behind his zipper. On Kaci's side of the coin ... well, I can't fully speak for her, but I can tell you that there was a lot of shame associated with her pregnancy.

We *were* super-excited to be parents, but this cloud hung over our heads.

We had both met each other's parents previously. I had gone to stay the weekend with Kaci's family near the end of January (in separate rooms, of course!) and had been back to visit them a couple more times after that.

The initial phone call with her mom was rough. We couldn't really blame them for being upset. We made the trip to their house that weekend, to see them face to face and discuss the future. We looked forward to that about as much as having a red-hot poker shoved into our eyeballs!

I was willing to endure it because I loved Kaci, and after meeting her family that first time, I loved them as well.

When we pulled up, we were greeted with hugs. Yes, everyone was disappointed, but they put that aside to show that they still loved us. It didn't mean we were off the hook; there were still some tough questions we had to answer, but first and foremost, we knew we were loved.

It was that weekend, around the dinner table, that Kaci's dad said to me, "It will be a blessing to have you as part of this family and as a son-in-law." That gave Kaci and I a peace that was well needed.

By the end of the weekend, our wedding date was set for May 5, only two short weeks later.

I was 21, Kaci was 20.

We also decided that neither of us would attend the University of Kansas. Instead, we settled close to Kaci's parents, and I started looking for a university closer to where we lived.

PART SEVEN

TWO BECOMING ONE-ISH

The Wall Is Built

Kaci and I were excited about our life together with a child. Others, not so much. It seemed like folks came out of the woodwork to derail our relationship. Of course, we had done enough damage to one another before we ever knew the other existed, and all of that would soon be on the table.

During my time as an NCA staff member, there was a young lady from Overland Park who I really liked. We worked on a lot of camps together and were inseparable for a while. I had even taken her home to Cosby for a weekend. She had lived in the city her whole life and had never experienced the countryside. She had never ever seen the stars! That was a city girl, right there!

She was a student at Kansas State University, and when I moved to Barton County, we were only a few hours away from each other. Smitten, I gladly took her number, thinking things would work out because we were closer geographically.

That fall semester of 1995, before anything had materialized with Kaci, I called her several times a week, leaving messages each time. Not once did I receive a return call. After several months, I took the hint. Wouldn't you?

Now that Kaci and I had announced our marriage, I got a surprise phone call. It was her.

Thankfully, I had been a complete gentleman with her, so the conversation, for my part, was much easier. However, she conveyed how hurt and disappointed she was that I had cast aside our relationship. I was probably a tad colder than I should have been, but as you've read, people had kicked me around and treated me like this my whole life. As far as I was concerned, she had played me and was the enemy.

Because that call came to Kaci's apartment, I had some explaining to do.

Yet, thoughts kept nagging me: *How did she even find out? How did she get Kaci's number?*

Over the next few weeks, 'friends' went out of their way to spend time with me and tell me all of Kaci's sexual exploits while at Barton County Community College. Without Kaci's knowledge. While I was crushed, I could see how that young lady from Kansas State found out. Someone had clearly called her.

Without a doubt, there was a concerted effort to break Kaci and me up. And it nearly worked.

With all of Kaci's baggage in my lap and a little over a week to go until our wedding, I was hurt in the worst way possible. I confronted her. The look on her face was one of complete horror. We both sobbed uncontrollably. It was the deepest form of hurt either of us had ever experienced.

Kaci can tell you that, at the time I confronted her, she felt me distance myself from her. That distance grew over the years as I built an emotional wall that I would not allow her to penetrate. While I still loved her, she had hurt me just like all the others, and I would not allow her to ever get close enough to do that to me again.

The look of horror on Kaci's face that night was because she had hoped no one would ever know. She was deeply ashamed. Years later, I found out that every instance was date rape. She had made her 'no' clear to the guys in question, but they had forced themselves on her anyway. Sadly, Kaci blamed herself, reasoning that she'd been drinking and placed herself in bad situations. I guess that's how some women deal with it. All I know is that she was trying to sweep everything under the rug and not deal with it.

Many times, early in our marriage, she would feel like the walls were coming down, but just as she was getting close, I would give her an emotional stiff arm, keeping her at a distance.

Sin Splatters

The last few chapters will feel like a magical day at Disney World compared to what I have to write here.

While I want to give you an unabridged look into my life, I also want to protect others involved from being dragged through the mud. So, I will be keeping details to the minimum.

It's true that Kaci made the mistake of putting herself into situations that did not play out well, but what happened to her wasn't her fault. And let's be clear, it certainly did not give me the license to do what I did. As a matter of fact, what I accomplished was to simply pile more anguish onto the person I love so much that I cannot fathom life without her. She's so incredibly amazing that she has given me her full permission to tell this part of my story, even though it exposes just how much I hurt her. Like me, Kaci wants you, the reader, to see and understand the redemptive and healing nature of Jesus Christ in our lives individually and in our marriage. If it weren't for Him, our marriage would not have survived the damage I did to it.

Pastor Ron Bowell, the pastor of the church we later joined, uses the phrase, 'sin splatters.' Meaning it never only affects just you. In this case, the sins of others splattered all over me, and I did not have the tools to deal with it in a healthy manner. Thus, the hurt nearly broke me. I've heard people say: 'Hurt people, hurt people,' and that was my situation. I was hurt, and I wanted everyone around me to hurt, especially Kaci.

The other thing I've learned about sin from Pastor Ron is that sin distorts logic. In the aftermath of a person's sinful actions, they always try to make sense of it, but I can tell you first-hand that they won't find any logic to it ... the path to sin is not logical at all. And it's a slippery slope. With one seemingly small step, sin will suck you in and ensnare you.

So, how did I get sucked in?

After the fallout and hurt of my first girlfriend, I had abstained from sex. I had plenty of girlfriends, and we did push the limits, but when it came to sex, I never crossed that line. Not knowing that Kaci's sexual past was date rapes, I believed that she had consented, and I was deeply hurt that she had not made the same choice to abstain.

With every minute, hour, and day that passed, the deep, deep hurt turned into an anger that eventually boiled over into rage and the desire for vengeance.

Even though I had a ring on my finger, having entered the covenant of marriage with Kaci, there were plenty of pretty women who paid me more attention than I should have received and accepted.

And I exacted revenge.

That revenge was in the form of casual adulterous flings. I wanted Kaci to feel every single incident the way I had been caused to relive every one of her incidents. In my anger, I was even so brash as to tell Kaci that I would get even. And by 'even' I meant that I would have the same number of sexual partners as she did. No more, no less. We would be 'evenly yoked.'

As I type this, I am shaking my head in shame. I can't believe I even thought that way. Yet, at the time, it seemed so rational, so logical. However, logic was indeed distorted.

Ironically, while I was the one cheating while married, I would bring up the past, remembering when Kaci had been 'unfaithful' that first Christmas we were together, and I would hurl accusations at her. She denied what happened. There were all kinds of shame and pain attached to it for Kaci, and it ran incredibly deep. No doubt, my behavior wasn't encouraging her to open up, either.

After each incident, I was overcome with guilt and shame, but after a while, the anger would set in again and slowly boil to overflowing, and then I'd find another willing girl.

I know Kaci was somewhat aware of my misdemeanors when they occurred, but once they were behind me, there came a time when I confessed. I will never forget the look of hurt on her face. I suddenly realized what I had done and how deeply I had hurt the person I loved more than life itself. My sin had splattered over her.

Concurrent with my anger towards Kaci was anger directed elsewhere. For years, I kept it hidden until men began coming up to me after our concerts and events telling me the thoughts and urges they'd had in similar situations.

I'm not just talking one or two men over the years. I'm talking dozens, if not hundreds of men who were in the same boat!

What is that boat? For ladies, this may be horrifying; I know Kaci was horrified when I told her. For men, it may be freeing to know that others have these horrific thoughts. Men – you are not alone.

The thoughts? They were thoughts that put the well-being of others in danger.

Let me explain. Because of the small-town nature of Great Bend and those so-called friends who divulged all the gory details of Kaci's past, I knew each guy Kaci had been with by name, and I knew where they were from. With technology advancing, it was not long before I knew where they lived, and I knew all about their spouses, children, and families. As the men who spoke to me after concerts also conveyed: the thoughts of subduing these men and forcing them to watch unspeakable acts done to their loved ones constantly dominated my thoughts. The rage played in my mind, and I'd invent scenarios that would make those men understand the deep hurt and pain they had inflicted on me. I wanted them to feel it for the rest of their days, never escaping the images, as I could never escape what I saw them doing with my wife.

This is why I am pretty passionate about giving young people the best possible information before they become sexually active. If young men and women knew they were potentially putting their future spouse, children, and families in danger, would they make better choices?

It's only a matter of time before we will read or hear in the news of a man snapping. We likely already have, but the reasons were

129

withheld or unknown. This is especially the case as our population continues down the road of promiscuity, denying the truth and value of Jesus and His teaching.

You see, there's a lot that no one is saying about sex! As I've already stated, there are valid reasons God says 'no.' It's not just a generation of old folk being prudes. God tells us to abstain until marriage to protect us. At the risk of appearing overly dramatic, it is a case of life and death.

And this is common to all men and women.

I wish I could say that all my hurt, anger, and rage was something that plagued me only in my BC days (Before Christ), but sadly, I cannot. Just because I came to know Jesus, I didn't immediately begin skipping through green pastures. The anger, the hurt, and the unforgiveness were all so raw. And let's also not forget that every one of us are human beings, and even the best of us are a mess on the greatest of days.

Even as of this writing, both Kaci and I feel pain from the bad choices we made beginning in high school. To paraphrase the writer of Proverbs, 'When a man goes the way of the harlot, it will follow him to the grave' (see Proverbs chapter 5). In other words, the hurts of sexual sin will only leave us when we leave this world.

Pipe Fitting

Following our shotgun wedding, Kaci's family put out feelers on my behalf for summer employment.

Her Uncle Rick owned a gas station in Bennington, KS, and he turned out to be a great resource as he had access to a steady flow of patrons at the station. Uncle Rick found me a great-paying summer job with an outfit of pipe fitters who were working on an expansion project at the Russell-Stover plant in Abilene, KS.

Pipe fitting in itself is a very physical trade. However, the pipe fitters were part of a trade union, and I was not a member of the union. I was there to do all the non-union support work, which turned out to be very physically challenging, but the pay was great.

One such job was punching holes through an explosion-proof concrete wall between the new expansion and the boiler room with a hammer drill. Temperatures outside in the Kansas heat were over 100 degrees so you can imagine what it felt like in the boiler room. On top of the heat, there was a heavy ammonia odor around the boiler room. It took me weeks to make those holes. It was brutal.

While I've since heard horror stories about union and non-union workers fighting, that was not the case on this job. I was very respectful of those men and their work, and they gladly included me in all of their conversations during break times. Collectively, as well as individually, they encouraged me to work hard in university, and they warned me not to let the high pay of their profession, or others like it, lure me away. There was a lot of male bravado and crass jokes around the break table, but those men were also very serious, and they lamented the fact that their employment took them away from their families.

Their words, as well as the back-breaking work, were not lost on me, and I came out of that summer job with a renewed vigor to work hard at my education. While I would still struggle with anger, I had a deep sense of making a good life for Kaci and our child. I knew I couldn't do that by screwing around and leaving university with a low GPA.

Added to that, the words of my former guidance counselor at Savannah High School were playing in the back of my mind, "You'll be lucky if you can get a job at McDonald's," and I was adamant to prove her wrong.

"I've Got Music in My Head..."

For the life of me, I can't remember the exact date I bought my first guitar. I do know it was sometime between the winter break of 1995 and my 21st Birthday in February 1996. It was an inexpensive, but beautiful, Sunburst Gibson Epiphone electro-acoustic. It was special for many reasons, but mainly because it was a *playable* guitar.

I had acquired two other guitars during my first two years of college. One was an old Silvertone that belonged to Grandpa Heckman, which my parents gave to me as a Christmas gift in 1993. It had no strings and was in pretty bad shape. I acquired the second guitar at the TKE house. It was a cherry-red Ibanez electric guitar. I had no amplifier or working knowledge of the instrument, so it was worthless to me. Who knows, with a little know-how, either of those instruments could have been amazing.

I traded that cherry-red Ibanez guitar in for the Epiphone (I had to part with some cash too). I also bought a couple of Mel Bay guitar books, thinking I could teach myself. The guitar was a good purchase, but with my learning style, the books were worthless.

The summer job helping the pipe fitters not only gave me the drive to succeed in education, but it also gave Kaci and I a nice financial cushion. One of the things we knew we would spend money on was guitar lessons. While there was a lot of hurt in our relationship, she was still very supportive of my dream.

We couldn't listen to the radio in Central Kansas without hearing a particular advert with a raspy voice: *"Hi, this is Steve Hanson from S. M. Hanson Music..."* and Steve would continue by talking about the joys of learning guitar. These ads seemed to be on every radio station and played multiple times every day. As I asked around, this was the consensus: Steve was not only a legendary guitarist, but he was also THE best guitar teacher in Central Kansas.

That was all I needed to know. Steve was going to teach me to play the guitar!

In July of 1996, I pulled up outside of S. M. Hanson Music in Salina. I was a nervous wreck.

I entered the store, and a salesman by the name of Lonnie greeted me and asked me what he could do for me.

"I need to talk to Steve Hanson about taking guitar lessons," I replied.

Lonnie was in the middle of telling me how Steve's schedule was completely full and that he wasn't taking any more students when Steve walked out of his studio. He stopped, introduced himself, and asked what he could do for me.

"Sir, I need you to teach me to play the guitar."

Steve replied, "My schedule is completely full, and I've got a list of people waiting."

"Sir, I have music in my head, and I need you to help me get it out," I said.

Steve looked at me incredulously, "Son, come into my studio. I've never heard anyone say that before."

Once in his studio, he asked me to sit down and said something to the effect of, "OK, give me a taste of some of the music that's in your head."

I knew this was a sink or swim moment. I took a deep breath and belted out a country song I had written about Kaci called *Man, Did I Lie*. It was a catchy, upbeat song that I wrote expressing my love for her.

Steve's jaw nearly hit the floor.

"You wrote that?!?! My Lord! That is a great song! Wait right here!" he said as he dashed out of his studio, rounded up everyone in the store, and ushered them into his studio.

"Sing that song again for these folks!"

I did.

The response was nothing short of amazing! Immediately after finishing, everyone clapped wildly and showered me with praise and encouraging words. Some stuck around, waiting to shake my hand and introduce themselves to me.

Once all the hubbub died down, and everyone had left the studio, Steve sat down next to me, looked me in the eyes and said, "I'm making a spot for you. We will start next week."

From decades of teaching guitar, Steve had designed and refined a simple method that got students quickly strumming recognizable songs that were currently playing or had been recently played on the radio. At the same time, he snuck in the mandatory lessons where students learned simple nursery rhymes. Steve's method fed right into my style of learning, and I soaked it up like a sponge! It didn't hurt that my guitar went with me nearly everywhere I went.

It's pretty amazing when I look back on it. Between family, work, and university, I learned the guitar so quickly that after one year of lessons, Steve approached me to teach his overflow of beginner and intermediate students. All the while continuing lessons with him.

Kansas Wesleyan University

I had three university options: Brown Mackie College, Kansas State University – Salina Campus, or Kansas Wesleyan University. For weeks, I poured over their degree offerings. Finally, I chose to study computer science at Kansas Wesleyan University.

This was new territory for two main reasons:

First, I grew up in an era where it was uncommon to have a personal computer at home. Shoot, no one I knew had even heard of the Internet! I had typed out some school papers on an old mainframe system at Northwest Missouri State University, but it was always with help from a librarian or some other staff member. I was completely computer illiterate!

Second, Kansas Wesleyan was a private Christian establishment, which meant it was expensive, and scholarships would not cover the whole expense. So, for the first time in my college career, I was going to have to take out student loans and actually pay for my education.

Back then, transferring course credits between educational institutes took much longer than today because it was not the electronic age. If my transcript was done on a computer, that was it. From there it was sent snail mail (via the United States Postal Service).

With my transcript in hand, I walked into the registrar's office to begin the enrolment process. As the lady looked over my transcript, she began glaring at me. I later learned the reason for her glare – she had been a young, single mother who fought and clawed her way through school to provide for her children. She could clearly see from my transcript that I had treated what she had to fight for as a ticket to party.

Through the process, I found out that I had too many credits in one area: physical education. I had taken so many messing-around courses like golf and target shooting that I had 19 credit hours that would not count towards my degree. It was literally a full semester wasted.

Moving forward, I couldn't afford that kind of a waste.

I needed to take a certain number of elective courses, and the good news was that I could cover that number with music courses. With a music program that had fallen into shambles and some fresh blood in the music faculty, I was accepted into the music program and told that I could graduate with a Major in computer science and a Minor in music.

Regrettably, I fell short of getting my Minor in music by two classes – Music Theory I and Music Theory II. At the time, I was not ready for those courses, and I would have failed them miserably.

Since it was a private Christian university, two of the required courses for all students was Old Testament Prophets and New Testament. The problem: the professor who taught those courses taught from a whacked-out perspective that furthered my disdain for Christianity.

However, I had wonderful professors for my science and math courses, and I later found out that they were both believers in Jesus. They utilized the courses they taught to prove the existence of God without ever preaching or proselytizing. Simply using their disciplines of science and math, they equipped us with the ability to critically think through problems. One problem they helped me solve without my even knowing I was doing it: the existence of God.

It took years for the light bulb in my head to go on and for me to realize what they had done. They helped me overcome the barriers in my mind. The hard part would be to overcome the barriers in my heart.

All in all, Kansas Wesleyan was a blessing. I was surrounded by amazing professors and members of staff who really helped me through two intense years of education. As a young married father, I maintained over 20 credit hours per semester (the average was 18), worked two, sometimes three, jobs, performed with the university choir, and did piano recitals (I took four semesters of piano, which I have all but forgotten). Plus, I played my guitar every moment I could pick it up, and during my second year of studies, when Steve Hanson approached me about teaching his overflow students, I began teaching 15 – 30 beginner and intermediate guitar students every week.

Those two years, with all of that on my plate, I was a straight-A student earning the honor of being on the President's List every semester.

There was one problem. I was on a college campus, and I quickly sniffed out where I could get drugs. As the hurt over Kaci's past settled deeper, I turned to drugs and alcohol again so that I didn't have to feel.

Allison

Kaci discovered that our baby would be born near Christmas. This was a relief as my finals would be over, and I'd be able to focus on Kaci and the baby.

Along the way, Kaci developed some pregnancy-related health issues. She had something called preeclampsia. Basically, Kaci had high blood pressure, swelling in her hands and lower legs, and impaired vision. Tens of thousands of women and children die from preeclampsia in the United States annually. It was pretty serious, and the doctor was very concerned. I remember the stress and fear of losing my wife and baby. The hurt had already taken hold by then and developed into anger, but this was a wakeup call. I realized that I might lose my beautiful wife.

It was my first but not my only wakeup call regarding Kaci. I received many more after this one, and I ignored them all for many years.

After my summer job with the crew of pipe fitters, I took a job at a local restaurant chain as a waiter/server where Kaci worked. This was actually great for our relationship. We loved working together and made a great team when it came to looking after each other's sections when busy times hit. After all, happy customers generally meant better tips, and better tips meant our family survived. Plus, it took our minds off all the other junk.

Waiting tables is a rather demanding job, and it required Kaci and myself to be on our feet for long periods. This didn't fare well with her preeclampsia diagnosis, but Kaci knew she couldn't stop working, so she pushed through it.

While I still looked very physically fit on the outside, I was not healthy at all. Not only had I resumed my drug and drinking habits to numb the pain, but my nutrition was horrible, my stress was through the roof, and I was smoking cigarettes like a chimney.

Around the beginning of December, as I was working through my finals and getting little to no sleep, I began to get sick. I tried all the over-the-counter remedies, but it kept getting worse. It got to the point where it hurt to breathe, like I had needles in my chest. Worried, Kaci took me to see the doctor. The doctor was visibly worried. She said, "You have walking pneumonia." She wrote out a prescription as well as a to-do list, then said, "You are very, very sick. If you want to see your child born, you better follow these instructions to the letter."

I followed the doctor's orders rigidly. There was no way I was not going to be present when my first child was born.

Thankfully, the sickness broke, and I made a full recovery. When I returned to the doctor, she was relieved and pleased. And I was relieved and pleased that I would be able to be with Kaci in the hospital.

The doctor may have been pleased with how I was doing, but she was not pleased with what was going on with Kaci as a result of her preeclampsia.

On December 12, 1996, the doctor told us that Kaci had to be admitted to hospital. She and our baby girl were in danger, and Kaci needed to be induced immediately.

Shortly after Allison was born, she was whisked away from us. She was jaundiced and had low oxygen levels in her blood due to some fluid on her lungs. Kaci stayed in a small room in the hospital for the next several days as Allison was kept under constant care. Allison was under an oxygen bubble to increase the oxygen in her blood as well as special lights to help with her jaundice.

I was at the hospital every chance I could get. But without Kaci working, I had to pick up double shifts. This was doubly exhausting, not only because I was at the restaurant from opening to closing time, but also because it was the Christmas season, and the restaurant was constantly busy.

Unfortunately, there are some pretty mean people out there, and they seem to take joy from being mean to restaurant staff while being overly demanding. While Kaci and Allison were in the hospital, I had the distinct pleasure (not!) of waiting on one of the worst couples I have ever met in my life.

Because the restaurant was busier than usual, there was a long wait for people to be seated. My section was, as we would say in the restaurant, 'slammed.'

Up until this point, my day had been great. All of my customers were jovial and very interactive. Being a people person, I would try to have fun with the customers at my tables while remaining respectful of their privacy.

As one of my tables cleared, and I bid those customers farewell, a new couple was seated. I greeted them and asked how they were enjoying their day. Nothing. Just glares. So, I proceeded to ask them if I could start them off with something to drink. The way the lady spoke to me startled me. She was full of pure hatred ... I had never before experienced somebody treating a perfect stranger, let alone myself, that way in public.

I continued to serve them happily, which I imagine just made them angrier. The nasty comments continued, as did their demands. Every time I fetched them something, I was met with another demand for something else. Even my other customers noticed. One older lady grabbed my wrist and said, "I'm so sorry you're being treated like this." Yet, the mean couple was oblivious to the fact that they were making fools of themselves.

Eventually, the stress of Allison being in intensive care, Kaci staying 24-7 at the hospital, and me trying to be there while working double shifts broke me. I don't remember what the couple said to me, but my response was something like this: "My wife just gave birth to our first child, and our little girl is now in intensive care. I'm working double shifts trying to make ends meet, but all I can think about is being at the hospital with my family, not here being treated like this. Is there anything else I can do for you before I bring you your check?"

Finally, they were speechless. And they had a look of shock on their faces. The customers at my other tables beamed, and a few of the older gentlemen gave me a wink and a nod as I continued to make my rounds serving them. After that, the manager on the floor (I had kept her in the loop about the situation, and she had also visited the table to catch a few angry insults herself) dealt with the couple.

My tips were pretty amazing that day. I'm sure those folks who witnessed that angry couple constantly berating me and heard my declaration made some pretty hefty contributions towards that.

I don't recall how long Allison was in the hospital. I do remember the relief of taking her and Kaci home to our little brick apartment not more than a block away.

Now came the most terrifying part: raising the child.

I wanted the world for Allison, and that meant her not following in the footsteps of Kaci or myself. This ended up being a big challenge because Allison was strong-willed to the max. On a scale of 1 to 10, Allison was about 32 or maybe 63.

It was so bad that, years later, after we came into a relationship with Jesus and we were attending a church in Salina that would be described as 'Spirit-filled' in churchianity terms, we took her to a man to see if he could 'pray the demon out of her.'

Hey, don't judge! Desperate parents take desperate measures!

When we walked into the church to meet the man, Allison caught wind that something was up. She bolted.

She ran up and down the rows of chairs in the church, screaming, "No! No! No!" over and over.

After several minutes of observing us chasing her, desperately trying to catch her, the man said to us, "That child don't have no demon. What she needs is a good spanking!"

As she grew, we tried that, and more. But the real problem was not her; the problem was that Kaci and I were a divided front. Allison, just like any other child, sensed that and ran wild with it.

Our First Home

Despite the hurt, Kaci and I were a great team. We really were made for one another. She is a great researcher, and when she is on a task, she will turn over every stone until she finds an answer.

Somewhere along the line, we heard that Kansas had a first-time homebuyer program and that mortgage payments were generally less than rental amounts. Of course, we would rather own than rent, especially if we could save money!

So, Kaci began making inquiries and eventually found out that what we had heard was true. We could buy a home, and our monthly payment would be nearly half of what we were paying in rent.

It didn't take us long to find a little starter home on the west side of Salina, a cute two-bedroom house with an attached garage. It was slightly less than 700 square feet, around twice the size of the tiny one-bedroom apartment we had been renting.

Kaci's dad, Ken, was a former carpenter, who co-owned a construction company. This house was the beginnings of my learning to do fixer-upper projects. The days in my dad's garage may have made me a good assistant, but I had no idea how to plan out or dig into a project. My father-in-law would cure me of that over the next decade.

I have fond memories of blowing insulation into the outer walls, putting on a new roof, and gutting the bathroom. Ken was always calm, cool, and never really got rustled. He would take something apart and put it back together however many times it took for it to fit perfectly. He was patient and precise. Everything I wasn't!

Kaci and I have fond memories of that home. Equally, we have some horrific memories.

Burnt Toast:
Deep Hurt, Fierce Anger

K aci carried the extreme hurt and pain of her date rapes. Having made a vow in high school to be pure for marriage, only to be verbally and physically pushed beyond her limits, completely wrecked her and pelted her self-worth. She continued to sweep the past under the rug, trying to pretend it never happened. And she made no effort to talk to me about it.

I took her silence to mean something different.

I believed that her silence meant she was not sorry for her actions, and that just made the hurt dig in deeper.

I felt worthless.

With no knowledge of what she had endured, I began to believe that she didn't care about me because I wasn't worth waiting for. I felt like she was laughing at me, the poor nerdy kid who was awkward around girls. Her past screamed at me, saying that she had gone out and sowed her oats while I was too much of a loser to do the same. I became paranoid and jealous. My thought process was: "You obviously didn't care enough about me to abstain before marriage, so what's going to make you stop now?" Of course, that wasn't the truth, but these horrible feelings were part of the consequence of sex outside of marriage.

My self-worth took a sharp nosedive, and depression began to take hold of me.

On the outside, I held a calm, confident look, but on the inside, I felt like an unlovable, unwanted, and worthless pile of crap, like I was just one big mistake that should never have happened.

When a person has that kind of hurt and doesn't deal with it, watch out!

My sweet wife had to put up with all of my outbursts. Sometimes, just the mere sight of her caused those feelings to bubble up, and I would explode into a fit of rage. I would let out primal screams, punch walls, and throw household objects (no matter their value). Then there was also the verbal abuse.

On one occasion, Kaci was trying to hug me, to show that she loved me, and I couldn't handle it. I stormed outside and found an aluminum baseball bat. I beat that baseball bat against a metal pole for what seemed like 10 minutes. I hit the pole so hard, and for so long, that I finally dropped to my knees in exhaustion. If you've ever bought a high-quality softball bat, you'll know they are very expensive. The bat was completely ruined. Smashed nearly flat.

In later years, as we began to share our testimony around the country, I told stories like this one, explaining that men tend to pack their hurts down so deep that when they explode in a fit of rage over something as simple and silly as burnt toast, they aren't actually upset about the toast – it goes much deeper. Men are taught to stuff their hurt deep, so they turn into ticking time bombs ... and that was me.

It turns into a sick, unending cycle. It causes distance in the relationship, which only causes more hurt, which causes more anger, which causes more outbursts, which causes more distance, and thus, the circle is formed, and the cycle is perpetuated.

Because I had a horrible image of God from what I had been taught, I would constantly say, "Why did You do this to me, God?" But the truth was that God didn't do any of it to me. I was living with the aftermath of sexual sin and making it worse for myself.

Yet, a different story is portrayed in the media. The message that bombards us on the big screen and on television, in newspapers and magazines, and from peers is: *There's nothing wrong with exploring your sexual desires. It's just sex. The real problem is those prudish Christians who want to hold us back.*

The interesting thing is that millions have fallen prey to this train of thought, Kaci and I included, and it only served to hurt ourselves, hurt others, and put us in a personal prison that was literally a hell on earth.

Yet, I stand back and look at those who trusted God and knew that what He asked of them was good for them. Their marriages, while not perfect, are filled with so much peace.

You can argue until your face is blue, but you cannot deny the facts.

I was in a prison of hurt, and the sick cycle of anger was in motion. My views of life, love, and sex became perverted, meaning they were out of line with how our Creator designed them to be. While my hideously sinful behavior toward Kaci has long since been dealt with, I am still in the process of unraveling some of these unhealthy views in an effort to become what my Creator intended me to be.

Kansas Cellular

In May of 1998, I graduated with a bachelor's degree in computer science. Now began the daunting challenge of finding an IT job in Salina, KS.

The job pool for professionals wasn't large in Salina, but for a computer guy, it wasn't even a puddle. Not only that, but compared to the money I could have made in another market, it was going to be a tough ride.

I looked through the *Help Wanted* section of the newspaper and submitted my resume to the handful of companies that were looking for a computer help desk technician, a programmer, or a system's administrator/engineer.

The problem: I'd been waiting tables at a high-end steak house as well as teaching quite a number of guitar students. I was making very good money, and all of the positions I applied for would mean a serious pay cut.

After several interviews, none of which I was very excited about, I got a call from Michael, the manager of the IT department at Kansas Cellular.

In 1998, cell phones were a novelty. Not many adults had them. Most cell phone companies were small and operated within equally small regions. There were not many large companies covering the whole United States. In fact, back then, there were two classifications of cellular carriers and where they could cover: metro and rural.

Kansas Cellular was one of the few that saw the potential for covering the large rural landscapes while the other companies clamored to get a foothold in major metro areas where the population was dense.

As companies in those metro areas equipped their sales teams and executives with mobile phones, they began to travel, and those who covered the rural areas cashed in on the roaming charges above and beyond their growing customer base.

The growth of cellular usage in rural areas meant that Kansas Cellular grew and needed to expand its IT department.

The interview process was interesting. I was in a room with Michael, Lee (the director of the IT department), and their system's engineer named John, who was several years younger than me.

I made it clear that I knew I was underqualified for the kind of technology at Kansas Cellular, but I also expressed that I was a quick learner and a hard worker. John made it obvious that he disliked the very sight of me in the room.

While at Kansas Wesleyan, my education focused on programming in several computer languages. I did some work with the IT director at the university to learn PC repair and computer networking. Still, I was way behind the curve. At that time, there were two different technologies: telephony (the standard telephone service) and data. There were racks and racks of expensive equipment to connect those two worlds and bring telephony into the data realm for all kinds of reporting and billing.

Despite John's objections, Michael lobbied for me to be hired, and Lee agreed to give me a chance. The offer: $9.62 an hour, or the equivalent of $20,000 per year.

To this day, this is one of the big gripes I have with companies in Kansas. Kansas Cellular was owned by a management company that owned another company as well, and both occupied the same building. The other company was KINNET Fiber Optics, which had several huge fiber optic rings that covered the whole state of Kansas. Between the two companies, they had around 200 employees and had an annual income that exceeded $250 million and was growing. We had it hung over our heads that for every minute the systems were down, the company would lose $20,000+ in revenue. Yet, I was making less than waiting tables.

Oh, but Kansas has such a low cost of living! Uhm, better check that.

The people of Kansas pay property taxes on their land and homes that are on par with folks I know in New Jersey (which is known for its high taxes). As of this writing, I have as much house in Nashville as I did in Kansas, and I pay only a third of what I used to pay in property tax. Then there is the property tax on vehicles. Every year, not only do folks pay registration fees but a depreciated tax on their vehicle. So, if they own a new vehicle, they'll be paying thousands per year in property taxes for numerous years (and many families in America have multiple cars, so that figure is doubled or tripled). Not to mention that if they sell their vehicle years down the road, there's a sales tax, too.

Yet, the powers that be in the region can't understand why there are no middle-class citizens or why folks won't relocate to Central Kansas. I guess someone will have to draw them a picture.

So, the job offer was not something that Kaci and I took lightly. We talked it over a lot. Of course, she was super proud of me and supportive. She encouraged me that I could do it and would soon be making a better wage. Through it all, she was still by my side: loving, proud, and supportive. In my anger, I was just too blind to see how amazing she was.

I accepted the position and was quickly accepted by everyone on the team. Everyone, that is, except for John. He didn't know me nor my past, yet he managed to surpass everything I'd been through before. I can honestly say that I've never been treated so horribly on a daily basis by any individual in my life. John was great at 'drive-by beratements' – meaning he would say something super degrading as he was walking off to the server room. What he didn't know was how close he was to getting the snot beaten out of him. Several times, I was physically restrained from doing so by a few of my co-workers.

There wasn't one of us on the team who was working less than 70 hours a week. The workload was utterly insane. Plus, we were on rotation to be on call, which made it difficult to switch off at home. We were constantly forced to eat quickly at our desks while working, which generally meant fast food. Stress was through the roof, and my health was failing fast as I gained weight.

By the end of 1999, after 18 months of working at Kansas Cellular, I was well over 230 pounds (approx. 60 pounds heavier than when I started). I had irregular heartbeats, and I was bleeding badly when going to the bathroom. Again, showing a crazy amount of love, Kaci pushed me to go to the doctor. It was not good. He told me that I had to make drastic changes if I wanted a long and healthy existence.

There was something about the way the doctor said this that got my attention and scared me.

Immediately, we bought exercise equipment and a mountain bike. I also started taking weight-loss supplements and began to change my eating habits.

Aubrey

Our marriage was a train wreck before it ever happened, and it was getting worse with every passing moment. We had one child on the ground, I was in a high-stress, low-paying job, and my health was failing. So, what did we do to fix it? We decided to bring another child into the world.

We are super glad that we did. We just wish we had brought her into a better situation.

Aubrey came onto the scene in March of 1999. Thankfully, Kansas Cellular covered all of our health insurance, and we were literally zero out of pocket. At least there was no stress on that front.

However, 1999 was all ramped up to be the end of the world as we knew it with the infamous Y2K.

In a nutshell, back then, we didn't have all the technology we do today, and in an effort to streamline computing power, many code writers entered the year in a two-digit format. For example, instead of '1978', a program would process and store the data as '78'.

The problem was not knowing what would happen once we hit the year 2000. It was hypothesized that when the computers automatically used '00' instead of '2000', it would 'get confused' and just stop working. The fear was that programs would crash or spit out bad data because they didn't know the difference between 1900 and 2000, etc., thus stopping all commerce and thrusting society into the dark ages.

OK, that's probably an exaggeration, but the media made a big thing out of it to scare the life out of people. Why? Because that's what sells. Needless to say, nothing came of it.

Not only were Kaci and I stressed with life, but we were on high alert for preeclampsia or other health-related issues with Kaci and the baby because of her rough pregnancy with Allison.

We were not disappointed.

While carrying Aubrey, Kaci had gestational diabetes, which is way less serious than preeclampsia, but we still had to watch Kaci's blood sugar by taking daily blood samples as well as totally changing our nutrition. As I mentioned, I was gaining weight at an alarming rate, but at the time of the pregnancy and Aubrey's birth, I had not yet experienced the worrying symptoms or seen the doctor. Perhaps if I had changed my nutrition at this time, I would have stifled my weight gain, but then again, I was working 70 to 80 hours a week...

Aubrey ended up being the perfect balance to Allison. Allison is much like me. Growing up as the only grandchild and niece, she thought the universe orbited her. She is definitely her dad's daughter. Aubrey, on the other hand, was quiet, smart, and calculating.

If I could compare Allison and Aubrey to biblical characters, I would compare them to Esau and Jacob, respectively. Just as Esau sold his birthright to Jacob for soup, I saw similar attributes in Allison and Aubrey's dealings together.

Once such situation: when she was around 6 or 7, Aubrey asked for a gumball machine for either her birthday or Christmas. Not a toy one; a real one that took money. Why? Because she had witnessed Kaci and Allison constantly pumping money into gum and candy machines. In her mind, she thought, "Why not make some money off these suckers?"

Another example goes back to when Aubrey was just a toddler. On Christmas Day at Grampa and Grandma Boss' house, she and Allison were going to act out the characters in the Christmas story while we read it.

Of course, the two of them could fight over air, and Christmas was no different. They began fighting over who would play which character. I can't remember exactly how it went down, but it was something like this:

We started Allison off as a shepherd and Aubrey as one of the three wise men ... or vice versa. Aubrey wanted to one-up her older sister, so she said, "I, Mary," which interpreted from toddler-talk meant, "I will be Mary." Not to be outdone, Allison fired back that she would be the angel. They went back and forth until Aubrey put an end to it by saying, "I, God," meaning, "I will play God in this production."

She shut that one down, and the whole family had a good laugh. Wow, how we wish we had cell phones with cameras like we do today! The things we would have captured of those two.

Yet, they both had to grow up with a father who was akin to Dr. Jekyll and Mr. Hyde.

PART EIGHT

THE PRODIGAL RETURNS

Uncle John and Finding the End of My Rope

In December of 1999, I got a phone call at work on my direct line. I heard Kaci's voice on the other end. Breaking up in grief, she said, "Jerm, Uncle John died." I crumpled in my seat.

One blessing that I never stop verbalizing is Kaci's family. All of her grandparents, aunts, and uncles have loved me as one of their own from day one.

Kaci's Uncle John was, like me, an 'outlaw,' meaning he married into the family. He was a fun person to be around, an entrepreneur, and he was a great storyteller. I would like to think that those attributes are ones that I carry.

Uncle John was 52 years of age when he passed away. All of a sudden, 52 didn't seem so old to me as a 24-year-old who was severely overweight and having serious health issues.

That morning, their alarm clock went off. Aunt Carol got up and was getting ready to go to the fitness center. Uncle John told her he didn't feel well and was going to lay back down for a while. When she returned from the fitness center, he was lying curled up in bed, but he was gone.

My mind began racing with fear. The words of the doctor were on my mind. Then after the funeral, as we gathered as a family for a meal, Aunt Carol came up to me, gave me a hug, and with both hands on my shoulders she said, "If you don't take care of yourself, this will happen to you soon." She turned and walked off.

It was one of the most tough and loving things anyone has ever said to me.

It was shortly after Uncle John's funeral that I looked at my pitiful reflection in a mirror. Staring at the emptiness in my eyes that revealed the emptiness in my soul, I thought, "If I die today, my legacy will be rubbish. Surely there must be more to life than this."

Turning over Every Stone

The fear of death is an interesting motivator. The old saying goes, "There are no atheists in foxholes." As I stared into the face of death, I began to reconsider my atheistic position, and I asked myself questions, such as:

What will happen when I die?

Is death really the end?

Is there a God?

I could no longer bring myself to believe that humans cease to exist at death. In light of that, I wondered what the afterlife was like. I reasoned that there must be a higher power, but there was no way I was going to buy into that Christian garbage because of all the hurt I associated with it. No, I would unravel this 'God thing' on my own, and I was confident it wouldn't lead there.

There was a drastic change in both Kaci and me at that time. We both attest that our marriage was not far from being over. However, after Uncle John's death, we began seeking out answers ... together. Although I was obstinately against Christianity as the source of truth in regards to finding God, I began attending a church with Kaci and the girls because I was committed to us searching together.

I was still a handful to live with, but the fear of death and the fear of losing Kaci and the girls was enough to take the edge off my bad behavior. Plus, we were working together to find peace. Remember that cycle of hurt I mentioned before? There was something about working together to find the Lord that began to unravel that cycle. It was miraculous.

One night, as Kaci was watching TBN (I know there are some fruitcakes on there, but hear me out), a show came on called *The Signature of God* hosted by Grant Jeffrey. It was a televised adaptation of Mr. Jeffrey's book by the same title. As he began to show historical, archaeological, and scientific proof of God's signature in creation and tying it back to Scripture, my cynical mind began to clear up, and my hard heart began to melt.

I can't point to a specific day or time and say that was when the truth of Jesus Christ struck me. However, I can say that Kaci and I surrendered our lives to Jesus at some point during the summer of 2000. I can also tell you that Mr. Jeffrey's TV show and book were very important to my journey of discovery. No one had ever given me this kind of proof that the Bible is a real-life, historical document. Now I was hungry for more, and I began reading everything I could find to unravel this great mystery. And in the July of that year, Kaci and I were both baptized at Lake Wassy (which is more of a glorified pond than a lake) just south of Salina.

The prodigal had returned home! In my pain and brokenness, I once again accepted the faith I'd rejected as a teenager. My heavenly Father welcomed me with arms opened wide, and now my 'falling down' was straight into His embrace.

Immediately, my speech cleaned up. Prior to this, I cussed like a sailor. So much so that Allison had dropped the 'F-bomb' at a family gathering, and I am pretty sure other embarrassing utterances came from the lips of our daughters because of what they heard me say at home.

What didn't heal immediately was my addictions. I'm being honest here. Becoming a Christian meant that I was instantly restored into a relationship with God – this was a spiritual thing, and it was very real. However, restoration in the other aspects of my life (emotional, mental, and physical) was – and is – a process. After all, it took me years to get myself into the mess I was in. Any Christian will tell you that believing in Jesus is not like waving a magic wand and making life a bed of roses.

Looking back on that time, I understand that I had deep issues that could not be healed overnight. Primarily, those issues were anger and unforgiveness.

Yet, life *was* different. Brighter. I began to feel at peace.

Added to that, having changed aspects of my lifestyle, my weight was down to 170 – 175 pounds, and many of my health issues disappeared.

Amazing Grace:
Hearing It for the First Time

Kaci's Grandpa and Grandma Boss were a big reason we came into a relationship with Jesus. In my atheist years, I may have opposed and argued with others, but I could never cross Grandpa and Grandma Boss. It wasn't because they had some old-school authoritarian 'respect your elders' air about them, but rather, they were the kindest, most caring, and loving people I had ever met.

They were the type of people who really lived out the Christian faith, and it was 'sticky' – meaning, when I was around them, I wanted what they had in my own life. It was their example that continually challenged my beliefs and the person I had become. No one, myself included, could utter an angry word against them, let alone angrily challenge the faith they lived out so authentically. Eventually, it was their faith that won us over that summer. At first, we attended a church in Salina where Kaci's parents attended.

In 2002, we decided to attend Bennington Bible Church, which was founded, in part, by Grandpa and Grandma Boss in the basement of one of Kaci's uncles. At that time, the church met in the old pool hall (basically, the bar) in downtown Bennington.

Even before that move, we would sometimes go to church with Grandpa and Grandma Boss, and stay for dinner after church.

One of those Sundays, in early 2001, was especially meaningful to me.

Since I grew up in a church environment, I knew all the old hymns by heart. For years and years and years, I'd heard them sung several times a week.

On this particular Sunday morning, as the pastor was wrapping up his message, he asked the worship team to play a song. They began playing *Amazing Grace*.

I don't think I made it to the second word in the song, which is 'grace,' before I crumpled into my seat, sobbing.

Amazing grace, how sweet the sound
That saved a wretch like me
I once was lost, but now am found
Twas blind, but now I see

For the first time in my life, I really *heard* this song, and the truth of it penetrated my heart. I had been a lost and blind sinner, a prodigal who had intentionally turned away from a loving God, but His grace ... His amazing grace had found me, His amazing grace had received me gladly when I returned, and because of His grace, I could finally see the truth of His unending love and mercy.

I was so grateful.

A Purpose to Play Again

At a certain point during my employment at Kansas Cellular, when I gained so much weight, I came to the conclusion that my dream of being a full-time musician was over. I stopped doing gigs, put my guitar in the closet, and closed the door on that dream.

After I came into a relationship with Jesus, I was asked to play on the worship team at the church we attended in Salina. The worship leader was a student of Steve Hanson and had known me for several years. He was excited about my decision to follow Jesus and wanted to get me involved in the worship team. I was more than excited!

From there, I began playing on several different worship teams for events during the week. It felt good to play again.

I was drawn to the ministry and felt like God was telling me He was going to utilize my musical gifts for His glory. I was immature in my faith, so I thought there were only four roles in ministry: pastor, youth pastor, missionary, or worship leader. Since I felt called to ministry, and I was a musician, I reasoned that God wanted me to be a worship leader and write worship songs!

That was sort of, kind of, correct.

From the start, I felt called to 'go,' but I didn't know how or when that would happen. In the meantime, I was, at the very least, playing music again and writing songs. Admittedly, they were super-simple worship songs. As Grandpa Boss would say of some of the worship songs that came out at that time, "They are 7/11 songs. There are seven words, and you repeat them eleven times." It was a true assessment of some of the popular worship songs of that era!

Since it was the popular form, and I was eager to be a part of the movement, that's how I wrote music.

Those songs were not awful, but you'll never hear me play them for you.

They were a good starting point.

"Honey, If He Wants to Flip Burgers..."

I can't remember when I heard, whether it was at the close of 1999 or in early 2000, but the news came that Kansas Cellular was being sold to Alltel.

The news was taken with mixed review. Some people were excited, some worried, and some infuriated. Most of the worry was from those who knew that mergers like this would cost jobs. Just because the IT department was under-compensated didn't mean others were not. As a matter of fact, our department was the only one that was undervalued, and it was all because of our director. I can't tell you why he devalued us and our work, he just did. Other department leaders paid their employees very well.

Actually, let's back up a bit. Before the news of the Alltel merger, I began to sniff out that other departments paid their employees well. Above and beyond that, I was tired of working nearly 80 hours a week only to make the same amount of money as I made when I waited tables two nights a week and taught guitar. So, I took a look in the newspaper to see what IT jobs were available around town. What I found infuriated me and the whole team.

It turned out that the local hospital was looking for a computer technician to troubleshoot and repair PCs. All that was required was a two-year degree. Starting pay, nearly $18 per hour!

All of us in the IT department, except John, had a four-year Bachelor of Science degree in computer science. Many of those guys had been with Kansas Cellular since the company started, almost 10 years previously. Not one of them made more than $12 per hour.

We gave the director of IT the benefit of the doubt and presented this information to him. He hemmed and hawed around the subject and gave us some crap about budgets and performance. In the end, he wasn't going to budge. We came to find out that he was getting paid on par with the other directors, if not the vice presidents, of the company. He sure was taking care of himself.

After much cussing and discussing, I proposed that everyone in the team should write resignation letters and that we should deliver them at the same time. The team recognized that our strength was in numbers, and we knew (or hoped) that, collectively, we had the power to bring about a change.

So, we did just that. In a single-file fashion, we all laid our letters of resignation on the desk of the IT director. The color drained from his face, and he looked like he was about to cry.

Two days later, we all found ourselves in the office of the CEO. He began by taking the side of the IT director, but as we carefully stated our case, his jaw dropped, and he began to question our boss. In the end, the CEO could not believe that we, the team that kept the company running (data-wise), were so grossly underpaid. He promptly declared that all of our salaries would be evaluated. After the dust settled, our salaries were doubled!

Our boss knew that he had lost our respect. He could barely look us in the eye after that. So, the news that Alltel was purchasing Kansas Cellular was good news for him, because he would be treated as an executive and receive a lovely parting gift.

One thing a company does not want to lose during a merger with a company they've just bought is that company's IT staff. Alltel came in and offered us a bonus to stay for one year after the completion of the merger. This was a significant bonus because it was 40% of our annual salaries.

You just read that our salaries doubled, right? Well, Alltel came in and found that even at that new amount, we were underpaid according to IT industry standards. So, they effectively bumped our salaries again.

Not only that, but we would also be taking day trips every so often to Little Rock, AR, where Alltel was headquartered. There are no direct flights between Salina and Little Rock, but that was no big deal to Alltel – they sent their private planes for us! Believe it or not, even that got old pretty fast.

As you can imagine, I took the bonus and stayed on for a year with Alltel. Who couldn't use that kind of money?! Our team only lost three members during the merger. The rest of us had jobs for years to come if we wanted them. I only stayed with Alltel for a little over a year, and I had a plan to utilize their benefits while I was still there.

During that year, our amazing, pay-nothing health benefits were replaced with a different kind of benefit's package. We now had to pay a monthly premium, co-pay for doctor visits and prescriptions, and pay a deductible that was due annually. We did gain the benefit of a medical savings account, which we could use by setting an annual budget for ourselves and then the company would deduct that amount from our paychecks (meaning we avoided paying tax on that money).

Since I was blind without the coke-bottle glasses ... and I mean, I was couldn't-see-the-big-black-E-on-the-top-of-the-eye-test kind of blind ... and because there were no limits on what I could use my medical savings on, I elected to use the money for laser eye surgery.

When I went for my consultation in Salina, the doctor told me that my eyes were so bad that I would still have to wear glasses after the surgery. The best he could guarantee me was 20/30 – 20/40 vision. I still saw this as a win, because the correction for that vision does not require very thick, coke-bottle lenses like I had been wearing for most of my life.

In January of 2000, I went to an eye institute in Kansas City and had eye surgery. The process was fun for a geek like me. I enjoyed seeing where technology and medicine intersected. The best part was after they put the numbing drops in my eyes and began working. As the eye surgeon dried my eyes with Q-tip-like swabs, I could feel the pressure on my eyes and hear a squeak that sounded like a squeegee, but because my eyes were numb, I could stare straight ahead and watch it happen.

After the surgery was a different story. Once the numbness subsided, my eyes felt horrid. It felt like someone had taken a bucketful of sand and packed it into each eye. I took the drugs they gave me to ease the pain, and I passed out. That evening, I woke up and felt a little better, but it still felt like I had loads of sand grinding in my eyes. I took more of the drugs and passed out until the morning. Holy smokes, when I woke up, I could see!

Several days later, I made my way back to the eye institute for a follow-up visit. The doctors were ecstatic with the results. They scheduled yet another follow-up visit with my doctor back in Salina.

When the doctor in Salina saw me, he was excited beyond words. Remember he said the best I could expect was 20/40, maybe 20/30 vision? Well, I ended up with 20/10 vision in one eye and 20/15 in the other! 20/20 is perfect vision, so my vision was now sharper than perfect!

The only downside has been that my eyes produce more oil than normal. At that visit, my doctor explained that it meant I would always see halos around lights at night.

I told him, "Doc, I had that issue with glasses and contacts! Only now I don't have to worry about broken glasses, eye infections from contacts, and other irritations."

Finally, I was rid of one of the big sources of low self-esteem in my life. All thanks to Alltel.

The rest of 2000 brought more changes at work as the merger completed. My role within the group increased, and I traveled more, whether for training or to support other regional call centers.

I discovered that big trading corporations love accounting and reports. And that meant our team had to work harder to justify our existence, whereas before, no one questioned our existence because they knew that without our IT group, the company would have problems.

The accounting mindset brought in a cumbersome process of 'IT trouble tickets.' We would have to log into a program, create individual entries for everything we were working on or had worked on, and log a 'time in' and 'time out' entry to show how long we had worked on that job.

Issues arose because some jobs took longer to log than they actually took to complete. For me, another issue occurred because my role as a system's administrator/engineer meant taking regular trips through to the server room to monitor the servers, server logs, etc. just to stay ahead of potential problems. That kind of maintenance was hard to log for it was just one of those routine things I did.

The trouble tickets were a constant source of stress. Our manager, based in Harrison, AR, constantly badgered us to complete more tickets and threatened that we would face cuts in our department if we didn't. We pushed back, saying we were so busy that we didn't have time to log every little move we made.

That stress, along with the hours I was working (which did not decrease after the merger), along with the increased travel, was making me absolutely miserable.

Not only was that happening, but now that I was a Christian, I was convicted by my lifestyle. Constantly at the front of my mind was my substance abuse, my hurt and unforgiveness, and how I was treating my family. I just didn't want any of it anymore. Not in a suicidal sense, but in the sense that I concluded that I'd rather take a less professional job at a restaurant and have more time with my lovely family. Money didn't really matter to me anymore.

Because my salary had more than doubled and the bonuses were pretty nice, Kaci had grown to love the financial freedom we enjoyed. While she was concerned about me, her mindset was: "There are not many jobs this good in Central Kansas – you can't leave."

It wasn't really a fight between us, just a continuous dialog. Continuous, because I truly was miserable. On the one hand, Kaci was supportive of me and felt my pain, but on the other hand, she was anxious that if I left my job, we would lose everything.

Thankfully, Kaci was a part of a Bible study at the church we attended in Salina. One day, at the end of the study, the group leader asked for prayer requests. Kaci told of my situation, her fears, and asked for prayer.

At the end of the study, an older lady came up to Kaci and asked her if she had a minute. Kaci said, "Of course," and they sat down for a chat. The lady proceeded to tell Kaci her story. Her husband had also been in the telecommunications industry and worked in a very high-stress job. On several occasions, her husband expressed that he would like to change careers because the stress was unbearable. Her reply was always the same: "The money is too good, and we would lose our home." Then, in his early 40s, the stress caught up with him, and he had a massive heart attack. Amazingly, he survived. The lady already felt guilty, but then the doctor told her, "If your husband doesn't cut the stress out of his life, he won't survive another year."

She looked at Kaci and said, "Honey, you can replace a house, you can find an inexpensive used car, you can replace almost anything, but you can't replace your husband. Honey, if he wants to flip burgers, and it makes him happy, you let him flip burgers, and be happy with him."

When I got home from work that day, I knew something was different, and Kaci told me what had transpired. Now we both had peace about me leaving Alltel, and I delivered my resignation letter at the end of the week. Because of my position and responsibilities, it was not two weeks' notice, but months of advance notice. And it took Alltel those months to get someone up to speed to fill my role.

As soon as I handed in my resignation, a huge burden lifted from me. I know it sounds weird, but it felt as if my soul was floating. Consequently, my alcohol and drug abuse subsided a little, although it was still there. Without that stress in my life, I simply didn't think about numbing myself as often.

Granted, we were a little stressed about what we would do for income, but we also knew we could easily wait tables a couple of nights a week to make ends meet if that's what it came to.

Then our church started a campaign to get to know everyone and their needs. We got a call from a couple, and they set up a time to meet with us at our home.

As I mentioned before, there were a few professors at Kansas Wesleyan University who gave me the tools to see God where others may miss Him. This was one of those situations where the mathematical odds were astronomical.

The couple who came to our house were Colin and Connie Cristy. Colin was an electrical engineer and part-owner of a small international manufacturing firm in Salina. Keep in mind, I knew none of this until much later.

After some small talk with Colin and Connie, they asked how we were doing. Kaci piped up and told our story; I filled in the gaps and answered their questions. We had a lovely conversation, and we all prayed together for each other's needs. We never thought much more about it. We were just pleased to know another couple from church.

About a week later, I got a call from Colin. It was then that he told me where he worked and what he did. Next, he said, "We have been praying about bringing on a person to manage our IT needs. Would you be free for a lunch meeting with me and one of my partners? Then we can give you a tour of our facilities, and you can meet the other partners."

Wow! Talk about an answer to prayer!

I found out that the company was formed years previously by two former missionaries. Later, they each brought in a brother as a partner, both of whom were also former missionaries. So, four Christian men, all former missionaries, owned and operated this business. Every Monday morning at 10:00am, they held a devotional time that was open to all employees (but not required). The devotions included one of the owners sharing a piece of scripture and talking about what God had put on his heart, and then everyone prayed for the week. In addition, a group of male employees organized their own weekly lunchtime Bible study. All in all, the atmosphere was one of a family. Oh, and working there would mean never being 'on call' again!

I was offered a job, and I accepted. I told them the commitment I had made to Alltel and that I intended to honor my word, and they totally agreed. My last day at Alltel was December 21, 2000. I was expecting to take some time off to spend Christmas and New Year with my family before starting my new job. Until one Sunday at church...

Kaci and I had signed up to work in the nursery at church, and I was having a blast with the kids. That particular Sunday, as we finished cleaning up and were heading out of the door, one of the owners of the company stopped me and asked, "When are you starting?" I told him that I hadn't yet set a date with the owner who would be my boss. Then that owner told me how their company's retirement program worked, and he suggested that I started before the 1st of January so that 2001 would count towards my retirement fund (starting later would have meant that I wouldn't be eligible until 2002).

My jaw dropped. Did one of the owners of the company just tell me a loophole in their retirement process? Yes, he sure did.

So, I left Alltel on December 21, 2000, and started with a company named Kejr, Inc., known by their industry name of Geoprobe Systems, on December 26, 2000.

That experience taught me just one of the many business lessons that I learned from those former missionaries over the next several years, this one being the biblical principle: do unto others as you would have them do unto you.

It all started with, "Honey, if he wants to flip burgers..."

PART NINE

THE BEGINNINGS OF
A MUSICAL CAREER

"You Can Sing?"

As my new job was underway in 2001, I continued to serve on various worship teams. At some point during the year, a simple yet significant event occurred.

I was at home, sitting in my chair, guitar in hand, practicing worship songs. Because our house was only 700 square feet, Kaci was always in and out of the room. There really wasn't any place to hide in that little house!

One of the big changes we had already made in our lives was how we consumed media in general. Music was huge for us, so it was the biggest change. We boxed up hundreds of CDs and took them down to a local business that bought used CDs. Because I'd kept them in good condition, we got a couple of hundred dollars out of it, and we took that money and went to the local Christian bookstore looking for new music. It was pretty easy for Kaci to find music that she liked, but it was too 'poppy' for me. It took me more time to find some music for my taste. Our radio dials also became fixed on Christian radio stations. We were completely immersing ourselves in the 'Christian culture.'

Because of this change, the songs I was practicing that day were familiar to both of us. I could hear Kaci humming along as she worked around the house. Then, just as I was in the middle of a song, she walked up beside me and began singing along. I was shocked! I stopped singing and looked at her in surprise, I never knew she could sing like that! As I remember it, I even stopped playing.

"You can sing?" I exclaimed with a huge look of joyful surprise on my face.

Realize that we'd been married for five years at this point, and I had no idea that my wife had such an amazing voice. Yes, you can let the man jokes fly right now.

Kaci was shy about her voice, but I gave her an enormous encouraging nudge, and she started singing in the worship teams that I was already involved with. Even now, Kaci is shy about her voice, and I continue to encourage her to shine for her voice is mega amazing.

The moment when I realized Kaci could sing was the beginning of our music career, the birth of the husband-wife duo that would one day be known as NEELY.

The Viaduct

My daily commute to Geoprobe was super easy. It usually took between 5 – 10 minutes, depending on traffic. The worst traffic to be found in Salina is two vehicles driving side by side going 25 miles per hour in a 40 mile per hour zone. That is more common there than you'll ever know! Otherwise, there is not a rush hour. I jokingly say there is a 'rush minute.' It is small-town living at its best.

About a quarter of a mile from what is now known as Geoprobe's Broadway campus is a viaduct that goes over the top of a rail yard. Believe it or not, the trains had an uncanny practice of rolling through Salina, cutting off all north/south traffic at 8:00am and 5:00pm. So, this viaduct was a blessing from the heavens for the inhabitants of Salina.

That, however, is not why I will forever remember the viaduct.

You hear many people say, "I remember where I was when..." such and such event happened. I know I say it. I remember being in Ms. Meade's 6th-grade classroom when I watched the Space Shuttle that was taking the first teacher, Christa McAuliffe, to space explode on live television.

I also remember where I was on September 11, 2001. I was in my car on that viaduct, a quarter of a mile from Geoprobe. When I heard the news on the radio about the first plane that had hit the World Trade Center, I put my foot down and rushed to the office. I skidded into my parking space and sprinted into the building and to my desk. I announced the news as I fired up my computer to see what was going on. No one else in the office had heard the news yet.

The office was in shock.

I remember the chaos at gas stations that day, the phone calls that flooded in from families, and the uncertainties as business crept on as usual.

It taught me a lesson that stuck with me, something that the Lord has used in our music and ministry. After 9/11, people flooded churches by the droves, searching for answers, for truth, for peace. Sadly, the surge in numbers wasn't sustained long-term for people did not find the answers or the peace they were looking for in the place they believed they would find it. Why? This question bothered me because these institutions carried the name that pointed to the only source of peace: Jesus, the Christ.

Lunches at Crossroads

My employment at Geoprobe began with several months of work in the shipping department. This excited me. It allowed me to learn everything about the entire manufacturing process, from how raw materials were brought into the company to how those flowed through different departments and became a product that ended up on shelves in the shipping warehouse ready to be shipped to customers around the world. As a system's administrator/engineer, this was a highly valuable opportunity for me. Many times, companies hire IT staff or contractors who may have some insight into the industry and/or the business they are working in, but they don't necessarily have the hands-on experience to know how the systems work. Therefore, they don't know how changes to those systems will impact day-to-day operations at the ground level.

While working in the shipping department, I met a man who became one of the most influential people in regards to my music and faith: Tony Bowell. After nearly a decade in Nashville, I can honestly say that Tony is one of the best singer-songwriters I've ever had the privilege of knowing.

One of the first things I learned about Tony was that he was the worship leader at a local church that his dad, Pastor Ron Bowell, founded. It was called Crossroads Church.

Hungry for Christian friends and fellowship, as well as a potential musical partner to jam with, I invited Tony to lunch at my house. We had a blast, but two rambunctious kids in a small house didn't make it a great fit for playing music.

So, Tony invited me to have lunch with him at Crossroads. He cleared it with his dad, and I was totally cool with it. Little did I know how much of an impact those lunch trips would have on my life.

First, the spiritual impact. Pastor Ron is a very laid back, loving man with a wealth of knowledge about the Bible and the history surrounding it. Pastor Ron is also a musician. Back in the day, he spent years on the road with his band *Friar Tuck and the Monks*. In the 2000s, Ron and his bandmates were inducted into the Kansas Music Hall of Fame.

Back in the 1960s, Pastor Ron was not a believer in Jesus. As a matter of fact, he was an alcoholic who farmed with his father during the week and then played all over the region on the weekends. His wife, Kerry, who came to faith in Jesus, prayed for her husband. Over time, the grind of farming, touring, boozing, and all the junk of life became too much to bear. Yet, through all of it, Kerry had peace and joy. Ron wanted that.

He became a Christian, and a short time later, he was called to pastor the church he was attending, and he left farming. I'm not sure what happened first, the pastoring or leaving the farm, but what I can remember from Pastor Ron's testimony is that it caused a lot of tension between his father and him. I later wrote a song inspired by Pastor Ron's father's last day on earth and the emotions he must have felt as he reconciled with his son in the last moments of his life. The song is called *Don't Tell Me It's Over*.

Pastor Ron became a spiritual mentor of mine, and he has been one of my biggest cheerleaders and sources of encouragement when it comes to my music. When most people around me were saying, "You can't," Pastor Ron was saying, "God has given you an incredible gift, and you *can*."

Second, the practical impact. Tony didn't just take me to the church to play music, he also taught me about the sound equipment and how to hook up my instrument. Then he made me play and sing through the PA system. There are countless ways Tony's input helped me as a musician, but I'll state two of the most important. Firstly, hearing my voice through a PA system for the first time shocked me. It sounded slightly different to what I heard in my head and completely different from how I perceived myself sounding in everyday interactions. This knowledge, combined with the second most important way Tony helped me, has proved to be invaluable. Secondly, then, Tony showed me how to properly set up monitors if they are needed. Monitors are the speakers that are positioned on the stage in front of the musicians and singers. Sometimes, each person on stage is connected to a separate channel, meaning everyone can hear exactly what they want to hear through their monitor. However, most of the time, there are only one or two channels, which means people need to know how to carve out their space because everyone else will fight to hear more of themselves. Tony knew his voice and instrument well enough that he didn't really need monitors. Sure, he'd like to hear himself if he could, but ultimately, he knew his skills and was completely in control. This spoke to me, and over the course of the next 10 years of my life, I gained sufficient confidence in my instrument and my voice, and it freed me from what is known as 'the monitor wars' – the war in which band members fight for more of themselves to be heard in the monitors. The ultimate climax of this war is a stage volume so loud that it overrides the need for a PA system, and because the music and vocals are not running through the proper sound equipment, it all sounds like crap to the audience.

To this day, whenever Kaci and I are ready for a soundcheck, most sound guys fall out of their chair when we ask them to turn off the monitors. We can hear the room just fine. Plus, we know that most monitor systems are not EQ'd (run through an equalizer), so our vocals come through sounding very thin and sometimes with different frequencies being highlighted, making our voices sound unnatural. By listening to the 'house sound' (i.e., with no monitors), we can hear the final product as the listener hears it and sing with a lot more confidence. It also allows us to give the sound guy feedback about our vocal EQ as we know what we sound like naturally. As my musical mentor and long-time friend, Brett Maltbie, used to say, "There's no talent knob on any of the gears, so you better know your instrument and your voice."

Crossroads Church has deeper roots in our music and ministry than those lunch meetings. For example, the associate pastor, Bob Lister, and his wife, Mary, started a Friday night coffee shop at the church with live music, and they encouraged me to play at open mic nights. This helped me to learn how to keep my nerves under control while projecting confidence and authority to the crowd. Those were valuable lessons, but I will also say they were the hardest attributes I've ever had to learn in my life! Also, I played on the Crossroad's worship team, which allowed me to hone my guitar skills.

Crossroads would continue to be a part of our lives, but at the time, our sights were set on a small town just north of Salina.

Bennington: Building a House

Salina is by no means a major metropolis, but it is a city just the same, and we were small-town, country kids. Kaci and I wanted our kids to experience that small-town life as well.

We had begun attending Bennington Bible Church and spending more time with Grandpa and Grandma Boss. Both Kaci and I felt at home in that church and were quickly accepted. Over time, I began sitting in on the high school youth group and helping out wherever needed. After some more time, I began organizing events. Eventually, I became the unofficial youth group leader.

It was hard to maintain this while we lived in Salina. Granted, it was only a 20 – 25-minute drive to Bennington, but that distance made it hard to be available for the kids in the youth group while balancing work and family life.

By that time, Bennington Bible Church had begun the process of building a brand-new church on a plot of land they'd purchased just north of town. The lot they chose left a stretch of land between a row of houses and the church. The city of Bennington decided they wanted to expand and bought that land, plotting it out into city blocks with lots for sale.

Kaci and I had been searching for a house for months in Bennington, but we simply couldn't find anything that wouldn't require us to gut and completely remodel it. While we could buy a house like that at a low price, the renovation cost would put the overall price in a comparable range to the cost of building a home.

Both sets of Kaci's grandparents had built new homes in Bennington. Beyond that, we also had the experience of Kaci's parents who had built and remodeled numerous homes over the years.

Taking all of this into consideration, we began researching factory-built homes. No, not trailer homes. Actual stick-built homes engineered in such a way that they could be built in a factory, safe from elements such as rain that can ruin the subfloor and cause squeaks and spongy spots years later.

We traveled to Clay Center, KS, and Stratton, NE, to visit two companies that built homes in factories. In both places, we poured over options and costs. Finally, we decided to go with the company in Stratton because the majority of their business focused on building larger homes for wealthy clientele. I loved the technology involved, as they built these homes in sections, trucked them to location, and put them together like Lego blocks (with the help of a crane). In the end, you simply could not tell the difference between a home built on site and one of their factory-built homes.

Because of their clientele, the company in Stratton used higher-end products than the company in Kansas. They were also a new company that was hungry for business, so I negotiated a cost that came in quite a bit lower than their competitor. This allowed us to purchase a bigger house, which was exciting for us as we wanted to grow our family.

Kaci and I bought a lot directly across the street from the new church. Shortly after, in January 2002, we broke ground and began the process of building. Kansas weather is an interesting beast. In most areas, one would never think of excavating, forming, and pouring cement for a basement in the winter months. Yet, in Kansas, while there may be a blizzard with negative temperatures one day, the next day may bring 70 – 80-degree weather lasting for a week. Thus, we began our building process early in 2002.

Not long after, on a cold, overcast, and windy day, two trucks came down the road carrying our new home. They were followed by a huge crane, which lifted the two halves of our house and placed them into position on the foundation. I think half the town of Bennington showed up to watch. Even a couple of my bosses from

Geoprobe came to watch as they were all accomplished engineers themselves and were curious to see the process.

The process was rather intense, and the crew that came from Nebraska were very skilled and hard-working. Kaci, ever the servant, not only made snacks but also catered lunches and kept hot coffee available.

If you've ever been around a construction site with multiple companies in the mix, you'll know there's generally some sort of jostling for position and always plenty of cursing. Being hands-on like I am, as well as a good project manager, I kept abreast of every aspect of the project and diffused each situation before it got out of hand, keeping the project moving forward and smoothly.

Day one: Get the home off the trailers, in the correct place, secured to the foundation, secured together, and then get the roof dried in (covered in multiple heavy tarpaulins to prevent moisture from getting in).

Day two: Raise the roof and finish shingling it.

Part of the engineering feat of taking two halves of a home down the road is the hinged roof system. If you think about it, the pitch of a roof would not fit under most bridges or overpasses, maybe even some power lines. So, the company from Nebraska figured out a way to hinge each side of the roof, which meant they could lay them flat, thus allowing for clearance on the roadways. Once each side of the roof was raised and connected at the peak, truss pieces were added, completing each side and giving it the strength and stability of any standard-built roof. Then the crew put down the tar paper and shingled the roof in no time.

Near the end of the day, the crew's leader approached me. "Are you a Christian?" he asked. Shocked by the question, I replied simply, "Yes, why?" His reply was something that has been at the forefront of my mind ever since that day, sometimes convicting me of my actions. He said, "I could tell by the way you handled yourself."

I've certainly failed at this more than I've succeeded, at least that's how I perceive my life. Yet, this one instance became a source of encouragement to me. Not as a pat on the back, but rather as a life goal. Over time, the Lord continued to teach me, via that interaction, what His desire is for my life. It even became a foundational principle of our careers, influencing how we have conducted ourselves in the music industry.

After the crew finished their work, we still had a lot of work to do to get our home ready for us to move in. From working on our first home, my father-in-law taught me the value of 'sweat equity,' and we definitely sweated on this project.

My dad and Uncle Terry made the trip from Missouri to help me install the electrical meter and run all the wiring needed to connect the meter with the circuit breaker. At the same time, Ken and I worked on installing our heater in the basement while fabricating sheet metal parts as we connected the ductwork to the heater. We also ran all the black pipe for the gas lines and installed the compressor for the air conditioning system.

That was just to get the electric and HVAC going in the house. Dad and Uncle Terry also tackled the plumbing from all the stubs coming through the subfloor into the basement. Then Ken and I moved upstairs and began laying the wooden floor.

While we hired in people to do the framing and truss work on the garage, Ken and I put on all the house wrap, siding, and roofing. We made sure that the siding and the roofline tied into the rest of the house seamlessly so no one could tell that it was factory-built after the fact.

All in all, Kaci and I built a 1,600-plus-square-foot home with a full basement underneath (complete with 9-inch walls), giving us a little over 3,200 square feet of liveable space. Besides, we built a 28-foot square garage with an extra 14 by 28-foot extension running along the end of the house. My garage was the envy of a lot of men. Because of the extension, I could pull a car straight through the north garage bay and into the extension, pull another car and position it between the two garage bays, and then pull a car into each of the garage bays. Thus, I could easily fit four vehicles into my garage in the event of inclement weather.

Because of the work we did on our own, and the help we got from family members, Kaci and I gained over $20,000 in sweat equity! Many years down the road, when God told us to sell our home, move to Nashville, and become full-time musicians, this was a huge blessing.

Stroke

There were a few guys from Crossroads Church who worked at Geoprobe, and they were all big lovers of music, which led to fast friendships. Now, some folks say they love music but never listen to anything other than what is popular on the radio or TV, and then there are folks who LOVE music. The latter tend to find great music, no matter how well-known the artist may or may not be.

That's how these guys from Crossroads were, especially Mr. Lee Shaw.

Lee fed me a constant source of good, independent Christian music. He was a lot like me, in that he grew up in the late 70s and early 80s and loved big, dirty electric guitars with huge solos. While we didn't necessarily find all those attributes in modern Christian music, whether it be signed or independent artists, we did find some music that rocked. Which was good by me, because that kind of music was seriously lacking on Christian radio.

Every once in a while, he introduced me to a group that had pop undertones but with a really good sound and lyrics that grabbed my soul. One such group was an independent band from Texas called *Mercy Me.*

Their early albums had some songs that cut me like a knife. They were so raw and honest. I thought to myself, "Man, if only I could see those guys live."

A little while later, one of their songs miraculously played on the radio. It was called *I Can Only Imagine.* As their popularity skyrocketed, *Mercy Me* began touring a lot more, and we discovered they were coming to Salina.

That night, they performed at Kansas Wesleyan University. I honestly can't tell you anything about the performance because it was overshadowed by something that I never thought or imagined could happen: Grandpa Heckman passed away.

Grandpa Heckman had been in full-time care at a rest home because he had suffered a stroke that took all his abilities away from him. I'll never forget when that stroke hit. It took all the energy I could muster to walk into the room to see him. It took my grandfather, one of the strongest men I'd ever known, nearly a full minute to say, "Hi, Jer." I held his hand for a while, then left the room and crumpled into Kaci's arms, sobbing.

Now, the night of the *Mercy Me* concert, I got a phone call telling me the unthinkable had happened. My superhero had died.

His funeral took place days later, and I was asked to be a pallbearer. Grandpa had served in the military during World War II, so there was a military presence with a gun salute. From the time we were in the chapel and my cousin, Amanda, read a poem she had written about Grandpa, to the moment those shots were fired at the cemetery by his casket, I sobbed.

I had spent my whole life selfishly running away and living life on my own terms. Once I hit high school, I began dodging family get-togethers. And if I was there, I spent more time paying attention to my girlfriend and planning where we would have sex later. If I did engage with my family, it was always topical; I'd tell them what I thought they needed to hear so they could think I was an all-American success story.

Now my Grandpa was gone. Thankfully, he spent any chance he could talking to me about the Lord and the importance of having Him in my life.

The tears weren't just because Grandpa was gone; the tears were because I realized my youth was also gone. As I sat there at the funeral, I looked around at my cousins. We used to look forward to our families coming together so we could play. Now, they were all adults, married, many with children of their own, and I had seemingly little to talk to them about. I had squandered the time I had been given with my family, and I could never get it back. The regret stung with unimaginable pain.

"You'll Always
Have a Place to Play"

At the same time, Kaci and I were still playing with various worship teams as well as doing special song items at our church and finding open mic nights at coffee houses. Believe it or not, in Central Kansas, it's pretty tough to find a place to play music that is not in a bar.

Because of the timing of my grandpa's death and the fact that it is a great song, Kaci and I began learning the song *I Can Only Imagine*. After a while, we had the opportunity to perform it as a musical item at Bennington Bible Church. After church, we had lunch, as was our long-standing custom, at Grandpa and Grandma Boss' house. Grandpa couldn't say enough about how much he liked that song, which surprised both Kaci and I because Grandpa and Grandma were pretty big Gaither lovers, and if it wasn't Bill Gaither or a hymn ... was it really Christian? Anyway, Grandpa encouraged us, telling us that we did a great job with the song and he loved it, which did a lot to boost our self-esteem.

Yet, there just weren't a lot of opportunities to play in Central Kansas. I knew God was calling us to do this music thing, but man, it seemed like a pretty insurmountable hurdle. So, we resolved to spend time in prayer.

Now, I'm going to preface what happened next. I'm not a hyper-spiritual, wacky sort of Christian who does crazy things that freak people out. With that being said, I heard the voice of the Lord, seemingly audibly: "You will always have a place to play. I will give you at least one place to play every month."

I know it sounds crazy. Plus, that specific 'once a month' deal sounds a little over the top, right?

Well, it happened. I'm not pulling your leg. Shoot, I can also tell you that the whole "I heard God say…" thing is not a common occurrence for me. I can count on my hands how many times that has happened. But it wasn't something I imagined. It happened!

Out of the blue, I got a call from a pastor in Abilene, KS, who wanted Kaci and me to perform *I Can Only Imagine* as a special musical item at their church service. No joke. I'd never met the guy. Abilene is about 30 – 35 minutes east of Bennington, so who knows how he found out that we had even played that song. It was one of those moments when I could only say, "Thank You, God."

From that moment on, Kaci and I found ourselves with more opportunities to play music than we could shake a stick at. These opportunities eventually led us to western Kansas and to our very first band.

Floyd

There was a group of young men in the Bennington area whose lives had been radically transformed by Jesus. We were all drawn to each another and got together as often as possible for prayer, study, and accountability. One guy, in particular, was kind of the ringleader who brought us all together and kept us all meeting. His name was Nate Wood.

Nate grew up in the church as his dad was a pastor in the Southern Baptist denomination. That meant he had a whole realm of people and resources open to him.

One Sunday after church, while we were hanging out, Nate approached me and said, "I have been meeting with a guy every Wednesday morning for discipleship. Why don't you join us this Wednesday? He will buy you breakfast."

If you know anything at all about me, you'll know that I am not a morning person. Not at all. As a matter of fact, I like to say, "I wake up at the butt crack of noon!" The idea of getting up at 5:30am to eat breakfast and do 'discipleship' (at the time I scoffed at that notion for some reason) was not enticing to me at all.

Yet, I found myself telling Nate, "OK, I'll be there."

I thought to myself, and even verbalized to Kaci, "I can't believe I said I would go!"

Wednesday morning came along. I got up at 5:30am and made my way to a truck stop at the north end of Salina. I walked in and saw Nate. Nate is a big ol' boy, and there's no missing him, especially when he starts waving one of his big ol' paws over his head to get your attention. You just can't miss him.

FALLING DOWN

Sitting next to him was a short, squatty old guy wearing a pair of old, worn-out, blue denim overalls and work boots. The man stood up, stuck out his hand, grabbed my hand with a rock-like grip and said, "Hi, I'm Floyd," in a slow southern-Kansas draw. While I was always taught that you can tell a lot about a man by his handshake (and I was comforted by Floyd's that he was a good, honest man), I looked at his common work attire and thought to myself, "What is this guy going to teach me that I don't already know?"

Then Floyd said to me, "You want to see my pride and joy?"

"Uh, sure." What was I supposed to say?

He dug out his wallet, pulled out a picture, and handed it to me. It was a picture of a bottle of *Pride* dish soap sitting next to a bottle of *Joy* dish soap.

He sat there chuckling with a big smile on his face.

I thought to myself, "What have I gotten into?" But the truth is that I have the same kind of quirky humor that Floyd exhibited. I was just mad that I had to wake up before 7:00am.

Recently, Floyd called me and sang *Happy Birthday* over the phone for my 43rd birthday. In our conversation, he reminisced about that Wednesday morning that occurred over a decade and a half ago. He said he would never forget the first time I walked into that truck stop. He said, "Jeremy, I looked at you and thought to myself, 'What a punk!'"

By the end of that first meeting, both of our minds would be changed about the other. Ultimately, Floyd took an angry young man who desperately loved the Lord but was floundering in life under his wing and spent the next six years discipling him. This meeting was one of the top three defining moments of my life.

Floyd is an extraordinary man, with an extraordinary journey. The son of an itinerant Baptist pastor, Floyd developed a love for Jesus at an early age. What drew Floyd and I together was the common thread that neither of us could take anything at face value and just go with the flow. Floyd began asking questions, no one had answers, so after he married his high school sweetheart, Mildred, he headed to Bible College where he earned a Master of Divinity degree.

In Floyd's own words: "After I graduated, I walked out of that school, looked at the horizon, and said to myself, 'What I am looking for that I did not find here?'"

Over the next few decades, Floyd followed his calling and became the pastor of several small Southern Baptist churches. Eventually, Floyd came to terms with the fact that he was a teacher, not an administrator. Instead of trying to run an organization, such as a church, he moved into college ministries and began working in the Baptist Student Union at Emporia State University in Emporia, KS.

During that time, Floyd's life was forever changed, and thus, years later, my life was forever altered as well.

While a leader at the Baptist Student Union, Floyd began the practice of memorizing scriptures. I know what you might be thinking, "I memorized scriptures in Sunday School." No, I'm not talking about a verse here and a verse there. Floyd began memorizing the entire book of Matthew.

Once he had most of it committed to memory, he stumbled across an old Revised Standard Version Pew Bible that was falling apart. Because of the paragraph format and the size of each page, Floyd found a system of placing the pages side by side on long reading boards so that he could just "flow through the words."

As he began another wave of memorization, not only did the words go deeper and become more solid in his mind, but he also began to see things in the writing. Floyd started to see what he calls 'sections' and 'parenthesis' as he read through the scriptures in a flowing fashion.

In the end, Floyd discovered that the book of Matthew was written as a discipleship manual. It was not written in chronological order, but rather in an order that guides new believers through God-breathed life skills that will restore their lives to what God had preordained mankind to look like: Jesus Christ.

After the initial section of 'who Jesus is' in chapters 1 – 3, followed by Jesus' public calling, His posturing of 'obedience unto death', and our call to be 'fishers of men' in chapter 4, readers of Matthew's gospel find the most foundational teaching that a believer in Jesus could ever have in their arsenal – the beatitudes.

I'm not diminishing the rest of the Sermon on the Mount, but the beatitudes are the single most important teaching I have personally experienced. They have allowed me to take a moment by moment account of where I am in my spiritual walk. I liken them to a spiritual barometer.

Never in all my years of being in the church had I ever heard anyone teach the beatitudes in such a manner as Floyd did that day. Shoot, most times when I asked, "What are those beatitudes things?" most people had no idea how to answer, other than, "It's part of the Sermon on the Mount," or some cheesy statement such as, "They are called the beatitudes because that's how our attitude should be." What? Really? That tells me nothing.

So, on that first Wednesday morning, as I ate my breakfast and heard Floyd unpacking the beatitudes, I knew this was a huge answer to prayer and that there was hope. I understood that God didn't just leave us down here to flop around in our pain and shame. He left us the tools we need to live the way He created us to live!

While Floyd took me into each beatitude in much greater lengths, here's a brief summary of how he unpacked them:

Blessed are the poor in spirit. Floyd asked me, "Are you poor in air?" Without thinking, I answered, "No, I've got all the air I need." He said, "Let's test your answer. Pinch your nose, cover your mouth, and count to 500." I quickly understood. Air may be all around me, but I needed it to survive. In the same way, we are poor in the Spirit of God. We need God's Spirit to survive. Unless one comes to this understanding in life, they simply will not see healthy growth.

Blessed are those who mourn. Floyd told me that once you come to the end of yourself and see your need for God, then comes the next stage in growth: mourning. He asked me, "What are you doing when you mourn?" I gave him some shallow answer describing grief. He explained, "Mourning is looking at your current situation, not liking it, and deeply desiring it to change." He then told me about some friends who lost an infant, and he described how they mourned for the loss of their child and wished that the child was still with them. Likewise, he explained, we mourn that we didn't have the Spirit of God present in our lives, which made our lives toxic, and we desire that to change more than anything.

Blessed are the meek. "Jeremy, define meek for me." I answered with the same answer that almost every Christian I have ever known has said: "Humble." He leaned forward, and with loving correction said, "Teachable." He told me that coming to a place of recognizing our need for God, desiring Him, and mourning what our lives have become without Him is not enough – everything comes to a screeching halt if we are not teachable.

Blessed are those who hunger and thirst for righteousness. After we hit rock bottom and come to the point where we are teachable, there must be a heart-level desire for God's righteousness in our lives. The danger in this is that sometimes we find ourselves eating from the wrong buffet. This happened to me. I came into a relationship with Jesus in the summer of 2000. Yeah, I read my Bible daily, but I used the insights of other writers and scholars to understand it. I'm not saying that these guys didn't have some great teachings, but Floyd helped me realize that I could go straight to the source and feast at the feet of Jesus who has made it very clear what He wants from my life and how I should operate.

Blessed are the merciful. If we're eating from the wrong buffet, it squashes our growth, and we never mature into this beautiful part of life: mercy. I'm not talking about receiving mercy. We all have amazing access to that from the Lord. I'm talking about dispensing it. This is where we begin to understand what Jesus meant when He said, "It all hinges on these two things: Love the Lord your God with all your heart, soul, and mind. Then love your neighbor as yourself" (paraphrased).

Blessed are the pure in heart. We can begin to see how all the beatitudes flow from one to the other, back and forth. At any given point, we can find ourselves needing to humbly re-establish that we are, indeed, poor in spirit. I confess that I sometimes take a look at this 'pure in heart' beatitude and realize that my heart is not pure. Oh, this one slaps in the face of modern Christianity. We all find ourselves doing a variation of the following: serving the poor, expecting the Lord to then pay us back with some miracle that we've been begging for, maybe a new car, a new home, or that the cancer would go away ... you name it. Whatever it is, we aren't operating out of a pure heart, we are trying to manipulate God into giving us what we want.

Blessed are the peacemakers. We have all kinds of skewed views on peacemakers. From the wild west where 'peace officers' such as Wyatt Earp dot history to modern UN peacekeepers occupying the Middle East and Africa. In God's kingdom, a peacemaker doesn't enforce social values or a political agenda. In God's kingdom, His peacemakers are doing just that, making peace in the hearts of men by mercifully and purely living out the life of Jesus Christ in front of them. And when others desire to know God for themselves, God's peacemakers are ready to disciple them. These are the true peacemakers. They disciple people after Jesus Christ. Not a denominational doctrine or some teacher of Jesus, but simply the Son of God Himself.

Blessed are those who are persecuted because of righteousness. I wish I could tell you that persecution comes only at the hands of those who have rejected Jesus Christ. Unfortunately, this is not the case. When you begin to radically change your life to align with how God desires you to live, and you interact with Him through the day and follow His lead, people will notice, and they will either want that peace, or they will want to squash it. Why? Because light exposes darkness. The church is made up of people, and when people are threatened, they lash out, and that takes us to the next beatitude.

Blessed are you when people insult you, persecute you and falsely say all kinds of evil against you because of me. Over the years, I've heard people say a lot of slanderous things about Floyd: that he is a heretic, a false prophet, etc. In the years to come, I would follow the calling of the Lord on my life, and I would be called a 'sell-out.' I would have pastors call me and tell me that what I was doing was evil and not in God's will. I would have churches cancel concerts at the last moment, throwing our whole tour in disarray because a member thought our music was satanic. All the while, we were seeing lives changed and receiving messages of how God was drawing people back to Him through what we were doing. Thank God that Floyd gave me a firm foundation in the beatitudes that saw me through those times.

Like I said, this is the abridged version. When Floyd teaches them, he shows how they tie into Scripture and how Jesus lived them out.

When I left that truck stop restaurant that morning, I knew that I had experienced something amazing. However, I still had loads of old teaching in me that kept my mind churning and saying, "That is just too far outside the box. That guy is nuts." Because we can let those voices run out of control, and I did, I decided that I was going to enjoy my sleep and that Floyd could find someone else to 'disciple.'

Next Wednesday rolled around. I didn't set my alarm because I just wasn't interested in drinking the Kool-Aid that Floyd was offering. Plus, I hated waking up before 7:00am.

Didn't matter. I was awake at 5:00am.

Again, I'm not a super hyper-spiritual person. What I am is a man who truly loves God and wants to live the way He wants me to live.

The only way I can describe that morning to you is this: I had a wrestling match with God, and He won.

Begrudgingly, I got up, got dressed, and made my way to that truck stop restaurant. Floyd was sitting there, waiting. For the next six years, I didn't miss a Wednesday unless I was out of town. As a matter of fact, in the following years, we would not only meet on a Wednesday morning, but multiple times a week, either for breakfast, lunch, or evening Bible studies.

He has been one of the most influential people in my life, and his influence has overflowed into my marriage and in my family. In Floyd, I found someone I could confide in, someone who would counsel me, someone who would let me be me without any judgment. The only way I know to honor Floyd and repay him is to pray that the Lord would bless me with the opportunity to disciple a hungry young punk after the life of Jesus Christ. Just as he did for me.

Oh, and just to brag on my mentor, he didn't just memorize the book of Matthew. He also memorized Romans, Hebrews, 1 Peter, and James. At the time of this writing, he is 77 years old and has just retired so he can focus on discipling several groups of young men throughout the week.

Wur'ship Project

From the moment I sensed God calling me into ministry as a musician, I began writing songs, performing, and actively seeking out other musicians in order to 'go.' My vision was to use my gift to connect people with Jesus, and the best way to do that was to create a big, professional sound with a band. However, the pool of musicians wanting to play Christian music for a traveling band was almost non-existent in our area of Kansas at that time. There were worship teams here and there, but those folks were not interested in playing outside of their church groups.

There was one guy at Geoprobe who went to Crossroads, and he loved music. The only problem was that he had quite a chip on his shoulder. While he claimed to be a believer in Jesus, he was really unpleasant to be around. I knew he wasn't a great person to be yoked with, but at the same time ... as I've said, the talent pool in our area was pretty thin.

There was another guy at Geoprobe who had a passion for recording and producing music. He bought a live recording device, and Kaci and I went to his church where he hooked it up, and along with our angry young musician friend, we tried our hand at recording. It was horrible.

Even in a bad situation, a person can walk away with the knowledge to get better. What I learned from this situation was twofold. First, if you are going into a studio, you better practice until you hate the song (just like the days when we would practice our cheerleading routines until we couldn't do it one more time without a mental breakdown). Second, don't yoke yourself with someone who isn't in the same space as you are. Let me clarify – I was still hurt and angry, but I didn't treat everyone I came in contact with like trash. You couldn't look across a crowd, pick me out and say, "Gees, that guy has a chip on his shoulder." Yeah, that's how bad this guy's attitude was.

To add insult to injury, he pushed to make our band name 'Acts 29'. The thought process behind it sprang from the fact that there are only 28 chapters in the book of Acts, which is an account of the Early Church. The name 'Acts 29' was a statement that we were picking up from where the Early Church left off. The problem I had with this name was that it was extremely cheesy and we weren't picking up where the Early Church left off. Leaving his problems to one side, I had my own hurts, addictions, anger, unforgiveness that I was dealing with – I knew that I was *not* continuing where the Early Church left off. I was still at the beginning stages of learning and healing.

A while later, we received an invitation to lead worship at a weekend retreat for a Christian campus group at Fort Hays State University. The angry young man came with us. When we got there, we were blessed to have the leader of the ministry, Micah, play drums with us, and a friend of his from Great Bend, Mark, play bass. There was an immediate connection, not only as friends and brothers in Christ but also as musicians. We just clicked.

Micah and I kept in touch, and we brainstormed ways of playing together as a band. There were several hurdles that we had to overcome to make this happen. One was that Hays was about a 2-hour drive away. And if we were going to travel, we would have to solve a bigger hurdle: Micah was a drumless drummer. He didn't own a kit, and if you know music, good drums are stinking expensive.

I can't remember exactly how it happened, but we started playing together more and more. Once a month, we gave the worship team at Bennington Bible Church a break and led worship, but it wasn't long before we found ourselves traveling and playing all over the state of Kansas.

After the weekend retreat that started it all, Micah pulled me aside and said, "Man, that guy you have with you is toxic. You can't have him with you, or he will ruin every relationship you try to build." I knew he was right. So, as we made plans to continue playing together, we just didn't include that angry young man. Interestingly enough, he didn't care.

That opened the door for Micah to introduce us to Jeremy (yes, another one!). He was a young home-schooled student who played in the same worship team as Micah, and he became our new electric guitarist.

Now that we had a band, we needed a name, and there was no way it was going to be 'Acts 29'! Micah had a degree in marketing and design from Fort Hays State University, so he and I got to work on ideas. Because we played worship music, and knowing our call to live a life of worship, I came up with the idea of 'Worship Project.' Micah took it a step further to set it apart visually and give the name a quasi-phonetic look, and we ended up with 'Wur'ship Project.'

About that same time, I had begun writing music with a super-talented young lady in our youth group at Bennington Bible Church called Emily After praying and talking to her parents about it, we asked Emily to be a part of Wur'ship Project. Still, to this day, I'm in awe of the talent this young lady has, not only as a vocalist but also as a songwriter, and when she joined us, she was only 16 years old!

Now we were starting to play at bigger events around Kansas. To advance what we were doing, we needed some extra money because most places generally gave us only enough money to cover the gas. Our solution was to create some merchandise to sell.

Jeremy's mom offered to loan us the money to make our first run of t-shirts. Micah took the lead on that and came up with a super-simple and super-popular design. It was simply the word 'wur'ship' across the chest of both regular and women's fitted t-shirts. They sold like hotcakes, and we were easily able to pay Jeremy's mom back and place a new, larger order.

In the meantime, my musical mentor, Brett Maltbie, and I planned a 'live to two-track' recording at a studio in Salina.

A 'live to two-track' recording is raw. Every instrument is played at the same time; hence, it's 'live,' and 'two-track' means only two tracks are being recorded. There is no room for errors because there's little to no room for editing.

Our recording featured six tracks, three of which were our own original works. The process was stressful and exhausting, but it didn't turn out half bad. It was nothing that I would make public nowadays, but back then, it was a major step forward.

The Fumes of a Two-Track Recording

We had no idea about the process of recording or publishing ... or anything in the music industry for that matter. All we knew was that we had a measly couple of hundred dollars to work with, and we wanted to make a few bucks so we could go to a bigger studio and record an album that only had our songs on it.

Because of our ignorance, we did the only thing we knew to do. We converted the recording files into WAV format, put them on a computer with a CD Writer, and began making a bunch of CDs.

Because we didn't want a bunch of CDs with 'Wur'ship Project' written in a sharpie on the CD face, Micah came up with a cool idea. He found CDs that had a blank white surface, and then he created a couple of stencils that we could lay over the top and spray-paint our logo and a title onto the face of the CD. Now, remember, Micah had a degree in this field, so the stencils were made of a thick, high-quality material, and they were designed in a way that we could line them up on each CD and get the same outcome. It was our own version of quality control!

My huge 28 by 28-foot garage became our workspace. The band came over one weekend, and we knocked out a run of CDs. It was a lot of work for not many CDs, and we quickly sold out.

This was one of those times when I found out who my real friends were. My good friend and cubicle partner at work, Kevin Collings, came over every week and helped me make batches of CDs while Kaci and his wife were at a Bible study.

There were a few times when the fumes built up in that old garage to the point that Kevin and I got a little loopy. By the time our wives were finished, we were a little out of it!

There are a lot of things in life that will probably put my body in the ground before it should be there. I'm quite certain inhaling all those paint fumes while making that first Wur'ship Project CD will be among the list of those things.

When we weren't out in the garage spray-painting CDs, we were inside, cutting out the glossy inserts that Micah had designed. We'd fold each one and put it in a slim jewel CD case.

After all of the weekends and weeknights in the garage, after all the cutting and folding, after the burning of CDs, we only made a couple of hundred bucks from those stupid things. Never again will I go down the 'do it yourself' route!

"You've Got to Get a New Guitar..."

Kaci and I were huge fans of Garth Brooks. Takamine guitars made a model especially for him, the GB7C, which had a cool odd-shaped sound hole. I saw so much of me in Garth Brooks, from his small-town background to his love of storytelling songs. Also, he didn't have a super-amazing voice, which I could relate to.

Many of us make the mistake of trying to imitate someone else instead of aiming to be the best version of ourselves, particularly when we're young. I was one of those youngsters. I wanted to be Garth. So, naturally, I wanted a GB7C.

The main problem: the guitar cost $1,500.

No matter how long and hard I saved, it seemed like we always needed to use our savings for something else. Steve Hanson had a GB7C right on his showroom floor, but owning it seemed light-years away.

Then, one day, Steve approached me with an idea. He had a similar model of Takamine that was not the Garth Brooks version but was half the price. Steve suggested that I compromised by buying that guitar instead and trading in my Epiphone acoustic-electric to cut the cost even more. He would reserve it and let me make payments towards it.

I regret letting my Sunburst Epiphone go. To make matters worse, Takamine guitars are generally a high-range guitar, meaning their high frequencies tend to be very bright, producing a cutting sound instead of a warm and even sound. And that's not a good fit for my vocals and style. On top of that, I constantly fought 'feedback' issues when playing that guitar live, which meant the monitors made a piercing ringing noise. The feedback was mostly because the sound guys didn't understand they needed to adjust the frequencies on the EQ, but still, my guitar seemed to have more problems than any other guitar.

I bought this guitar about a year after I had started taking lessons, and the issues it gave me followed me into playing live with Wur'ship Project. It was a constant source of frustration for me as well as the other band members.

After a while, Mark approached me and said, "Brother, do you have a moment? I need to talk to you about an issue that me and the guys are having."

I expected the worst and thought, "Oh, no! What have I done?"

We sat down and talked over a few things before Mark finally got to the point, "Jeremy, you've got to get a new guitar. The guys and I feel that your guitar is problematic to us sounding great when we play live."

Kaci, who was sitting there listening, agreed. That was all I needed. I began researching and playing every acoustic guitar under the sun.

One brand that I'd never considered was a high-end brand carried by Steve Hanson: Taylor Guitars. The starting price for this range was $3,500. That was the first drawback. The next was that the higher-end models had spruce tops and a high-end sound that I don't like in a guitar. Lastly, they have all kinds of pearl inlay artwork on the fretboard and around the sound hole, and I am more of a simple and sleek kind of guy.

But there was one hanging on the wall that got my attention – a Taylor 514CE with mahogany back and sides, a western cedar top, and none of that gaudy inlay work. It had a rich, warm tone that sounded like the guitar was already 20+ years old.

The problem? Well, I already told you that Taylors started at $3,500. I thought there was no way in the world I could talk Kaci into it!

Roll back the clock a few years: I was at a ministry event put on by the church Kaci and I attended. I can't remember what was said that night, but I do remember God convicting me of my lifestyle. The guy said something to the effect of, "Have you accepted Christ already but just need prayer for a change in your life?"

That was me right there!

I headed down that aisle like my pants were on fire and there was water up ahead. When I reached the front, a couple of men surrounded me, and I shared some of my hurts and how they had affected me. They prayed for me. When the smoke cleared and everything was done, I looked over and not too far from me was Steve Hanson. He was giving his life to the Lord.

Back to the search for a guitar: I was sitting in Steve's shop, playing that Taylor 514CE for the umpteenth time. Steve walked in and said, "Jeremy, I'm so proud of you and what you've done with your music. Look, that 514CE is last year's model, and I need to make room for the newer models. I want to bless you and your ministry. I'll sell you that guitar at cost with an extra ten percent discount." Beyond that, Steve would reserve the guitar like he did the previous one and allow me to make payments on it when I could.

I went home to tell Kaci about this incredible blessing. The closer I got, the less I was confident that Kaci would see this as a blessing at all.

Wrong. She had heard me play that guitar on several of those umpteen occasions and knew it was an excellent guitar. Plus, she was in agreement with the band that I needed a new one. She encouraged me, saying that we would dig in and figure out a way to pay it off.

Then we received our tax return. Would you know that our tax return was the exact amount as the price Steve wanted for that guitar? And we had no other plans for the money.

I still have my Taylor 514CE. Anytime I'm on stage with an acoustic guitar in my hands, that's the guitar you'll see. She's played thousands of shows and is the envy of nearly every musician who hears her.

Be Still and Know

We called our live to two-track spray-painted recording *Wur'ship Project: Demo*. Simple. Because that's all it was. A live to two-track demo recording. It helped us to raise some money to get our drumless drummer some drums, and it bought us time so we could begin writing our own material for a real studio-recorded release.

For me, writing songs is a process, and that process never seems to happen the same way twice. Only one song on the live to two-track was written by me. Two were by Emily. We sure had a way to go before we had enough good material for a full-length CD.

Kaci and I had not dealt with our pasts yet. Things were definitely better, but our deep hurts were still there. There were good days, and there were bad.

One particular windy and rainy Saturday morning, I was sitting in my chair in our living room with a fire going in the fireplace, writing in my journal. It seemed like all the hurt, pain, and consequences of our choices were slamming down on top of me, and I was sinking into depression. I've never really had any suicidal thoughts in my life, but at that moment, I was so low that I thought to myself, "If this is all life has for me, it would be better to be done with it."

Months prior, as a surprise for Kaci, I had bought a picture that I had hung over our fireplace called *Peace, be Still* by Stephen Gjertson. It's a magnificent piece of art depicting the outline of a boat on a large body of water. There are several silhouettes of individuals on the boat, but one is standing with outstretched arms. In the background, storm clouds swirl in retreat as the sun begins to shine through on the now calm waters.

I had already written these words in my journal: *Lord, the winds are strong, and I'm sinking fast. The waves of life have got me down.*

It was my own personal pity party with my three favorite people: me, myself, and I.

That's when I looked up at that painting, and as sure as I've heard any person talk to me, I heard God audibly say to me: "Be still and know that I am God. As I can calm the storms and raging seas, I can calm your hurt."

That's when my writing turned from a pity party to an exchange between God and myself. The next words I came out were: *Every time I start to fall, You never fail to comfort me.*

Then I penned God's response:

Peace, be still
It's My will that you stand in awe of Me
Peace, be still
Call My name, you will find your rest
Peace, be still

Later that week, when Emily came over for a songwriting session, I shared these words with her, and she helped me compose them into a song. Together, we finished the lyrics and put music to the song.

As the band rehearsed the song and we prepared to play it at Bennington Bible Church, Kaci made a request that redefined our ministry once more. She asked, "Can I sing that song?"

This was the first time that Kaci had ever sang lead vocals on a song in her entire life. She was always passed over in her high school choir and wasn't considered as a vocalist by anyone else, but now she was stepping out and taking a shot at it. I'm so glad she did. Today, Kaci is recognized as one of the most solid vocalists in the business. She doesn't sound like anyone else, and she has super control, amazing tone, and perfect pitch. Not to mention that she is one of the very few people who can complement nearly any vocalist by picking out a harmony – she strengthens their sound without stepping on their vocals to the extent that people don't realize her voice is even there. Recently, a long-time producer who has worked with singers like George Strait, Dolly Parton, Emmylou Harris, and Ronnie Milsap gave Kaci one of the biggest compliments by putting her vocal abilities in the same league as those greats. From a student who was overlooked in high school to a vocalist who is categorized by a great Nashville producer as one of the greats, I can't begin to tell you how incredibly proud I am of her! It all started when she requested to sing *Peace, be Still.*

You've Called Us Out

Shortly after we recorded *Wur'ship Project: Demo*, Emily began courting a guy in Wichita, KS, by the name of Brandon. Once Emily introduced Brandon to the band, he was instantly one of us.

Brandon, an amazing singer-songwriter and worship leader, quickly got us involved with his church in Wichita. This introduced us to a whole new pool of musicians who were brothers and sisters in Christ.

For me, it was a cool season of growth, spiritually, musically, and as a writer. Brandon, Emily and I began writing songs for a new album, but it was still slow going for we were all very critical of our own work and wouldn't allow just anything on the album. All of which is kind of funny because there are a few songs on the album that I wrote, and I sure wish they would have spoken up and had us cut them out ... but perhaps that's my insecurity speaking more than anything.

I was really excited and hopeful for the project to take wings. We had all kinds of talent:

Micah was a monster on the drum kit! He had an impeccable sense of time, and he could play to the room – meaning, in a huge room he could play big, yet in a tiny room, he could play intense while making the volume just right for that small space. Above and beyond that, he could feel the music like no other drummer I've ever played with – he could follow any spontaneous changes I made, and it was totally seamless, appearing like we had rehearsed it that way.

Mark, our bass player, was also a student of the instrument. During the day, he was a pumper for an oil company, checking oil wells. Once he was off work, he was either playing his instrument or reading articles about it. He and Micah were one of the most solid rhythm sections I've ever played with.

Our guitarist, Jeremy, was super-talented, and he had a knack for musical arrangements. One weekend, while the band was staying at our home in Bennington, Jeremy and I were sitting in the living room just talking generally about music. Somehow, the topic moved to old hymns and making them relevant. I blurted out, "Like the old hymn 'Holy, Holy, Holy' – that song could really rock if it had a solid rock beat under it." Jeremy picked up his guitar and started chugging out a thick rock beat. He said, "Sing it."

If you listen to the *Wur'ship Project: You've Called Us Out* album, there are three old hymns we remade on there. All three arrangements were by Jeremy.

After the demo, we learned that we couldn't simply put other people's songs on our CD and sell them. Like I said, we had no clue what we were doing. Now that we had this knowledge, we knew we could not just throw random songs on our album that we didn't write. With a little research, we found that the hymns Jeremy had arranged were in the public domain. This meant these songs were not subject to copyright laws and anyone could record them. Since we fell under the banner of 'anyone,' we added the hymns with Jeremy's new arrangements to our album.

Brandon brought a lot to the table, especially when it came to the *You've Called Us Out* album. He introduced us to Josh Racchini, a talented guitarist, who created all the lead guitar parts on *You've Called Us Out*. Later, Josh even played a few live shows with us. Another person Brandon introduced us to was super-talented producer Moses Kostamo, the owner of MOKO Productions. Moses had worked on some major projects with Vineyard Worship and was excited to work with us. Moses became an invaluable resource as he led us through the recording process and taught us much about the music industry from the recording standpoint.

Then there was his music. Brandon brought two songs to the table that are absolutely out-of-this-world fantastic, and he allowed us to record them. The two tracks, *By the Hand* and *In the Valley*, ended up becoming the songs that opened doors for Wur'ship Project, both in the realm of touring as well as the realm of radio.

All these factors led up to the recording of the album, but we still had one huge problem: recording a full-length album cost a lot of money, and we didn't have much.

A few people came alongside us with some contributions, but it only amounted to a couple of hundred dollars, and we needed nearly $5,000 for the whole project. Back then, it seemed like an insurmountable sum of money. Now that we are in Nashville, that amount of money is not quite enough to record two songs!

Emily's parents were farmers up towards Minneapolis, KS, and they'd had an excellent year with their crops and cattle. They found out about our need from Emily, and out of the blue, they wrote us a check for the whole amount.

Moses booked the studio space in Wichita, we all bunked at Brandon's house, and we got to work. The whole process was a paradox in so many ways. Amazing, yet terrifying. Exhilarating, yet exhausting. For nearly a whole week, we worked from early in the morning until well into the night.

This was all new to us, so we had no idea what to expect. After recording, we thought the worst was over. Nope.

Next was the mixing process. Each song had to be 'mixed' – meaning that each vocal and instrument track was brought together ('blended') to create a final version. After mixing, the songs were sent to us to be reviewed. We burned a CD and listened to it in the car, at the church, through earphones, on a home stereo, and through just about any other device possible to get a good overall feel for the mix. Then we sent back our critique, and the mixing engineer made the tweaks, sent it back, we burned another CD and started all over again. We did this over and over and over until we felt like each song was as good as it was going to get.

Granted, we have matured so much as artists since that point, and we don't even sound remotely close to that recording anymore. Yet, we are still pretty proud of our first studio album.

Even ten years after recording it, Kaci and I still receive messages from people telling us that they have our *Wur'ship Project: You've Called Us Out* CD in their car and listen to it regularly. That is one of the most fulfilling things an artist can ever hear.

The Wheels Fall Off

Looking back over my life, there are several things I would love to go back in time and do over. Especially relationship-wise.

After *You've Called Us Out* was recorded and released, we traveled to every corner of the state of Kansas and beyond. Because we were immature and idealistic, we allowed people to say to us, "Well, you are a ministry, so you should be willing to come and play for free." After a while, 'free' ends up costing someone, and it began hurting our budgets. Because any profit we made from selling our merchandise was used to restock, or to increase our web presence, or to pay whatever operating costs there were, there wasn't anything left over for anyone. Even with my good job, Kaci and I were struggling financially.

Generally, Micah and Jeremy had to travel the furthest, and because of the amount of equipment they had to travel with, they had to use Micah's truck, which I'm sure drank fuel like it was going out of style. Plus, it was post 9/11, and fuel prices had doubled, if not tripled. So, not surprisingly, they began to ask for fuel reimbursement and suggested we all took a small wage. In hindsight, I should have started putting a value on what we were doing. Yes, it was a ministry, but a ministry shouldn't kill the ministers.

Ultimately, due to the financial situation, Micah and Jeremy said they wouldn't be able to be part of some of our events. Our frontline of singers now consisted of Brandon, Emily, Kaci, and myself. Brandon, Emily, and I could hold our own with guitars, so we simply contacted the places we had booked and asked if it would be OK to do acoustic shows. The folks didn't care. They were getting us for free anyway.

Then we had the opportunity for another photo shoot in Salina (we had done our very first photo shoot shortly after recording *You've Called Us Out*, but they weren't good enough to send to the press or other media outlets). Micah and Jeremy said they didn't want to drive out for it. We needed some decent press photos badly, so Brandon, Emily, Kaci, and I went ahead and did the photo shoot without them.

A couple of months later, a photo from that shoot found its way into a news article in the Savannah Reporter, a local newspaper in Savannah. The article was about the whole group, but because I was a graduate of Savannah High School, it mostly focused on me. When Micah and Jeremy saw the article and the photo, they were upset. Thus, the tension over money that no one was addressing started to build to pretty serious levels. Then a tipping point happened.

To set up that tipping point:

The very first time Jeremy came with Micah to be a part of Wur'ship Project, I gave him a microphone to sing. I was just so excited to have a band! But when I heard him sing, I knew it was a mistake (we all did). He had an amazing ear and could play anything on the guitar by listening to it, yet his singing was not on pitch, and even though he was singing backing vocals, his voice severely rubbed against the lead vocalist. Being so excited, I was a pushover, and I didn't address the problem there and then.

To make matters worse, Jeremy's personality was such that, in his mind, because we gave him a mic the first time, he should have one all the time. And since he is one of the sweetest people you'll ever meet, no one wanted to be blunt with him, so all our hints and explanations were lost on him. As time went by, it seemed easier to just not allocate a microphone for him.

Jeremy's whole family was on his case, saying he should be singing, telling him he was the best, etc. He did do a good job of leading worship at the small church he attended, but this wasn't a small church, and our ambitions were very high.

Jeremy constantly bugged me about this, asking, "Why aren't you letting me sing?" but I didn't have the guts to be straight with him. Then his mother started confronting me as well, and not just privately, but publicly too.

Sure, I shouldn't have been such a coward, but there was another legitimate reason I held back. Only a few short years before this, I couldn't read music or play an instrument, I only had music in my head. People liked my voice, but I knew I still had a long way to go (it was certainly nowhere near as solid and strong as it is today). So, I really struggled with the whole leadership thing and having to be the 'dream killer.' I reasoned that with his ear and love for music, his voice might improve. After all, mine had changed and gotten stronger.

Yet, with the stress of work, the demands of parenthood, the constant hurt and pain from mine and Kaci's past, the growing conviction of my continued (albeit very diminished) substance abuse, the youth group, *and* trying to grow a full-time music ministry, I cracked.

Instead of following the scriptural model that Jesus set forth (as seen in Matthew's gospel), I shot off a lengthy and firm reply to an email Jeremy sent me in which he had once again asked, "Why am I not allowed to sing?" Now, the problem with written responses is that they lack all of the personality that one receives with face-to-face interactions, and because they are one dimensional, they are subject to the reader's interpretation.

Jeremy's interpretation of said email was pretty negative, and it hurt him badly. In turn, he forwarded the email to Micah and unloaded his hurt on Micah. Although Micah had agreed with us from the start that Jeremy should not sing, because of the building tension, he sided with Jeremy, and it all blew up. I got an angry phone call from Micah, and it was done – he and Jeremy would never play with us again. Sadly, I haven't spoken to either of those guys since.

From the get-go, I took full responsibility for those failed relationships and hurts. And I'd do anything to go back and change what happened.

"I Want to Puke You Out!"

Through the process of recording *You've Called Us Out*, God was convicting me of the fact I had not fully dealt with my addictions. I wasn't using every day; it might be a few months before everything in life became so overwhelming, and then, boom, I'd have to get my fix. Still high-functioning, no one seemingly knew.

At that time, I was following a daily Bible reading plan that took me through the entire Bible in a year. This was my second or third time through the plan.

Now, any time we had a family gathering when I was a youngster, Grandpa Heckman and all of my uncles would talk endlessly about the Bible and all things Christian. Plus, my parents had me in church constantly, so I was very, *very* familiar with certain Bible passages and Christian teachings.

One particular day, I had to read the third chapter of Revelation as part of my Bible reading plan. I was familiar with the chapter because it contains a very common passage in Christian circles: Revelation 3:15-16. Contextually, Jesus is speaking to the church of Laodicea. In the well-known verses, Jesus is recorded as saying, "I know the things you do. I wish that you were hot or cold, but because you are lukewarm, I want to spew you out" (paraphrased). When I read those familiar words, something about them hit hard in the core of my soul for the very first time in my life. I grabbed a couple of resources that my mentor had given me and looked up the word 'spew' to find the original Greek meaning. I discovered that 'spew' actually means 'to vomit.' And I've often driven this point home by expounding the meaning to: 'gagging to the point of puking, violently throwing up.'

It felt like I had been punched in the gut!

I will totally take responsibility for my own actions and choices. At the same time, I want to point out that I was following the lead of the church in regards to being lukewarm.

What do I mean?

On any given Sunday, I saw happy people and their happy families walk into church with smiles on their faces. All across the sanctuary, I heard people speak about how things were going so well in their personal lives, I saw them raising their hands in worship and knew that some of them led Bible studies during the week. Yet, outside of the church, I saw (or heard about) the screaming matches that went on in their homes, not to mention the drinking, how their kids were out of control, their adulterous relationships or failed marriages, addictions, etc. It was like everyone put on a 'Christian mask' at the church doors, and it was acceptable somehow.

I thought, "If that's how these fine Christian folks are living and everyone is turning a blind eye, then I'm good, right?"

But that day, when I read Revelation 3, I realized that my life might look good to others, but my lifestyle was not OK in the sight of Jesus.

From that realization, I understood that if my life had a flavor, it was such a taste in the Lord's mouth that it made Him gag and vomit violently. I knew He still loved me, but I recognized that His response to my life at that time was: "I want to puke you out!"

I knew He wasn't expecting me to fix everything, but I also knew that I shouldn't be OK with the hurt that manifested itself into anger. I shouldn't be OK with my alcohol and drug use. I shouldn't be OK with anything contrary to His will.

Around this time, I wrote the song *In the Middle*. It artistically shows how I was being pulled in different directions and how I was stuck 'in the middle' – my addictions were pulling me one way, but God was drawing me another way. The chorus goes like this:

I've got to get out of this place now
In the middle is not where I am meant to be
I've got to get out of this place now
Chew me up, spit me out, or set me free

God used that scripture in Revelation to get me to move, to make a choice. I couldn't stay in the middle. I could return to my life of darkness and full-on addiction, or I could scratch, claw, and fight to become the man He designed me to me.

I did give up alcohol and drugs following the day God spoke to me through His Word. It was at this eye-opening moment that I put my foot down and finally said, "I'm done." However, I didn't 'put the ax to the root,' as Jesus would say. The underlying problems were still there, and they continued to play out in angry outbursts.

Emma Grace!

One reason for building our new home in Bennington was that Kaci and I wanted to expand our family. At our home in Salina, Kaci had conceived, but we lost the baby through a miscarriage. While we were devastated by this, we were still determined to grow our family.

We had been spending time with a few larger families, and there was just something about them that we wanted for ourselves. Each child had a different and unique personality, and the family dynamics were simply chaotic bliss.

We continued to try to grow our family, and finally, in 2003, we found out that Kaci was pregnant with our third daughter, Emma Grace.

Each child is indeed different and unique. Emma is our smiler. Kaci's mom calls Emma her 'sunshine' because Emma seems to bring a smile to every face in every room.

Emma is also a good source of laughter. Sometimes, she says things in public that make Kaci and I want to crawl under a rock and hide ... although we usually have a good laugh about it later.

Two incidents stand out in my mind:

First was the time Emma described her birth. Actually, I'll recount her birth and then share what Emma said that made us cry as we laughed so hard.

Those who know us know that we rarely turn down an opportunity to play music and minister. On May 5, 2004 (our wedding anniversary), we were playing a concert in Topeka, KS. Kaci was heavily pregnant, and by the end of the show, she began noticing light contractions.

Three days later, we were at her parent's house, and Kaci jumped up suddenly to announce, "My waters just broke!" This got all of us moving because we knew from previous experience that once Kaci goes into labor, there's not much time to wait before the baby arrives.

Thankfully, we were in Salina, only a couple of miles away from the hospital.

I drove her to the hospital in a flash and took Kaci to the waiting area to check in. I left her for a few minutes to park the car, and by the time I got back, the nurses were ready to wheel her to a room.

Immediately, a midwife came in to check Kaci and see how far along she was. I knew the midwife from Kansas Wesleyan University, so we all chatted happily as she examined Kaci. Then, all of a sudden, her expression changed and became serious. "I need to get a doctor ASAP. We will be preparing you for surgery!" she said.

"Wait! What? What's going on?"

"The baby is coming and coming fast. I felt feet. The baby is breech!" she explained.

"Are you sure? I don't want a c-section," Kaci cried.

"Trust me," said the midwife. "I know what a foot feels like!"

Then she ran out of the room.

Everything from that point happened so fast that I can't clearly recall it! The midwife must have sent the hospital into DEFCON 4 because all kinds of people in scrubs and masks started swarming around us and herding us towards the operating theater.

I was allowed to stay with Kaci, and I held her hand as we talked and joked. Then we heard our baby cry. Emma was cleaned up, swaddled, and handed to me. I began pacing around the room, talking to the new child in my arms.

Now, remember that I wanted to be a doctor earlier in my life? In my wandering, I found myself on the other side of the curtain that separated Kaci's face from the operation zone. Without thinking about it, I watched them put my wife back together. The doctors and nurses didn't even realize I was watching until towards the end of the procedure when a startled nurse saw me and said, "Oh my, are you OK watching this?"

Of course, Emma doesn't remember any of this, she only recounts the parts of the story that she has heard us talking about. What had us in stitches, though, was how Emma described her birth 5 or 6 years later.

I can't remember the occasion, but we were in a room full of friends. The subject of birth came up, and several folks were sharing birthing stories. Wanting to be a part of the conversation, Emma piped up and said, "I came out of the wrong hole."

Not a person in the room had a dry eye. Tears streamed down every face as we laughed and laughed and laughed!

If you want to get technical, Emma was not wrong. It's just that a surgeon had to make precision cuts to make that hole. We still love to tell this story, and every once in a while, we remind Emma that she came out of the wrong hole!

Another instance that we still laugh about happened in Tampa Bay, Florida.

Because our kids have grown up on the road, we would set aside time to do special things as a family. On our first tour in Florida, we decided to splurge and take the kids to Disney World for a day.

It was special in a unique way: first, because my parents flew down to join us, and second, it rained for nearly the whole day. The rain actually worked to our advantage because the park was practically empty. On popular rides, such as Space Mountain, we could get off and be riding it again within five minutes. On a 'normal' day at Disney World, visitors are fortunate if they get to go on the main rides once in the entire day because of the long lines.

Kaci and I thought everyone loved everything about Disney, including our children. We soon found out otherwise. After getting off Splash Mountain, we walked past the photo stand where they displayed the pictures of everyone going down the big slide. We spotted the photo of our family and saw that Emma – aged 9 at the time – had a look of sheer terror on her face. Clearly, she did not like the big rides!

Fast forward a couple of years, and we were back in Florida playing concerts and serving churches. After leading worship at a church in Tampa Bay, the pastor and the leadership team took us out to lunch.

As we were all sitting around the table eating our entrees, the subject of Disney World came up. The pastor began asking each of our girls if they like Disney, and he even asked them about a specific ride in the park.

When it was Emma's turn, he asked, "What about you? Do you like Disney World?"

"Yes," she replied.

"What's your favorite ride? I bet you like Splash Mountain."

"No, I don't like Splash Mountain," Emma stated.

"Really? Why not?" asked the pastor.

"It scares the hell out of me!" she exclaimed.

Kaci and I looked at each another, and both of us were horrified! If we could have dived under the table to hide, we would have.

The pastor, his wife, the worship leader and his wife, and all the elders of the church burst into roaring laughter. They saw the embarrassment written all over our faces. Thankfully, every single one of them told us a similar thing: "It's OK. We have kids. We know what it's like. These things happen."

And they were evidently sincere for we were asked to serve that church again on several more occasions.

Emma definitely had a way with words ... she still does!

PART TEN

THE MAKING
OF A DUO

Revolving Door of Musicians

One of the reasons for the new press photos (the ones that Micah and Jeremy were not part of) was that we needed updated photos of the band. We had taken on a new bass player to replace Mark, and he wasn't in the glossy photos we were selling at our merchandise table.

Unlike the parting with Micah and Jeremy, we parted with Mark on good terms. He had begun courting a lovely lady and was getting married. While they courted, his fiancée came to our concerts and was very supportive, but in the end, Mark sensed that he needed to back out of the band so he could serve his family and church better.

So, we planned the photo shoot. As you know, Micah and Jeremy didn't turn up. But neither did our new bass player! It was just Brandon, Emily, Kaci, and myself. In frustration, I forged ahead, thinking, "We'll do the shoot with just the four of us. After all, we are the singers out front."

Now, we had photos with old band members and photos with just the singers, and every new band member who came along asked us to do a new photo shoot so they could be in the pictures! As if to rub salt into their already wounded egos, people at our concerts would ask our newest members to sign pictures – photos they weren't in! And if that weren't bad enough, some people would blurt out in front of everyone around them, "Why aren't you in any of the photos?"

I would've liked to have told them my answer: "Photo shoots are expensive."

The materials we printed and put on the tables were expensive, and the artists we hired to put those photos into a format to be made into those materials were expensive. And don't forget, traveling is a huge commitment, and most of the guys didn't last longer than 6 months. All of which meant that if we had done another photo shoot and produced more prints, we would have even more merchandise with faces of past band members.

So, we left everything as just the four of us, and it seemed like that was going to be the way it would end up.

Then an old acquaintance of Emily got in the mix. They had met at a Christian camp in the United States, but he was from Germany. In Germany, he was evidently a success in the music industry, and just like everyone else, he thought Emily was a rare talent.

He invited her to Germany, saying he wanted her to "see how it all works." Brandon didn't like it one bit, and it sounded kind of fishy to Kaci and I, too, but at the end of the day, it was her and her parents' decision.

So, she went, and she came back a different person.

Instead of showing her 'how it all worked,' this guy actually tried to sign Emily to a deal with a major record label. He told her she could be "the Britney Spears of Europe." He took her to photo shoots and into the studio, and he introduced her to all kinds of big-time music executives.

Beyond that, I really have no idea what happened, what was said, or what Emily even felt or thought about it. All I know is that she continued to sing with us for a while, but she wasn't really with us following that trip. And it wasn't too long before she pulled out completely. Brandon followed suit because he was courting Emily, and well, you can't blame him. Their relationship was worth more than a band.

So, now it was down to just Kaci and me.

Once again, I had to frantically call everyone that had booked us and explain the situation.

I wish I could tell you that right from the inception when I heard God's call to music ministry that I knew it was just going to be Kaci and me as a duo. I wish I could say that I followed

God's lead to set it up that way to save money on photo shoots, merchandise, and marketing. Or that the Lord showed me that by hiring band members as we needed them, we would save ourselves heartache on several fronts as well as save travel costs and provide for our family.

But the honest and messy truth is this: it was a bunch of hard, hurtful, broken relationships that paved the path of our becoming a husband-wife music duo. Any revelation that I had about the simplicity of being a duo was from the scars of becoming one.

"You Aren't Good Enough"

When it was just Brandon, Emily, Kaci, and I, we still had a band. Our bass player was based in Salina while Brandon, Emily, our drummer, and guitarist were all in Wichita. So, every week our bass player and I drove to Wichita and rehearsed with the others. Kaci would stay at home with the kids because the travel made for a very long night – it was about a two-hour drive to Wichita, making it a four-hour round trip in one evening.

Granted, this story could have easily been a part of the last one as this portion of our journey was deeply entwined in Kaci and I becoming a duo. Nevertheless, this part of the journey was probably one of the most hurtful and debilitating moments in our musical career.

When I said that I didn't know what happened regarding Emily's trip to Europe, I was telling the truth. However, when she got back, there was a tangible distance between her, Kaci, and myself. It felt like we were miles apart, even when we were in the same room. Many times, I wondered if I had somehow become invisible to Emily.

We did find out one thing from Emily before she left the band, and it cut like a knife. She said, "You are not good enough to make it without me."

That will flatten your sails quick. I don't care who you are.

Then she quit coming to rehearsals, then our events. For a time, Brandon stayed with us, and the bass player and I continued to travel to Wichita for rehearsals.

Several months later, on the drive home, our bass player told me the same thing in conversation, "You aren't good enough to make it without Emily or Brandon."

My reply didn't hide my hurt too well, "Then why has God called me to do this, and why does He continue to open doors for Kaci and me?"

There have been others along the way who have said, "You aren't good enough." Let me be the first to say that there are many artists out there who are way more talented than I am. I knew that from the very beginning.

Yet, God continued to open doors for Kaci and me.

From that point on, it was just Kaci, me, and a guitar. Back in those days, I wasn't nearly the guitar player I am today, and I admit that it was a struggle. But we showed up when we were booked, and we gave our very best every single time. Some nights that 'best' had patchy vocal moments, other nights had forgotten lyrics, and others were filled with a myriad of mistakes and missteps. Yet we smiled, sometimes made fun of ourselves, and always praised the Lord regardless.

Honestly, I don't know why He still chooses to use me. There are plenty of Emily's in this world who have voices like angels and can write catchy songs that people instantly love. Then there's me. My raspy baritone voice means that people can't tell if I'm a country or a rock singer. And I'm not a prolific songwriter. Heck, we only produce enough original songs to release an album once every ten years.

Yet, those words still echo in my ears. Sometimes, they hold me back from submitting our music to radio stations or services that may advance our career. Sometimes, they keep me from emailing someone in the industry to see if we could partner to utilize their services. But all in all, I keep my eyes on Jesus and the dream He placed in my heart decades ago at the tender age of four in the St. Joseph Civic Arena, and I simply say, "Here I am, send me."

At the time, the problem was that these same words were already haunting me from the baggage Kaci and I had in our marriage. In my state of low self-esteem, I already constantly heard the words "You're not good enough" in my mind. Now, I'd heard the words from two more people whom I had counted as friends.

Band 2.0-ish

There's just something about playing with a band. I desperately wanted to have a band again, but as I stated before, the pool of Christian musicians was slim in our area of Kansas.

One day, a co-worker at Geoprobe and a very dear friend of mine, Jon Terpening, called me and told me that he had met a new couple, Craig and Vanessa, at church that Sunday. They were pretty young and had just moved from California. Craig was going to finish his music degree at a local Christian university. Jon asked whether we'd be interested in meeting them and helping them get plugged into the music scene.

Of course!

We invited them over for dinner, and we immediately clicked. There was only one big drawback: Craig played the clarinet. Nothing else. We didn't have much use for a clarinet player in our band, and I couldn't imagine anyone else having much need for one, either.

After some small talk and getting to know one another, I shared with Craig and Vanessa my frustrations of playing without a band. I went so far as to tell Craig that even having a percussion musician playing hand drums and a bass player would be amazing.

Craig took the initiative and learned percussion through his coursework. Within a few months, he was playing djembe (a hand drum) more proficiently than anyone I've ever seen or heard. Not only that, but he also took the initiative to have his percussion instructor teach him using our music.

You don't often see people taking that kind of initiative, let alone following it up with the hard work necessary to become excellent at what they've taken on.

But that's what Craig became: an excellent percussionist.

Now, we just needed a bass player. And a good bass player is hard to find.

Enter a 16 – 17-year-old, 6-foot-three-inch, red-haired, fair-skinned, home-schooled kid by the name of Kelley Bowker. His parents were on the worship team at Crossroads Church, and they knew us well. That's why they allowed Kelley to galivant all around the countryside with us to play music.

If anyone ever asked him, Kelley would quickly say, "I'm a singer, and my main instrument is the acoustic guitar." Yet, he ended up being a darned good bass player.

It may have been more of an acoustic troupe, but by golly, it was more than just Kaci, myself, and a guitar. We had a band again!

Canadian TV

Moses was super-excited about how *You've Called Us Out* had turned out. While he would be the first to say that we had a lot of room for improvement, he would also say that we turned out a pretty good album that people seemed to really enjoy.

Not long after we had finished *You've Called Us Out*, Moses decided to move his family to British Columbia, Canada. It was part of a compromise he had made with his wife: he would live in the United States, close to her family, for so many years, then they would move to Canada to be close to his family.

This ended up working in our favor.

Because Moses lived closer to his family, they seemed more interested in his line of work. His sister worked for a TV station called *The Miracle Channel* in Lethbridge, Alberta, Canada. Via Moses, she heard our music and thought we would be a great fit for a TV show on their station. We just had to get from Bennington, KS, to Lethbridge, Alberta.

Not only would this be our first multi-state tour, but it would be our first international tour, and certainly our first TV show. All in one punch!

Do you know how hard it is to book a tour when your opening line is, "We are a husband-wife duo based in Kansas?"

Very hard.

The person I'm speaking to almost immediately thinks we must suck. That couldn't be further from the truth. While the musician pool of people wanting to be in a traveling Christian band was thin, the overall pool of musicians in Kansas was rather large and talented.

In 2006, we finally got a tour set up. Man, was it thin! Three stops: Steamboat Springs, CO, Sheridan, WY, and Bozeman, MT, before crossing the border into Canada to do the TV show and then driving straight back to Kansas.

For this trip, we decided to leave the girls with my family in Missouri. We met my dad and mom in Topeka, which was kind of the halfway point. This was the first time Kaci and I were traveling without our kids, and Kaci cried almost the whole way back to Salina where we picked up Craig and Kelly.

Kaci and I were already road warriors, and Craig was well-traveled, but Kelley was kind of clueless. As we drove across the plains of western Kansas and eastern Colorado, he kept slamming back bottle after bottle of water. We had already made too many stops, and I was getting irritated because part of the 'man code' is that you have to make the drive with the least amount of stops or you lose points on your 'man card.' Stupid, I know. The older I get, the more I'm getting over it.

I warned Kelley that Limon would be our last stop before Denver and that he better slow down or he would be hurting. He didn't listen to me. We stopped at Limon, everyone went to the restroom, and we hit the road again. Unfortunately for Kelley, we hit roadworks somewhere between Limon and Denver ... and we were right in the middle of nowhere! The lane closure caused a little stoppage and added a good 10 – 15 minutes to our drive. As the traffic began to creep through the construction zone, Kelley asked me, "Do you think there is any place to stop out here?"

I replied, "Yep, Denver."

"No, seriously, I gotta pee real bad!"

"You don't say? Funny how that works."

By the time we reached Denver, Kelley could barely walk. The poor guy shuffled slowly to the restroom. We stopped in Denver for dinner so Kelley could relieve himself some more before the next phase of our drive.

We never had that problem again. Not on that tour or any others.

The tour went great. Craig and Kelley really did a knock-out job. We sold tons of merchandise and received some good love offerings.

That gave us the ability to cover all of our costs as well as pay for the vehicle maintenance on Craig's car (he and Vanessa allowed us to use it for the tour).

When we got to the border of Canada, we met the crankiest border guard in the history of border guards. We had prepared our documents to avoid any problems, and everything was in order, but he continued to bark and yell at us. Shell-shocked after the grand inquisition, we were finally on our way to Lethbridge.

After we checked into our hotel, we went for dinner at a small Chinese restaurant. When they found out we were Americans, we were instantly promoted to celebrity status, and they treated us like royalty. We had a great time talking to them, and they even brought some Canadian currency to our table and gave us a lesson on the loonie and the toonie. If you've never been to Canada, the loonie is the Canadian one-dollar coin, while the toonie is the two-dollar coin. They were really sweet folk, and they just gushed over us and told us over and over how amazing it was to meet Americans. Maybe that border guard should let a few more through!

The next morning, we packed up and headed over to the TV studio. Wow! At that point in my life, I'd never been in a real studio. It was a huge warehouse with lots of little sets built for different TV shows. It felt like one big maze!

We were taken to the set where we would perform, and we were asked to set up and just start rocking. At first, it was weird. Not only was there no audience, but cameras were zooming in and around us, sometimes getting right up in our faces. It took a song or two to get used to it. The crew were gracious and coached us through it, and once we got over the cameras, we just settled into the groove and rocked. They were impressed that we caught on so quickly, and they were pleased with the live performance after only a few takes. Then they took us to another set for the interview portion of the show.

Months later, they sent us a DVD of the show. Wow, after the edits, cutting from one song to the interview, then to another song and back to the interview ... it was really sharp!

After we left the studio that afternoon, we drove over 20 hours to get back to Kansas. Montana is one of the most beautiful states

I've ever driven across. Just after dark, we came to Billings. Our path brought us to a cliff just north and above the city. The lights stretching across the plains was breath-taking. As were many of the buttes and a huge windmill farm that we drove through – windmills for miles and miles, right along the road. At one point, we were driving around a tight curve with a sharp drop off. Just as we entered the corner, a crop duster zoomed out of the depths straight up in front of us. It startled us for sure, but it was one of the coolest experiences.

As we drove across western Kansas, just past Oakley, we witnessed a hawk flying towards us, it swooped down, snatched a snake out of the grass, and lifted up again only feet from our windshield. These were just a few tastes of the interesting things we experienced on that trip, and many more followed as we lived life on the road. Little did Kaci and I know that we would eventually make several of those 20-plus-hour drives during our touring career. At the time, though, we swore we would never do it again.

Tater (aka Ella Mae)

That year brought us another surprise and blessing. Our fourth daughter, Ella Mae, was born in August of 2006.

The whole pregnancy process with Ella was interesting. Kaci did not want to go through another c-section, so she was desperately looking for a doctor who would support her in doing a VBAC (vaginal birth after cesarean).

After some research, Kaci found a birth center in Topeka, run by a group of midwives that supported VBAC and would coach Kaci through the process. The birth center was in a historic house that had been remodeled to have several examination and consultation rooms as well as several big birthing rooms. From the first visit, we were in love with our midwife and the center.

The biggest hurdle we had was not Kaci's past cesarean but the fact that when she goes into labor, we generally have a child in our arms within the next hour ... and the birth center was an hour and forty-five minutes away from our home.

In the early morning hours of August 11, 2006, Kaci woke me to say she was having contractions. While she was not in full-blown labor, we both knew it was best to make our way to Topeka. She called a friend who came over and stayed with our girls as they were not awake, and we were not about to take them with us. We wanted this to be a good experience, after all!

We grabbed our 'go bags' and left.

I don't remember what speed I was going, but I can tell you that I was flying. During the trip, Kaci's contractions became more intense, and she made her way to the backseat to lay down. She was getting pretty uncomfortable.

Then, lights lit up behind me.

I quickly pulled over, anxiously waiting for the officer to get to the vehicle. Per his training, the officer was checking out the vehicle, and I could see him do a double-take at Kaci laying down on our back seat. He didn't even ask me about my speed, he skipped directly to: "Sir, is everything OK?"

"My wife is in labor, and we are trying to quickly get to the birth center in Topeka as she is notorious for quick childbirth."

"Fair enough. From here on, try to be reasonable. No breaking the sound barrier."

"Yes, sir!" I replied, and we were on our way.

One never knows what to expect in life, and this time, Kaci's labor was much longer. It wasn't until later in the afternoon that Ella made her appearance.

That gave us time to call my parents. Excitedly, they drove to Topeka to be with us. They sat in the outer room, running to get a few things here and there for Kaci. This was the first time my parents were able to be present for the birth of one of their grandchildren.

After Ella was born, the midwife examined her and Kaci, and a couple of hours later, she said, "Well, y'all might as well go on home where you can be comfortable and rest."

With decades of experience, this lady knew that the best place for us to be was at home. Out the door we went. By 7:00pm, we were home and eating dinner with our family.

From the moment I first held Ella, I noticed an intensity in her eyes. It was like she was taking everything in, not missing one detail. I didn't think much of it at the time, but it's now well-known in our household – if you can't find something, ask Ella.

Literally.

Once, I could not find a set of miniature screwdrivers. Ella shot out of her chair, ran downstairs, rummaged through a plastic bin, and within a couple of minutes, I had those screwdrivers in my hands. That's just one example.

Most people who know us won't even know who I am talking about right now. That's because everyone knows Ella as Tater.

Here's why. When Ella got her two top teeth, she had a huge space between them. The movie *Cars* had come out, and her favorite character was Mater, who also had a big space between his two top teeth. Since her name is Ella Mae, we started calling her Ella Mater, and over time, it got shortened to just Mater. Later, it somehow changed to Tater, which stuck. Each of our girls has some kind of nickname: Allison is Alli Jo Jo, or simply Al; Aubrey is Bub or Toots; Emma used to be Goose, but is now simply Emzie.

As it has turned out, Tater's skills go beyond finding lost or misplaced items.

Here's another example. Many times, as we crisscrossed the country, we would drive by a feedlot, and the girls would all groan as the smell of cow manure flooded the truck. I would say, "Girls, that's the smell of money."

On one particular occasion, we were beginning to try our hand at eating healthily on the road. In an attempt to have healthy snacks on hand, Kaci bought several boxes of Fiber One bars, or as our family came to call them, "Fiber Fart bars."

This came back to haunt us at several concerts when Kaci and I were in pure agony from holding in all the gas. We couldn't let rip because there were people constantly around us. In the truck, all of us were gassed up like nobody's business.

One evening, we were driving to Farmington, NM. We had just left Bernalillo and were heading north on highway 550. The girls were all nestled in, and we thought they were sleeping. Then someone let one rip, and it stank!

That's when we heard Tater's tiny voice say, "I smell money!"

From the mouths of babes! We all erupted in laughter.

Tony Bowell: Live at Crossroads Church

I was and am a huge fan of Tony Bowell (the guy who taught me all about sound equipment). He's a super-talented singer with a high lonesome voice, a talented guitarist who has a knack for finding amazing chord voicings, and a songwriter with the skill to tell a story in a way that will melt you into a puddle of emotional jello.

I desperately wanted others to experience Tony's talent in the way I had experienced it. Recording in a studio was too expensive. So, in 2007, I set out to do a live recording of Tony. In hindsight, I feel like the project was a success in some ways but a failure in others.

My brother-in-law, Jesse Smith, and I worked hard to assemble teams of people to work on all the different aspects of the project: lighting, live sound, capturing the tracks from individual channels on the board to a computer, mic placement, promoting the live event so we could capture a room full of people clapping and cheering, etc. It was overwhelming.

The easy part was Tony. He got on stage and knocked it out. Because we wanted to take advantage of the momentum, we doubled the bill. Wur'ship Project played first, followed by Tony Bowell. I used that event to get tracks for the *Wur'ship Project: Live* album. That ended up being an album I really wish I hadn't released, but it's out there anyway.

As I said, Tony knocked it out of the park. We got good tracks and put them on a portable hard disk and shipped them to Moses in Canada. Moses imported the tracks and did his magic on them through the mixing and mastering process. All in all, the tracks came out sounding very organic, and they sounded amazing.

The downside: there are vocal blemishes here and there that came through on the recordings that would simply not be noticed at a live event. Being in a packing room with all senses firing, people simply don't hear those subtle things. I guess you could call it the 4-dimensional effect. When you take that recording and play it back in the car without any of the energy from the crowd and the other sensations of being at a live performance, every little nuance comes across loud and clear. It's very one dimensional. That's how I feel like I failed Tony.

To this day, more than a decade later, the one thing I dream of doing (if I ever become independently wealthy) is taking Tony Bowell into a studio with a great producer, engineer, and studio musicians to put his music down the way it should be. Then I want to release it for the world to hear and be blessed by it.

Another Bad Breakup

Take all my character flaws, wrap them in the simmering anger that was inside of me, and deep fry that in immaturity. Nowadays, I understand why some old people are so meek and kind. Imagine ... after years of leaving ruined friendships in their path, older people put two and two together and realize that there was one common denominator in every failed relationship: themselves.

I could have saved some beautiful relationships had I learned this lesson decades ago.

I have certainly not arrived in life, but I am at the point where I look back and realize the harsh truth: *I* was the problem.

Somewhere along the way, I rubbed Craig up the wrong way. I'm certain it wasn't just one thing; it was a culmination of all my quirks. And let me tell you, I've got a few!

Over time, I got to the point where I lost patience with Kelley and couldn't stand being around him. He was an amazing young man who loved the Lord, but I couldn't see that. All I could see was a kid who had the opportunity to travel the country playing bass and ministering to people but insisting that he was a singer and a guitarist. It made me feel like I was some sort of charity and that he was doing his part for the band as a favor to us. Because of my feelings, I believed that he didn't think much of me or my music, and what that said to me was that my music and ministry was worthless. It was the same old crap bubbling away under the surface.

One evening, we were all together for a writing session. I don't recall what happened, but Craig did something that Kelley and I found hilarious. No one likes to be laughed at. Couple that with all the festering junk, and it's no surprise that Craig popped. It almost went to blows.

And that was it. It was over.

Craig and I have never really hung out or talked since that day. Oh, we'll exchange small talk if our paths cross or chit chat on Facebook. However, the close bond of true friendship ... it was gone in a flash.

I lament that loss deeply. Such good folks. Such good friends.

Super Summer

Now we were without a drummer again. On the horizon was a two-week stint as the worship band for the Kansas/Nebraska Youth Camp called 'Super Summer.' It was held at Webster Conference Center where my mentor, Floyd Smith, worked.

We had to find a drummer! There was no way we could do worship for 500+ youngsters as an acoustic duo.

I can't remember how his name came up, but this was when we met our long-time friend, Kenny Schneider. The funny thing is: our first meeting at Chili's in Salina was almost a showstopper. Kenny was all business (and he still is; I've learned a TON from him!), and Kaci was totally turned off by all the talk about money. If I hadn't been persistent and we didn't absolutely need a drummer, I doubt our beautiful friendship with Kenny and his wife, Sara, would have ever made it off the ground.

So, we had a drummer. Whew!

We started rehearsing.

Everything was going great, but we were heading for a train wreck because of something that God did in my life that doesn't really gel with the 'industry' of Christianity: when I'm leading worship, there's no place for performance.

Don't get me wrong, I am a performer to the core! If I'm hired for a concert, I will put on a show! However, if I'm asked to lead a group of people in worship, I would rather hide behind a curtain where no one can see me. Not to mention that I painstakingly pray about what songs the Lord would have me do. I don't subscribe to any kind of formula.

That's how I walked into week one of Super Summer.

The first couple of days, you'd think I was standing on stage biting the heads off bats. But by the end of the week, the kids were really starting to open up. There were tears, and special moments were happening between individuals and the Lord. It was beautiful.

No Longer so Super

We got a new camp pastor in week two. Little did we know that he would become one of our dearest friends and biggest cheerleaders: Nate Dunman. He's one of the most fun people you will ever be around. Yet, if you mess up, he will lovingly bring correction. You know what? The youngsters, not only at camp but at every youth event he has led, LOVE this man with a love and respect I have never seen afforded to another individual in my life!

The week started off much the same as week one. The kids were like, "What the heck? Shouldn't we be jumping around?"

Nate was active in working through song lists. We were co-laborers. It was great!

Then the last night came around. There was supposed to be some time set aside for our band to do a 'mini-concert.' Of course, meetings always go on for longer than planned, and that evening was no exception. So, the camp director came up to me and said, "You've got one song. You'll be up in about 20 minutes."

Immediately, I began praying about what to play. I dragged Nate into it, and he prayed with me. After a couple of minutes of asking God to guide us in what song to play, I got an overwhelming sensation, and I knew what I must do.

Our time came, we took the stage, I told the story of the young lady who inspired the song we were going to sing, and then we played *I'm Alive*.

Before I tell you what happened next, let me share the story behind the song. Every Sunday at Crossroads Church in Salina, someone shares a testimony. It is simply the most powerful part of the service. One Sunday, a young lady got up to tell her story. Kaci and I knew her, and we would describe her as the type of person we would be OK with babysitting our children. So, we had a very high level of respect and trust for this young lady, and we didn't expect to hear what she said.

Her story revealed that she once looked like she had it together on the outside, but the truth was that she had been dying on the inside. She was everyone else's cornerstone, the person others would go to and share their hurts with, but she had no close relationships and no one to turn to. Eventually, she cut herself. Over time, she *needed* to do it. Then she needed to cut more often and go deeper. She described that, in a sickening way, the physical pain of the cut would wash away the emotional pain, and she became addicted.

She had been raised in a Christian home and had been active in the church all of her life, yet she was lost and hurting.

Then, one day, she cried out to God, "If You are there, I need You!!!"

She said, "What used to just be good words on a page came to life. For the first time in my life, I realized that God is a real being and that He is active in my life!"

As she drew on this very real relationship with a very real Jesus, she overcame a very real addiction.

Back to that night at Super Summer.

I shared the story, and we began singing.

Without being prompted, over a hundred kids left their seats and made their way to the stage. Many fell down weeping; others embraced each other, weeping. That's not to mention those who stayed at their seats, weeping and hugging one another.

However, there were a few who were bored, and they walked out of the meeting.

Nate, Kaci, Kelley, Kenny, and I finished, walked down to the front, and prayed with those hurting kids.

No joke, we didn't make it five steps out of that building before I had an angry camp director in my face!

"I'm going to tell you this out of love," he started, which told me that nothing he was about to say was going to be loving. Otherwise, he wouldn't have said that.

He began to chew my butt in front of everyone walking in and out. I'm not talking about a mild-mannered constructive criticism session. He was loud, angry, and irate, to the point that the campers and the leaders passing by were giving us some pretty strange looks.

The gist of his tirade: "A song about cutting? Are you serious? Did you see those kids leaving the room? The Lord wanted something upbeat there that would get them jumping and dancing!"

My reply: "Did you see the 100 – 200 kids who were weeping at the front?"

He huffed, waved dismissively, and walked off.

From that moment in 2007, until we became full-time musicians in 2010, we did not lead worship again.

You see, what was really at stake was money. Yes, you read that right, it's all about money. Christian camps are set up in a way that emotionally manipulates teenagers towards Thursday night, which is dubbed 'cry night.'

And that nickname was created by campers, not camp staff!!

What happens is this: the youngsters are pushed to an emotional point where they are scared of going to hell, and they say a magic prayer that will get them into heaven no matter what. All the while, the staff work like mad to count how many of the magic prayers were said, so they can report back to churches, tug on donor's heartstrings, and raise more money.

And the kids go back to their regular lives, and nothing has really changed.

Don't get me wrong, there are a few here and there who have life-changing encounters with the Lord, but what about the rest?

Later, I even got emails from some of the campers. They were all along the same lines: "At first, we really hated what you were doing. We wanted to dance. We wanted to jump around. As the week progressed, though, we saw what you were doing, and we began to follow. By the end of the week, we loved what you were doing. We had intimate moments with God that we really can't describe, and we long to have that again. Thank you for what you guys did for us at camp. We realize now it wasn't the popular path, and we didn't respond well at first, but now we are so grateful."

I forwarded those emails to the camp director. I never heard back. Honestly, I didn't expect to.

Over the decades that I've sat through church services and conferences, and listened to radio sermons, etc., I've heard many pastors describe Lucifer, aka the devil, as the angel God chose to lead worship. Lucifer was beautifully adorned to reflect all the glory to the Lord. Somewhere along the way, Lucifer became addicted to the worship he was reflecting towards the Lord. Subsequently, he was expelled from heaven, and the rest is history.

However, the problem of worship leaders becoming addicted to worship still exists. Today, we have worship leaders who dress trendy and sing at venues with huge lights, with hundreds, if not thousands, of people raising their hands and responding to the music they are playing in an act of worship to the Lord. Yet, those responses have become personal and addictive to the worship leader. If people don't raise their hands, they feel like they have failed, and so they begin manipulating song lists and formulating songs to ensure they get that response. It's a drug. It becomes an expectation.

It's the same spirit that ensnared Lucifer.

It has ensnared the church and its worship leaders.

I'll never forget Super Summer in 2007 because I do not want to be ensnared! I praise God that, for whatever reason, He spared me from that particular snare!

Gary Parr

Ever so slowly, God was changing how I saw ministry. As He ever so gently reminded me just how much of the sin nature was still at work in me, I began to have more of a compassionate heart for those who did not know God or was hostile towards Him.

As my compassion grew, I sought to minister at more public venues so that I could tell people about Jesus. One of which was the Kansas State Fair.

Of course, I knew we would not get to play on the grandstand stage. I had my eyes set on the side stages where I could gain the attention of the foot traffic.

We got accepted! Not just for one performance, but several. I don't remember how many exactly, but I know we played at least twice during the fair.

The company running the sound on all of the stages at the fair was Parr Sound and Lighting from Great Bend.

When we pulled up to the stage for our first performance, we were greeted by none other than the owner, Gary Parr.

Gary had been in the music business since his teenage years. Beginning as a drummer, he played in bars, and eventually traveled the US with a band that courted a recording offer from MCA Records.

Raised in a Christian home but going the way of the prodigal son, Gary fell into a lifestyle of sex, drugs, and rock and roll. Because of the dark side of the music industry, Gary had become a hard and confrontational man.

Kaci and I did not experience any of that, which shocked everyone who knew Gary. While everyone would say that he is one of the best sound engineers in the business, they would also say that he is one tough guy to work with and for.

As Gary later described it to me, and I paraphrase, "I was in a piss-poor mood when you guys pulled up. Anything that could have gone wrong did go wrong, and then some. As I was walking towards your vehicle, I had every intention of satisfying myself by crushing you. However, as I walked up to you, both of you greeted me with smiles and handshakes that melted me. From that moment on, I knew that whatever you two were involved with, I wanted to be involved in it as well. The funny thing is, I hadn't even heard you play or sing a note!"

That day, Gary did something else that just about made everyone who knew him fall out of their chair – he let us take a complete drum kit with us to be used by one of our drumless drummers. It was just a loan, but he didn't give us a time frame in which he wanted it back.

A couple of months later, I called him to say we had finished with his kit, and I told him I'd run it down to his warehouse. He was flabbergasted.

Gary himself couldn't believe that he let us walk off with a complete drum kit. He later realized that he didn't even take my contact information, although he could have tracked us down via the fair office. That we had the integrity to call him and deliver the kit once we were done just had him floored. Based on his past experiences, he assumed that the drum kit was as good as gone.

Little did we know, God was working through us to restore a relationship in Gary's life, but that's his story to tell.

Gary has been an active part of our ministry since that day. On special occasions, he has traveled all over the United States to haul gear for us, and for no other reason than the pleasure of blessing us.

He even does fun little things for us. For example, when he 'rings in' a sound system for a huge arena show, he will do it with our *Everything I Am* album. And he's called me several times while playing *Falling Down* so loud in an arena that it's louder than a 747 taking off ... all I can hear on the phone is a distorted version of our song blaring through the earpiece, followed by Gary laughing crazily.

Throughout our friendship, I've never viewed it as one in which I ministered to Gary. Because, Lord knows, that man has ministered to me and taught me more than I've ever given him credit for. He's been there for me at my worst and lowest times, and he's given me work when I needed to pay bills and feed my family.

Gary has become one of those brothers I can call in the middle of the night, and I know he would be on his way to help me within minutes.

If you ask any of those people who say that Gary is one of the best sound engineers in the business and that he is a hard guy to work for, they will also tell you that it is because he expects excellence. Not only that, they will state, categorically, that he has one of the biggest hearts and is quite possibly the most generous person they've ever met.

Band 3.0

It wasn't long after the (not-so) Super Summer experience that Kelley drifted off to do his own thing. Kaci and I easily transitioned back into being an acoustic storytelling duo. However, this time, the wheels didn't totally come off the bus. We had Kenny as our drummer, and he was excited about what we were doing.

Kaci and I kept on playing at live events, and Kenny and I got busy looking for band members.

An incident in the fall of 2008 gained us my dream-team lead guitarist...

All of the band members we'd had over the years had badgered me relentlessly about getting an electric guitar, an amp, and some effects pedals. The problem was that equipment like that was (and is) expensive, and I had a family to provide for. So, there was no way I was going to rush out and buy the first thing I found.

Instead, I made weekly trips to S. M. Hanson Music and tried different guitars, amps, and pedal combinations. The guy who helped me week after week, month after month, year after year was Ryan McClintock.

Ryan became my dream-team lead guitarist. And he still is to this day. He's also my right-hand man when it comes to writing music. Ryan just knows how to pull songs out of me.

From 2002 until 2008, Ryan saw me weekly! He patiently put together guitar, amp, and pedal combos for me to test drive, all the while knowing that I probably wasn't going to buy anything.

However, that changed one day in the fall of 2008. I had finally made up my mind.

I walked into S.M. Hanson Music, and Ryan asked, "What do you want to try out today?"

When I told Ryan that I had come to place an order, his jaw just about hit the floor. After 6 years, he had resigned himself to the fact that I would never make a decision and actually purchase anything.

That day, I ordered a custom-made PRS guitar with a gold top. I opted for the bolt-on 22-fret neck, and instead of all rotary dials, I chose a toggle switch to go between the front and rear humbucker pickups. It seemed more practical to me to slap the toggle in a live show environment rather than stopping in the middle of a song to turn a dial.

Ryan hemmed and hawed around a bit, but I could tell he was trying to deliver some bad news softly. Finally, he spat it out, "Special orders from PRS are taking anywhere from 9 – 15 months."

"No worries, I've waited this long. I'm not in any rush anyway," I replied.

The next day, Ryan called me, very excited.

"I've never seen God move in someone's life as much as I've witnessed Him in yours," he said, opening the conversation.

He proceeded to tell me that a salesman from PRS had just called and told him they had a gold-top custom 22 with my exact specifications sitting in their warehouse. It was the previous year's model; someone had ordered it, but they had either not picked it up, or they had canceled the order. At any rate, it had been sitting in the warehouse for over a year, and PRS were willing to make a sweet deal.

Can you fathom the coincidence of it all? Every last detail of my custom-order guitar was waiting for me at the PRS warehouse at a super-discounted rate. Both Ryan and I were blown away.

Now all I had to do was find the rest of my rig, meaning an amplifier and pedal combination that would create my tone (the way the guitar sounds).

At the time, I was really into rock music, and the popular guitar tones were coming from Mesa Boogie amps. The problem was, I could buy a very nice used car for what a Mesa Boogie amp would cost.

So, after I had saved some money, Kaci, Kenny, Gary Parr and myself drove to Overland Park (a suburb of Kansas City) where there was a music store that sold Mesa Boogie amps. Gary's experience in the industry meant that he knew how to tweak dials to get great sound, and we played with every Mesa Boogie dual and triple rectifier that was on the showroom floor.

I was overwhelmed. There were knobs and toggle switches on the front *and* back of these amps! But I'm simply not a tweaker, so they weren't what I was looking for. I just wanted to set my tone to perfection, as easily as possible, and get on with it.

The problem wasn't just the overwhelming number of knobs. It was also that I just wasn't completely satisfied with the tones I heard, no matter what we tried. And for as much as those amps cost, I wasn't going to settle for less than my perfect tone!

So, I had to step away and breath (whenever I get overwhelmed, a claustrophobic type of sensation grips me, and I begin to meltdown). While I walked away to regroup, Gary began fiddling around with other amps.

Soon he called out, excitedly, "Neely, check this out!"

I made my way over to Gary to find him messing with a used amp being sold on consignment.

Now, I must point out that while Kenny played drums for us, his main instrument and love was guitar. Kenny was kind of living vicariously through me and had his heart absolutely set on a Mesa Boogie rectifier amp. But the amp that Gary was getting excited about was a simple Marshall combo tube amp with a single speaker ... and it was used. Kenny was not impressed and objected before Gary even played a note through it.

At the first strum of the guitar through that amp, I was sold! This was my amp. This was my sound.

Plus, I got the amp for 25% of what any Mesa Boogie amp would have cost me!

Two down, one to go! Just an effects pedal needed...

At the time, I was using an Ibanez Tube Screamer pedal to get that 'crunch' in my overdrive tone, but I had often complained that the mid-range sounded like a wet fart. It bugged me, but there really wasn't another option available that sounded so close to what I wanted.

Then one day, Ryan called me, "Come over to the store on your lunch break, I think I've found a solution to your tone issue with the Tube Screamer."

I was skeptical. Mostly because I had played dozens of pedals, and the distortion was usually too heavy, even on the lowest tone settings. But I went to the store.

Ryan already had a rig set up for me. Granted, it wasn't my amp or my guitar, but he had it pretty darn close.

I always had other people demo products for me because I wanted to hear it from 'out front.' To me, what the audience hears and what a musician hears is always different.

When Ryan strummed the first chord, I could swear I heard angels singing. I shot out of my seat with excitement. When I returned to work that day, I had a BBC Green Screamer (their answer to the Tube Screamer) sitting next to me in the front seat of my car.

At this point, I had a drummer and an electric guitar rig but had yet to find a bass player or lead guitarist.

That's when I approached Ryan and asked him if he would play for us. He said yes, but we had to dance around the issue that he was already in a long-term band commitment that came first. I didn't see it as a problem; I was just happy to have my dream-team guitarist committed to playing in my band! Even if we were secondary, I counted it as a huge win for us.

In talking with Ryan, I mentioned our need for a bass player, preferably one who was a believer in Jesus and could actually play a bass line (most worship team bass players don't really get REAL bass lines). He mentioned a young man called Robert Finnell, an amazing guitarist who can also play pretty much anything he touches.

That was about the easiest conversation I've ever had. I think Robert said yes before the question was even out of my mouth.

And so, the band was complete. Now it was time to rehearse and make our live shows great!

Zodlounge: "I Want to Hear Neely!"

I guess I put the cart before the horse in this story. Let's back up to spring 2008.

Wur'ship Project had been with a management company that really did more artist development than managing. This company had put us in touch with top-notch vocal coaches, ran me through songwriting exercises and, most importantly, encouraged Kaci and me to take our recording to the next level.

The owner of the management company introduced us to a production company called Zodlounge in Nashville, TN. Zodlounge was comprised of three men who had played music together since their college days in Michigan. They told me how they came up with the name 'Zodlounge,' but I don't remember any of the details other than it had something to do with their time in the music program at university.

Brett Vargason was the contact person for Zodlounge as well as the drummer and programmer (the guy who put down synth sounds, beats, etc.). While on the phone with Brett, I made a startling discovery: I had seen these guys play!

It was early on in my Christian walk. There was a concert at Salina Central High School. A big-time worship band from Nashville was coming through town. I'll never forget that night because I remember how good that band was; they really made an impression on me. You have to know that I have seen hundreds and hundreds of concerts in my lifetime. I don't recall many of them because they were underwhelming. This was not the case!

Talking to Brett, I came to find out that the band that had me mesmerized was Zodlounge!

That night in Salina, I saw Brett Vargason on drums, Todd Shay on lead guitar, and Tom Michael on bass guitar. Now, I was going to record with them! Talk about a dream come true.

Although they had played in front of tens of thousands of people around the world, Brett seemed sincerely impressed by the connection.

The spring of 2008, Kaci and I drove to Kansas City to board a flight to Nashville for our first recording session in 'Music City.' As I've told people since then: standing there in the airport, it all seemed very surreal. I felt like I was on the edge of something great and that it was my moment to shine. There was no pressure or anxiety, just anticipation. Even as I write this a decade later, I remember how I felt like I was in 'the zone,' as athletes call it. You know, that space where time seems to stand still, everything moves in slow motion, but you are in a deep groove where everything you do falls into place perfectly? Yeah, that's the zone, and that's where I was from the time I got to the airport in Kansas City until we left Nashville to return home.

This was probably the single most defining moment of my life. Not because I was in the zone, and not because we walked away with killer recordings, but because I found my voice!

So many artists sound like someone else. Whoever their favorite artist is, their influence, they tend to imitate that person's vocal and musical style. Without ever saying it out loud, the thought process of hundreds of thousands of musicians around the world is: "Well, it's working for them, they are famous, and so I need to imitate them so I can become famous as well." I was no different. When I was performing, I would manipulate my vocals to sound like all the big names I admired in whatever genre I was trying to make the song fit into.

I'll never forget that Monday morning in the studio, which was literally the whole basement of Todd Shay's house that had been completely remodeled into a beautiful recording studio.

We all sat in the control room where Tom would record and layer all the tracks. First up, though, we needed to chart out the songs. So, we sat in a circle, and I played the songs on my acoustic guitar while Brett charted the song with all kinds of notations that a Nashville drummer uses.

Brett then went into the drum room and played all four songs. Perfectly, I might add. Without any other instrument. He just had the song and direction locked in his head and knew how to get it out. That was my first experience with someone so phenomenally talented.

Then Tom recorded a scratch bass track, which was followed by Todd's recording of some scratch guitar tracks. These gave us a very solid music track, which we used as a backing track to record our vocals.

The musical side of things took place from Monday to Wednesday, and the vocal parts were booked for Thursday and Friday.

When Thursday came around, Todd and Tom walked me through the process. Todd took me into the booth, set me up with a microphone and cans (headphones), and I heard Tom's voice come through the cans. He checked the EQ and levels, and then we were ready.

We had determined that we would record the vocals of *Falling Down* first. Tom told me to listen out for a certain number of clicks and then start singing along with the backing track.

I sang about 3 or 4 words, *"I'm falling, falling down..."* and the music stopped abruptly.

Tom's voice came in the cans, "What the hell was that?"

I had no idea what to say. Was it a trick question?

"Look, I don't want to hear any other artist today. I want to hear the voice that came out naturally when we charted out the songs. I want to hear Neely!"

You'd think I would be reeling. That I would be confused. That I would be all kinds of shaken up.

I wasn't.

As a matter of fact, the biggest peace fell over me. Tom had seen me. He had HEARD me! And now Tom was giving me permission to be me!

"OK, I've got this. Give it to me from the beginning."

"You want a minute?" he asked.

I took a deep breath and slowly let it out, "No, I've got this."

From that point on, Tom only needed to stop me to work through specific vocal parts, or to give my voice some time to rest because I was pitchy. After the first take of me singing in my own voice, I can tell you that the excitement and encouragement that came over those headphones set my soul on fire. I went back to Kansas a different singer. Confident. Controlled. Unique.

I'm not going to pretend that I had it all together from that moment. Throughout the past decade, I've continued to, as I call it, 'settle into pocket' and let my voice be my own.

You see, before that trip to Nashville, I could only sing around 4 songs before I began losing my voice. I'd tried all sorts to remedy the problem – certain teas, candy or cough drops, and I even tried eating small amounts of toothpaste to keep my voice from going froggy! After Nashville, so long as I'm properly hydrated, I can sing for hours without losing my voice. Because it's natural. I'm not putting undue strain on my vocal cords trying to be someone I'm not.

Oh, and shortly after recording, we cut ties with the management company. We realized the terms were ridiculous, and we couldn't afford to continue paying for nothing much in return. We were now 100% independent.

NEELY: Hanging on When God Says, "Let Go!"

We were still known as Wur'ship Project. Zodlounge had mixed the four songs we recorded, and because we couldn't wait to release them, we produced some download cards during the summer of 2008. The front of the download card read *Wur'ship Project: The Zod Archives*.

Yet, since the Super Summer event, God had been speaking to me about letting go of the Wur'ship Project brand. I knew deep in my heart that this was a good thing and would take me in the right direction to become what I was created to be. However, I was in familiar territory with Wur'ship Project. It was comfortable. People knew who we were. Our songs from *You've Called Us Out* were even being played on several radio stations. Excuses, excuses, excuses...

Finally, I couldn't take it any longer. I had to do what the Lord was leading me to do. After a lot of praying, I drew a line in the sand and decided that we would change our name that October, once we had kept our commitment to a Christian music festival. We just had no idea what we would change it to.

We made lists of band names. Oh my goodness, we made list after list after list! In the end, our minds kept going back to Zodlounge and something Brett Vargason had said to us: "Why don't y'all just call yourselves 'NEELY'? Y'all are a duo, it's your name, it's unique, and it sounds tough!"

Of course, if you know me at all, Brett sold the deal when he said, "It sounds tough."

Eventually, that's what Kaci and I settled on: NEELY. Not a moment too soon, either. We were about to go into the studio of secular radio station 92.7 *FM The Zoo* in Salina for an interview about the Christian music festival. The last show that we would be known as Wur'ship Project was only a few weeks away. Nothing like coming down to the wire.

So, we went on air and took part in the interview with radio personality Brother Ken as well as the director of the festival. At the end, we were asked where people could find out more about us.

"Well, for now, you can find us at…" and I gave our web address, "but this will be our last performance as Wur'ship Project. From here on out, we will be known as NEELY."

Pleasantries were exchanged, the interview came to a close, and we began to pack up and head out of the building. Pretty standard stuff.

We were just about to go out of the door of the station when we heard Brother Ken shouting, "NEELY! Hold up!"

He and the station manager were quickly making their way towards us. When they got to us, Ken said, "Man, I've been following your music for years. I genuinely love it! The problem has always been your name. If your name had been different, I would have been playing you on the air."

"Now that you're changing to NEELY, we wanted to run something by you," he continued. "We would like NEELY to become the official rock band of 92.7 *FM The Zoo*. We will play your songs regularly on the station, you'll be promoted in all of our materials and at all of our outings, and we'll give you live performance events. Your first performance will be next month, doing the opening set for White Lion (an 80s metal band that used to play to arenas full of people) when they come through Salina."

We accepted the offer!

Letting go of the Wur'ship Project brand was so simple, yet so excruciating. It had become my security, my identity. Not God. With one simple act of obedience, God opened the door for our music to be played across the Central Kansas airwaves, and with Brother Ken's contacts, it felt like the sky was the limit!

The offer of being *The Zoo's* official rock band was a permanent one. However, the station changed its format shortly after this, and the terms of our agreement fizzled out.

The Blue Goat and
the Anti-NEELY Crowd

You would think the mantle of *The Zoo's* official rock band and the opportunity to open for big-name acts would have generated excitement among our friends and supporters, right?

Not exactly.

Just the changing of our name from Wur'ship Project to NEELY brought cries of us 'selling out.' Oh my goodness, the hurtful things that were said! And this from within our church family and friends, those who supposedly knew our heart for ministry.

When we announced that we would be opening for White Lion at The Blue Goat, it was as if we had said, "God is dead," or something heinous! And all because we would be performing in a bar, and that meant alcohol would be served to our listeners.

Yet, we knew this is what God had wanted us to do all along. This was what He was preparing us for, stretching us and molding us for. Of course, everyone else was telling us that God was telling them to tell us ... ah, you get it.

Thankfully, I'm a stubborn, strong-willed rebel. When I know which way to go, I go for it, against all the odds. This was no different.

Our music began playing on *92.7 FM The Zoo*, and we opened for that 80s band at The Blue Goat.

Beyond all the 'hate mail' and 'anti-Neely' sentiment, two things happened that cemented our decision to take this new direction.

The first was a simple email we received via our website from a gentleman in Central Kansas. One of our songs had been playing regularly on *The Zoo,* and this gentleman heard it ... he *really* heard it!

It goes without saying, Brother Ken and the guys at *The Zoo* were not calling us a Christian band, nor were they giving any kind of presentation of the gospel of Jesus before or after any of our songs. They simply introduced us as the official rock band of *The Zoo* and played our music.

This gentleman heard more than that. I didn't keep the email, though I wish I had. He simply said, "Your music is so moving and powerful. As I listened to it the other day, I realized that my life is a wreck, and I need God." He wanted us to know that he was searching for a church to attend so he could reconcile his life with God.

We were floored! Our songs didn't say anything about God, and the station staff certainly didn't!

The second thing happened at the infamous Blue Goat show. Out of all our friends, family, and followers, only one person showed up to support us. She simply sat at the bar and drank a coke while we played.

Interestingly enough, she knew the bartender, and they caught up with one another before and after our set.

Again, there was no preaching. We just got up and put on the show that we had rehearsed for months.

Later the next week, our friend called us and said, "You'll never believe what just happened."

She proceeded to tell us that her friend, the bartender, called her to say that one of our songs was stuck in her mind and was tearing her apart. She told our friend that she felt her life was off track and out of control. Then she said, "I know you go to church. Can I go with you the next time you go? I need God in my life."

Amazing! And we never said a word. We simply showed up and did what God had gifted us to do. And here's the big clincher most believers in Jesus don't get: we trusted God to do what He was going to do.

I'm aware that these stories make us sound like we were perfect Christians, but that wasn't the case. At the time, the Lord was still maturing us, surgically cutting nasty parts out of our lives. I'm embarrassed to look back and see how I thought I had it all together.

I'm thankful that I'm no longer that person, and I'm thankful the Lord opened my eyes to how much I didn't (and don't) have it all together! Nevertheless, the Lord did use us, and He still does. We came to realize that it was our willingness and obedience that made the difference, though the Lord has mercifully helped us mature and overcome many of our personal issues.

Nashville Photo Shoot

October 2008 was a defining month for us. We shed the name Wur'ship Project, immediately became the official rock band of *92.7 FM The Zoo*, opened for a big 80s band, and received all kinds of hate mail. I'd say that's a pretty spectacular month in anyone's book!

Yet another milestone was reached that month: we had our very first photo shoot in Nashville.

Really, I don't tell this story for any reason other than my eyes were opened to the music industry through this process.

First, I came to realize the difference between independent artists, such as Kaci and I, and artists signed to a record label. For those of you who don't understand what an independent artist is – we are artists who do everything ourselves. We don't have a manager, an agent, or a team of people working on our behalf. It's just us. Independent. Alone. Hoping beyond hope that our friends, family, and fans will love us enough to help. For artists signed to a record label, it's the opposite.

If you want the quick version, it's like you or I buying a hammer versus the government buying a hammer. You and I can buy one for $5, but the government has to pay $400 for the same hammer. Why? Because the government can afford it and the seller can get away with charging more.

When I booked this photo shoot, the photographer's assistant read me the riot act to ensure that we were not signed to a record label because the price for independent artists was roughly $2,000 whereas the price for an artist with a record label was $6,000. Why?

Because the record labels can afford it, so the photographer can get away with charging more.

I guess it kind of makes sense, but still, at the time, the revelation was shocking.

Second, clothing. I had no idea what would go into our wardrobe.

Believe it or not, guys didn't wear men's jeans. If they did, they were the designer-labeled, custom-made ones that cost more than $300.

Now, this was before jean companies ever thought about putting stretchy spandex material in men's jeans so that mega artists could wear tight-fitting jeans without ripping out their crutch or showing their butt when they bent over. So, back then, jeans giving you this kind of flexibility, discretion, and comfort were custom-made and super expensive.

So, what did the smaller artists on a much tighter budget wear? They wore ladies' jeans.

For the first time in my life, I went shopping for women's jeans!

You know what was even funnier than that? It was so common in Nashville to see male artists buy them, that it didn't faze anyone in the store. It didn't stop me from feeling uncomfortable about it, though.

Then I found out about the sheer volume of clothing we needed to have on hand. I couldn't just have one black t-shirt. I had to have a crew cut as well as a V-neck black t-shirt. Oh no, it's not done there! Then I had to have multiple material types of those options. And then there was the different styles ... some baggy, some fitted.

That's just for the black shirt option! Six variations or more of black t-shirts!

So, the volume of clothing we had was astronomical!

The boutiques in town actually hired out clothes to artists! I can't remember the exact deal, but it was something like 40 – 60% of the entire wardrobe cost for X number of days, and then at the end of the shoot, you needed to have purchased at least one of the outfits.

It doesn't sound like a bad option until you consider their prices. The lowest cost pair of jeans I found was $325, and a simple black t-shirt was $60 – $80 (and this was back in 2008!).

Thankfully, our photographer's style of shooting didn't require the need of a makeup artist. Yes, I had to wear some makeup, but it was easy for Kaci to apply, so we were spared that cost.

At the end of it all, though, those photographs are some of the iconic NEELY photos that people still love to this day. And the cool part of that is: at the time of this writing, we are almost a decade past that photo shoot.

You and Me: Forgiveness

The momentum of 2008 was staggering. We had a lot of things going for us, but we had one big problem. And the problem was that we only had four songs recorded. There was no way we were going to spend our money on printing a couple of thousand CDs with only 4 songs on them. Yes, we had the download cards, but in 2008, in the center of America, digital media had not yet caught on.

Plus, every artist wants to release an album. Especially when the recordings sound as good as the ones Zodlounge was kicking out.

This brings us to a couple more fundamental problems:

Firstly, it cost almost $2,000 to record one song. Secondly, I didn't have any new material ready. Certainly, not enough to record 6 more songs so that our album could have an even 10 songs on it.

So, what did I do? I booked studio time!

Nothing like working under pressure, right? I'm glad I did it. It pushed me to write, and I wrote 4 more songs. But when we were only weeks away from recording, we still needed 2 more.

Both came right at the last minute, and the first one also brought with it something I didn't expect, something that I *never* expected to happen.

Forgiveness.

While our marriage had certainly improved, wholehearted forgiveness was something I'd still been searching for. I'd prayed and prayed, seeking to be able to forgive Kaci for what I believed were her sins against me. I sought out Bible studies and books about forgiveness. I constantly spoke to Floyd about it, asking him,

"How do I do it?"

Even though Kaci had opened up to me about her sexual past approximately two years before this, I was still struggling to forgive. I was gutted to realize the truth, of course, but after 10 years of imagining her frolicking with other men, it was difficult for me to change the scenes in my mind, and therefore it was difficult for me to let go of my hurt and anger.

In the end, my search for forgiveness brought me to this point.

We were two and a half weeks away from getting on a plane to Nashville to record 6 more songs with Zodlounge. They didn't know that we only had 4, and I was praying like crazy that the Lord would open up my creative juices.

I was still the IT Administrator at Geoprobe at the time, and I sometimes worked remotely, doing server maintenance from home. During the evenings, Kaci and I watched TV shows in front of the fire. We really enjoyed our time together, just being in each other's presence.

On this particular day, Kaci wasn't home. It was rainy, windy, and pretty chilly. I was sitting at my desk, logged into a router, checking something when an overwhelming urge hit me. I wanted to be next to Kaci. It didn't matter where she was, I wanted to be there. Even if she was out shopping (which I absolutely hate), I wanted to be there, just to be next to her.

Then words began to flow out of me, and I started writing. Then a melody formed, and it was good! Oh my gosh, 15 minutes later, I had a song. This had never happened to me before!

I ran out into the nasty Kansas weather, got into my car, and made a beeline for S. M. Hanson Music.

Ryan told me later: "Dude, I saw the look on your face, and I cleared a way for you to get to the acoustic guitar room."

Ryan joined me in the guitar room, and we knocked out *You and Me*.

Afterward, we just sat for a moment in awe and excitement. We couldn't believe what had just happened.

As quickly as I came storming through the door, I said, "I got to get back to work!" and I was gone.

When I got back to my desk, still thinking about the song, I heard the quiet, internal voice of the Lord. He said something to the effect of, "Jeremy, you know how you long to be in Kaci's presence right now? It would be cool if our relationship were like that."

That was all He said, but it rocked me to the core! He already longed for me, and He wanted me to long for Him in the same way that I longed to be with Kaci. Interestingly, when I looked back at the lyrics, I found hints of my longing to be with the Lord written into the song. He had His hand in the process even before I was conscious of it!

Then I realized something huge: this was a piece of art depicting my love and desire for Kaci, and it was the first time I'd been able to do that since the baggage of her past had been dumped all over us just weeks before our wedding.

It was a very uplifting moment for me because I realized that the process of forgiveness was actually happening. The anger, the rage, and the hurt were beginning to wane. It would still be a long road to total forgiveness, and more hurts did follow, but this was definitely a bright spot in the process of forgiveness between two hurt souls that desperately loved one another.

The Return to Zod: Everything I Am

Whew, with two and a half weeks until our next scheduled studio time at Zodlounge, we had *You and Me*.

But we still needed one more song to get us to 10 songs. To say that I was stressed is an understatement.

At least the financial side was not stressful. The Lord laid an idea on my heart – to ask family, friends, and fans to sponsor a song, either fully or partially. Wow, did people respond! I'm not sure when all the crowdsourcing websites began, but in 2008/2009, no one I was dealing with had ever heard of a concept like it.

With the financial stress a non-issue, it made the stress of writing songs ... more bearable, if that makes sense?

This trip to Zodlounge was different because we were taking Ryan McClintock with us. So, I had my right-hand man, in terms of writing songs, with me for the whole trip.

Leading up to the trip, I spent a lot of time with Ryan at his house. About 5 days before we were due to leave for Nashville, we had a breakthrough that set the tone for NEELY for years and years to come.

As we sat at Ryan's kitchen table, we were frustrated. We had hit a wall in the songwriting process, and we felt hopeless and helpless. Ryan leaned back in his chair with his old guitar nicknamed 'firewood' in his hands, and he began noodling with the E minor chord.

"Wait! Play that again!" I said.

And he did, over and over as I scrambled through my notebook.

Deep in my notebook were my writings from the previous Sunday's sermon at Crossroads Church. Pastor Ron Bowell had been teaching about Mary and the alabaster jar.

To this day, I can tell you where I was sitting that Sunday morning. I was stage left (the left-hand side of the auditorium), three rows back from the front and two seats in from the outer aisle. When Pastor Ron began speaking about Mary, who she was, her circumstances, and her humility as she sought out the Son of the living God, I was moved to the point that I was no longer in that room. Kaci can attest, I began writing furiously. Not notes, but rather emotionally-charged lyrics. Poetic in some ways, soul-deep outbursts in others.

I found it. Two pages of words. Full of emotions. Nothing more, nothing less. Until later that week when Ryan started playing that riff.

As he played it over and over, I began singing, *"Quietly, I walk into the room..."*

His head snapped up, and we made eye contact.

"Hoping for a chance to be with You..."

Ryan leaned forward to look at my notebook while continuing the riff. The verse continued to flow.

"Check this," said Ryan as he played into the chords that are now the pre-chorus to *Everything I Am.*

Then we hit a speed bump, and it seemed like we wouldn't make any further progress. Just as hopelessness started to loom over us, Ryan jumped up and shouted, *"They say, I'm not good enough! You say, come and take my hand..."* and the chorus began to take shape.

The song was still pretty rough, but my favorite part was about to come forth.

"How about we step out of time for the bridge?" asked Ryan.

"Let's try it!"

He then played through the chorus and hit a C major 7th chord, followed by an E minor chord, and he repeated the two chords at half the speed of the rest of the song. I began playing around with lyrics that went back-and-forth between Kaci and myself.

We were excited. We had a 10th song! We had no way of getting the rough cut to Zodlounge before flying out because we had not yet fully tied all the parts of the song together. We just knew we had a great song.

When we arrived at Zodlounge 5 days later, we played what we had for Tom, Brett, and Todd. They absolutely loved it. "You need to tighten it up quickly because we've got a lot to do in a short amount of time," warned Tom.

It's all a haze from there. I don't recall how Ryan and I pulled it off, but we did. In hindsight, I can see God's hand all over the process. In the midst of it, I was just trying to hang on.

At the time of this writing, *Everything I Am* has been the face of NEELY. Several years after the album was released, it went to number 18 on Billboard's Christian Rock Charts. Subsequently, it has been played on numerous radio stations, both Christian and non-Christian, all around the world, and the music video has been played in more countries than I can list. Not only that, but this song also took our social media following from zilch to hundreds of thousands. And all of this without a huge budget for radio promotions!

Granted, there were other songs along the way that helped build our identity and reputation, but this was the foundational song. This is the one that kickstarted it.

What makes me most proud: Kaci sang it, and she owned it. That fun-loving middle child from a small town in Central Kansas who was always pushed into the shadows and overlooked for lead roles in theater and solos in choir, that wonderful and sweet young lady who was abused by men who tried to destroy her for their kicks ... this song was the redemption of Jesus Christ written all over her life!

This may have been the last song written for the album, written at the eleventh hour. However, it became the title track of the album, and it became our battle cry.

Rewrite This Song While I'm at Lunch

This second trip to Zodlounge was intense. On the previous trip, we recorded 4 songs in one week, and it took every bit of that week to get those 4 songs done. This trip we were recording 6 songs!

Tom kept saying, "You can come back and finish anything we don't get done."

But I'm a total cheapskate! I always try to get the best bang for my buck. By golly, we were going to get all 6 songs done in one week and save a lot of money!

Yeah, we made it, but looking back, we could have done it in a much more relaxed fashion.

One of those intense moments came mid-morning on Tuesday.

All of my songs have a deeper meaning, and many are very personal because they tell my story. There was one I'd written for this album that was particularly intimate because it was written directly to my addictions. Up until this point, I had not admitted to anyone that I had been addicted to drugs and alcohol. This song forced me to talk about it. It's called *I Don't Need You.*

I've always tried out our songs with live audiences before committing to recording them. Mostly because it's so dang expensive to record. Now yes, I could record songs myself, or I could go to a local guy who has a studio and record for much cheaper. We hear stories like this all the time, right? "That song was recorded in someone's basement." But when you run the math, those artists may as well play the lottery. The chance of winning the lottery is like the chance of getting hit by lightning – it could happen, but most likely, it never will. Likewise, the chances of those artists getting a decent recording and making it in the music industry are very, very slim.

This is what I tell the people who vehemently attack me for recording in Nashville and paying a premium for it.

Back to the story. We had played *I Don't Need You* live for a whole year. In our minds, it was done. Ready to go.

But Tom walked in that Tuesday morning and said, "I feel like *I Don't Need You* isn't finished. With your other songs, I feel chills when we get to the chorus. I never get there with this song."

OK. What do I do with that information? How are we going to arrange the song to make that happen? Nothing ... yet.

We brewed some coffee and continued the work we were doing on other songs.

Around midday, Tom stood up and announced, "Well, I'm going to lunch. You are staying here. I want you to write a chorus for *I Don't Need You* that gives me chills by the time I get back, or we aren't recording it."

He walked out of the room and went to lunch.

Ryan and I were mortified.

"Well, Neely, I guess we better get to work," said Ryan.

He grabbed his guitar, and we started hammering through options.

"It just doesn't feel right!" I said.

"That's because you're in it too deep. Take a step back. What are you trying to say?"

"What do you mean 'in too deep'?"

"You can't see Tom's point because you've played the song for too long. You've backed yourself into a corner. What are you trying to say in this song? Let it out!"

Frustrated, I blurted out, "I'm declaring that I'm free. I'm free of me. I'm giving up my will so that I can be everything God has created me to be."

"It's about time. Now sing that!" Ryan ordered.

He began playing chord progressions for a hard-hitting chorus. I was digging it. When he looped around, the words flowed, *"Free of me. I can be everything I'm made to be..."*

We played it over and over until it was solid.

About that time, Tom walked in. "Yes! That's it!" he exclaimed.

Immediately, the tension broke. We called in Brett and Todd and began charting out the song.

Following that, you'd think that I would never 'back myself into a corner' again. But I still love to try songs out on audiences before I record them. I want to make sure they resonate with people.

However, I'm now more flexible. When I walk into a studio, I set my mindset to: "How can we make this song excellent?" And excellence is what I'm paying for. I'm paying for studio musicians to play and record tracks efficiently and amazingly, but at the same time, they also teach me something new. Likewise, producers create an excellent product, but they also challenge my creativity to soar to new heights. These are the unspoken things that one pays for when going into a professional studio.

Sure, I could record guitar tracks on my own. However, by hiring a professional who comes highly recommended and has done it for years and years as his day job gives me the benefit of gleaning from his knowledge. I get to ask questions, video his fingers, document chord voicings, hear his stories and tips ... all of that is part of the price of recording.

That day, as we worked on *I Don't Need You*, I came to understand the hidden value of being in a studio with talented people. This is probably one of the most valuable lessons I've ever learned. From it has come wisdom, tips, and tricks that have helped shape me as a musician, writer, performer, producer, and businessman in the music industry. Sometimes, I've just asked questions and listened. Believe it or not, I've also learned a lot about myself, my faith, God, and ministry from this principle.

"Who Is My Neighbor, Lord?"

Y ou've seen my pedigree. Born and raised by Christians. All of my uncles and aunts are believers. I was at church every Sunday ... until the day I chose, like the prodigal, to walk away. So, I had heard Matthew 22:37-40 many times:

Jesus replied: "'Love the Lord your God with all your heart and with all your soul and with all your mind.' This is the first and greatest commandment. And the second is like it: 'Love your neighbor as yourself.' All the Law and the Prophets hang on these two commandments."

All the Law and the Prophets hang on these two commandments? What?

In his gospel, Luke recorded more of this interaction between Jesus and an expert in the law, adding that Jesus was asked, "And who is my neighbor?"

I always thought to myself: "What an idiot! How could you not know what Jesus meant by this?"

Evidently, my thought processes prove that there was way too much pride in my heart. Yet, as can be seen from songs like *In the Middle* and *You and Me*, God was working on my heart, and I can look back on those years of struggle and failure and say that God was faithful. For I truly desired that He would radically change me. I desired more than anything to be free from all the junk and to simply love my wife as Jesus loved me. And by the way, although Kaci and I have come an incredibly long way, that's still my desire.

One day, it hit me like a ton of bricks: *my wife is my neighbor, and I am meant to love her as I love myself.*

My heart shattered.

And at the same time, I saw clearly: I was married to a beautiful person. A princess who was once so full of life that it was like a smile entered the room when she entered.

I could see her again.

I could see the sweet and precious woman who had captured my heart, the girl I had met and fallen in love with back in 1995. And I could see the weight of my sin on her. I could see the look of pain on her face every time I reacted in anger, every time I failed to forgive.

There is something from the world of addiction that relates to this. Many times, the family of the addicted person never allow that person to become more than a dirty addict. Even after Jesus has completely changed them, they still lash out. I came to the realization that I never allowed Kaci to be more than the dirty person I built her up to be. I didn't allow her to be who she really was. She had carried so much shame and pain, and instead of helping her to heal, I had acted selfishly.

It absolutely gutted me.

However, following this, my thought processes changed:

Would I want Kaci to treat me the way I treated her?

How could I hurt Kaci so horribly?

Kaci and I began to talk about the past again. But this time, it wasn't to hurl accusations or place the blame on each other. Rather, we talked with a whole new perspective: God's perspective.

We both owned our sin and how it had impacted each other. And, most significantly, we both forgave each other. Entirely. Completely.

Don't get the impression that we were instantly skipping through green pastures with flowers in our hair. We didn't say a prayer, and 'poof,' Jesus immediately made our marriage so much better. It took work, and we were willing to work towards restoration. As a result, we began to see changes: emotional walls began to come down, we began to laugh together, and we held hands more often.

This was also when my faith grew by leaps and bounds. This was when I finally understood that I hadn't given God all of my heart, soul, and mind. Consequently, *I* was the fool who didn't understand who my neighbor was, and I certainly hadn't been loving anyone as I loved myself.

Had God not placed Floyd in my life, had that man not invested in me for 6 long years, I may have never reached this place. There were many others along the way who invested in my life in spite of my sin, and I praise God for these folks every moment of every day.

In the subsequent months and years, God did a mighty work in me through the sermon I heard about Mary and the alabaster jar. He used it to continue breaking my heart for what breaks His. It wasn't enough to tear the veil from my eyes to see the beauty of Kaci sitting in front of me. He also wanted to cleanse my eyes of any film that had been built up under that veil. He wanted to take out the old tube screen and install a high definition image of the beauty I had forgotten. What an amazing, healing, restoring, forgiving Savior He is!

PART ELEVEN

GOING FULL-TIME
... FINALLY!

The Cosmic Neon Sign: "Move, Dummy!"

I have to lay some groundwork for this story. In 2007, God moved a mountain in our lives. Specifically, in Kaci's life.

Up until that point, she was a 'homegirl' and had no desire to live anywhere but Central Kansas, near her family. Yet, something changed within her when we were presented with an offer to be worship leaders at a church in Texas. Not only did she consider it, but she also went online to look for houses in the area.

This was a huge change in Kaci!

The opportunity ended up falling through, but God used it to lay the foundation for a move He called us to make several years later.

The following year, when we stepped off the airplane in Nashville for our first visit to Zodlounge, I felt a peace that I can't understand or fully put into words, but it felt like I was finally home.

During that visit, I asked Brett, Todd, and Tom (together and individually) what their thoughts were about singer-songwriters moving to Nashville.

They all replied similarly: "Nashville is a great place to live, and a great place to raise a family. However, the music industry is in turmoil, and it's a tough business. There are literally tens of thousands of dreamers pouring into Nashville each year looking to strike 'Nashville Gold.'"

They weren't trying to discourage me; they just didn't want to paint a picture of easy success.

But throughout that trip and for months following it, I sensed God telling me that He wanted us to be in Nashville. So much so that I believe He gave me a plan to present to my boss that would phase out my job over six months. I mean, this plan was detailed. Over those six months, my time in the office would incrementally decrease, while my remote hours would increase. Thus, giving my employer the security of having an administrator overseeing daily operations but taking my 'hands off' the in-house side of things.

Every so often, I presented the plan to friends and family. The response was always the same, "Why would you do that?!?!" Followed by a variation of, "You work for a company owned by Christians who give you the flexibility to make your music while providing a great life for your family."

In essence, they thought they were 'talking sense into me.' However, they were undermining God's desire for Kaci and me.

With that said, I will also say that I don't think God was wringing His hands together saying, "Oh no! This ruins everything!" After all, we're talking about the Being who spoke everything into existence. I'm quite certain that if He really wants something to happen, He can make it happen. That evidence is in the stories of *You and Me* and *Everything I Am* and probably hundreds of other occasions that I've forgotten or missed.

Because of the reactions of friends and family, I didn't act on God's plan. However, a couple of other things happened that pushed us in that direction:

Firstly, after our 2009 recording session, momentum in our ministry felt like it went from a snowball rolling down a mountain to a full-blown avalanche.

Secondly, from 2008 to 2009, the recession had really set into the heartland of America. Usually, the heartland is fairly recession-proof, but this recession was deep, and the company I worked for was not immune.

Hours were cut across the board to reduce costs and to weather the company through the recession. Unfortunately, the recession went too deep, and layoffs had to happen.

There were a lot of things at play that led to a meeting I had with my boss in mid-May 2009. For starters, I dyed my hair (I had some back then!). I also had gauged hoop earrings, a tattoo, and I dressed trendy. Overall, I was different. I didn't fill the Central-Kansas-farm-boy-churchgoing mold. Added to that, my boss frequently made sideways comments that insinuated that I was a thief – that I stole company time.

To top it all off, my boss was the head of the finance department. It is NEVER a good idea to have an IT department under a finance department. Why? Because accountants need numbers. They need to justify expenses. And the only time an accountant understands the need for thousands of dollars in an IT budget is when the whole system goes down. Then, they see value in that money.

I don't mean to brag, but when my system was running as I designed it, it simply didn't go down. It was solid. My philosophy was to research, fight for, and then implement a system that allowed me to do daily maintenance and administrative tasks rather than running around putting out fires.

But in Kansas, the old-school mindset is: "If you aren't running around working like a madman ... you aren't really working." And this meant my work ethic and integrity were also questioned.

However, my colleagues, who were mechanical and electrical engineers of the highest caliber, spoke highly of what I did. They understood the value of what I had achieved. I'm only saying that to point out that the question mark over my head wasn't a company-wide view of me.

With all those factors at play, I attended the meeting with my boss.

Basically, the meeting started with: "We really don't have any idea what you do, and we can't justify the expense of your position right now. Plus, we see that your music ministry is increasing, and we sense that we are standing in your way."

That was my first inclination that God was totally at work. How? It was the statement, "We can't justify your position."

Without getting into all the nitty-gritty technical details, what I accomplished during the 10 years I worked for this company, developed and improved their IT beyond recognition. So, for my boss to utter these words ... yeah, God had to have totally blinded him.

I'm not saying this from a place of bitterness, but rather a place of astonishment. Especially because of what happened next.

My boss proceeded to say, "So, we've been praying about it, and we want to propose phasing out your job over the next 6 months..."

OK, do you remember the plan? Well, as my boss continued speaking, he laid out the exact plan God had given me a year earlier, the one I didn't take to my boss because everyone 'talked sense into me.'

I was so overwhelmed by the presence of God in that meeting.

"I accept!" I said, almost interrupting my boss and definitely startling him.

"Well, don't you need to talk to Kaci about this? Pray about it?" he asked.

I replied something to the effect of, "Nope. I see the Lord in this."

I walked out of that office feeling very encouraged. I may not have said it out loud, but I knew beyond a shadow of a doubt that we were moving to Nashville!

"You Aren't Good Enough" (Episode 2)

Between the name-change fiasco of 2008 and the time we announced we were moving to Nashville in late 2009, things settled down quite a bit.

Well, we thought things had settled.

The last two months in Kansas were some of the hardest we've ever been through. Mostly because friends and family came out of the woodwork to once again 'talk sense into us.' And that always ended up coming down to one point: "You really aren't good enough to be in Nashville."

You think I'm kidding? Let me give you an example of a conversation that happened at work.

It all started when I needed a mid-afternoon pick-me-up. So, I went to the break area to get myself some coffee. As I was pouring it, in walked one of the company owners.

"So, you're all set with your move?" he asked.

I nodded.

"How is that going to look? Do you even have a plan?" he enquired.

"Yes, sir, I do."

"Well, what does that look like?"

I laid out my vision, which was a rough plan and told him how I intended to execute the plan.

"Do you really think you are that good?" he asked point-blank.

I didn't reply. Other than a sarcastic chuckle, a cocky grin, and a stare.

"You really think you are talented enough to compete with the artists who are on the radio?" he persisted.

With intensity, poise, and anger that I can't even begin to describe, I replied, "You evidently haven't listened to our album."

And with another cocky grin, I walked back to my desk.

You see, I learned to go toe-to-toe with bullies at a young age. On the outside, my boss saw what I wanted him to see – a man dripping with confidence. However, on the inside, my soul ached from the attack.

The old saying, 'Sticks and stones may break my bones, but words will never hurt me,' is the biggest load of crap I've ever heard in my life.

Thankfully, the Lord gave me a rebel spirit along with a strong will. I turned that hurt into "I'll show you..."

Make no mistake, that's not what people intended me to do. They were not using reverse psychology in the knowledge that I would turn that hurt into fuel. No! They were trying to tear me down. Why? Because if I did succeed, they would have to answer the very real challenge to their own hearts: "Why did I never chase my dream?"

Everyone has a dream, and we each make daily decisions that either take us towards our dream or away from it. The reality is that many people operate out of fear. They believe all the negative influences around them, and they never make their move. They never chase their dream.

So, they join the ranks of the nay-sayers and try to cut the legs out from under other dreamers.

I bet I had at least 20 conversations like the one I shared with you. If it were not for Jesus holding me through this, I would have never walked into the dream that He birthed within me as a youngster watching Charlie Pride at the St. Joseph Civic Arena.

Music City, Here We Come!

I returned home on the day of the meeting with my boss and excitedly relayed the story to Kaci. She panicked for a couple of minutes. Then she calmed down and showed me something she had bought recently – a 'For Sale by Owner' sign.

We put that sign in the yard and posted on Facebook that our home was for sale.

Now, here's where the story just gets crazy miraculous.

Remember, the recession had set in deep. Two of the houses in our new development (several other homes were built after ours) had been on the market for over a year. The owners had reduced their prices time and again trying to attract a buyer, and both houses were listed with very successful realtors.

Just two weeks after we put the 'For Sale by Owner' sign in our yard, we were signing a contract with buyers who had agreed to purchase our home for the full asking price.

No price reductions, no realtors, just the good Lord opening doors for us.

We had several months to get the house in order before everything was finalized, which helped us out a lot.

Over the next six months, we moved from our home to Kaci's parents, and from there to Kaci's grandparents. All the while, we made several trips to Nashville looking for our new home.

During that time, I worked through all the mixing, mastering, and marketing processes as well as every other detail you can think of to prepare for the release of our debut album *Everything I Am*. It was a busy time, but I wasn't stressed. I was at peace.

In November 2009, we asked some friends from Nashville to join us in hosting a 'CD Release Party.' Gary Parr brought the sound and lighting equipment and helped us put on a first-rate concert.

But hardly anyone came.

There we were, excited about this new chapter in our lives and how God had opened the doors for us to take our music and ministry to the next level doing it full-time ... and nothing.

As the old saying goes, 'Actions speak louder than words,' and we heard loud and clear: "We don't care."

Yeah, it hurt, but through it, God confirmed that it was time for us to exit Kansas and follow Him.

Shortly after the CD Release Party, Kaci and I finally went on honeymoon! We went to a small town south of Cancun, Playa Del Carmen and spent 5 days together, just the two of us (something we hadn't experienced since Allison's birth 13 years earlier). I continued to see the beautiful person that I became friends with and fell in love with all those years ago. It was an incredible time on our journey of healing.

For those 5 days, we forgot everything.

We returned to snow and below-freezing temperatures in Kansas, which woke us up to reality! And the reality was we had to get our skates on – there were only two months left of my 6-month phase-out plan, and we still hadn't found a home in Nashville!

I don't recall how many trips we made to Nashville. The drive between Kansas and Nashville is a mind-numbing 13 hours. We were burned out. Our realtor in Nashville had shown us so many homes that we were overwhelmed. None of them was 'the one,' and we were beginning to feel discouraged.

About a week into the New Year of 2010, we made our 'final house hunting trip' to Nashville, though nobody knows why we dubbed it as such when we had no guarantees of finding something suitable. Regardless, my job was coming to an end, and we needed to find somewhere.

Our drummer, Kenny, and his wife, Sara, decided to move to Nashville as well. They wanted to support our ministry in whatever way they could, plus Kenny would have better work opportunities in

Nashville. To make the move financially viable for all of us, we chose to live together, which meant the house needed to be a decent size. In light of that, Kenny joined us on this trip to Nashville to help with the search (due to work commitments, he hadn't been able to join us on the previous house hunting trips).

For an entire week, we spent our days looking at house after house with our realtor, then spent our evenings at the hotel searching for houses online.

Finally, our last day in Nashville dawned. We packed up our vehicle early that morning because we had to head straight back to Kansas following our final viewings. Both Kenny and I had to get back to work.

All of the properties sucked. We were disheartened.

Yet, there was one house that Kaci had found online. She kept saying, "I'd like to look at this one."

To be fair, she'd been saying this for at least two days. When we mentioned it to our realtor, she balked at the idea of us seeing the house. Thankfully, Kaci was persistent, and our realtor relented, "OK, I'll call the realtor it's listed with, but don't expect to see the house on such short notice."

When she got off the phone, she looked surprised. "The realtor got in contact with the family, and as long as you don't mind them being there, we can go and see the house now."

Off we went! By this point, we were hours behind our schedule of leaving Nashville. The only one who wanted to see the house was Kaci, but I wanted to support her, so I put a smile on my face and said, "It's just one last house, let's do it."

The moment we walked in, we knew it was the one.

The house needed some work, but the structure was solid, and I could do all the cosmetic work myself.

In the end, it was the last house, the one we almost didn't even go to see, that was 'the one'!

We told our realtor that we wanted to make an offer, but she asked us to talk it over on the drive home and call her on Monday morning. On the way home, the only discussion between us was about how great the house was and how good God was to provide it for us.

As soon as we got back to Kansas, I emailed our realtor and began the negotiation process. Two days later, our offer was accepted, and we began signing documents and taking trailer-loads of stuff to Nashville.

What a whirlwind month we had between sending that email and taking possession of our home: Gary Parr and I flew out to Bakersfield, CA, to purchase our tour vehicle, a Ford Excursion with a 6.0L diesel engine, and drove it back to Kansas; we also made several more trips to Nashville to transport our trailer-loads of items (thankfully, the sellers let us store things in the basement before they moved out), to sign documents and to make other arrangements.

March 13, 2010, Kaci, the girls, Kenny, Sara, and I loaded up our vehicles and moved to Nashville.

Thus, It Begins: Life on the Road, the Baptism by Fire

We had two weeks to settle into our new home, and then Kaci, the girls, and I headed off for our first tour as full-time musicians.

I didn't book a two-week tour or something easy for us to get used to life on the road. I booked a 3-month-long tour!

Talk about a baptism by fire.

Prior to this, our gigs or events meant being away for only one weekend at a time. Almost always, we were back in our own beds by Sunday evening.

The tour had its ups and downs. Some of these 'down' times were self-inflicted. Others were things we just had to deal with and work through.

One instance was towards the end of the tour when Allison had a breakdown. She just sobbed uncontrollably, saying over and over, "I want to go home." It was understandable, really. We'd gone from weekends on the road to a full 3 months on the road, and that shortly after uprooting our family and moving to a new city.

Because we were just starting out, we took each and every opportunity we were given to play, and this meant that we sometimes had to drive 12 to 15 hours between shows. We were not exactly used to that kind of travel.

One occasion comes to mind, which directly preceded Allison's breakdown. We had booked a house concert on a Friday evening in San Antonio, TX, but we had to be in Omaha, NE, to lead worship on Sunday morning. Sounds like no big deal until you think it through.

Friday evening, our show began at 7:00pm. We had an awesome crowd who wanted to buy tons of merchandise and have us autograph every bit of it. By the time the crowd left, and we had taken down and repacked our equipment and merchandise, it was 1:30am.

Here's where I made the huge miscalculation. We would have to get up at 5:00am and be on the road as fast as we could because we had an 18-plus-hour drive ahead of us.

Now, many of you may be checking your map application to verify this, and it will tell you it's around a 14-hour drive.

But have you ever made a 14-hour drive with four young kids? Have you ever sat still that long? Have you ever made that kind of drive on 3 hours of sleep?

Neither had I.

We actually woke up before 5:00am (and shot out of the door in record time), but we didn't pull into Omaha until a little after 11:00pm.

To make matters worse, the big flood of 2010 hit Nashville that very day. We were getting phone calls from Kenny and Sara as they were frantically working to divert water from our basement door. Plus, we were hearing stories of trailer homes floating down Interstate 24, not far from our home.

Would we have a home to go back to?

Thankfully, we stayed with some of the most gentle and loving folks in Omaha. They were real salt of the earth people and beautiful believers in Jesus Christ. They totally loved on our family and ministered to Kaci, our girls, and me through all of it.

Another defining moment in this tour happened in Farmington, NM. For the first time since the (not-so) Super Summer experience in 2007, Kaci and I led worship. It was beautiful. It was right.

We found family in Farmington on that trip. They took us in, much like the family from Omaha did. However, these folks invested in us in a way that I'm not sure I could ever fully put into words.

The pastor, Andy Fine, immediately took me under his wing. He sensed the hurt in me. He listened to my story about that summer camp. With tears in his eyes and a love and passion that I had never experienced before, he put his arm around me, prayed for me, and prayed with me.

The plan was for us to do a concert for Calvary Chapel, Farmington, but when Andy finished praying, he asked me, "What do you think? Time to get back in the saddle?"

I sensed it was time, but I was hesitant. Andy sensed my reluctance but knew it was born out of hurt. He also knew that the folks at the church would be a gracious crowd, and he assured me that they would support and encourage us.

He was not wrong at all.

I will say this: it was probably the absolutely worst worship session we've ever led. However, the chains that were binding us broke right there on that Sunday morning. In turn, that started the process of healing. The Lord began to heal the hurt and anger as well as the nasty taste we had in our mouths for what worship had become.

Andy was correct. The church family loved us. They immediately organized a return date. That spoke volumes to me, but not as much as what Andy did next...

Before we left, Andy called me into his office and told me that he would contact every pastor in New Mexico in the Calvary Chapel denomination plus a few he knew outside of New Mexico. He also said I could use him as a reference and that other pastors could email him or call his cell phone directly for a reference.

Months later, we got a call from Vertical Radio in Farmington, NM. They wanted our music because so many people had called in requesting that our songs be played on their station. Eden Fine, Andy's son, organized the whole thing. A born leader, Eden rallied the folks at Calvary Chapel and had them call the station daily until the station agreed to play our music.

I've never told Eden this, but because Vertical Radio is a 'reporting station' (at least, it was at the time), their efforts were instrumental in having *Everything I Am* played on other radio stations and landing at number 18 on Billboard's Christian Rock Charts.

Many of our relationships today can be traced back to that first tour, and specifically, Calvary Chapel, Farmington, New Mexico.

Sturgis and Lakeshore Christian Church

Even though we were full-time musicians, I still had to pick up side jobs to make ends meet. I made sure these jobs were part of the music industry for I was keen to network.

Most of my side jobs were with Gary Parr. He flew me to locations to do rigging and lighting, particularly for high-profile shows. Setting up a huge stage with row after row of lights is extremely hard work, and if it isn't done in a certain order ... it can be disastrous and end up costing too much in labor. With my attention to detail, and having experience of project managing in IT, this type of work was a perfect fit.

Without a doubt, the Sturgis Bike Week was high-profile and paid a great deal of money. The only problem was keeping the guys in line.

It's the same problem that plagues all business owners: since the equipment and the business do not belong to the workers, the general attitude is "I don't care." And that attitude breeds all kinds of other issues, one of which is not paying attention to details or processes.

This attitude came to bite me just before the Sturgis Bike Week. We were loading the 53-foot semi-trailer full of equipment to head out, and the crew had just loaded the stage decking into the front of the trailer. Gary and I were in the trailer surveying the space because the 'truck pack' is the ultimate game of Tetris.

The stage decking was made up of large pieces of welded aluminum frames with sheets of half-inch-thick plywood on top. Very heavy duty. Once on site, the decks would be assembled together.

After surveying the pack, we turned towards the back doors and called out for specific equipment. Then we heard a quick hiss and a BANG!

A millisecond later, the pain hit, and I screamed an expletive.

Several of the crew later told me that a horrible fear arrested their hearts when they heard me shout that word since I never cussed or engaged in nasty talk. Their fear was followed by a rush of adrenaline, and many of them raced into the trailer.

One of the decks had fallen and landed on my ankle.

Unfortunately, it took a trip to the emergency room and a lot of stitches to close me up.

Fortunately, I had been standing just far enough forward, and I stress *just far enough forward*, that the deck missed severing my Achilles tendon or perhaps breaking my leg. God had to have been watching out for me.

I was not excited about having an injury like this on the eve of Sturgis, but I praised God that I did not need major surgery. After all, being a small business/ministry, our family did not (and still does not) have health insurance.

If you've ever been to Sturgis, you'll know why I was not excited about this. For those of you who have never been, let me describe it to you. It's literally on the plains of South Dakota in the middle of July. It is hot, dry, dusty, and windy. Keeping a wound like mine clean would be hard, especially when my role required me to be on deck from before sunrise until 2:00am the next day ... every day.

This was only two months after our big 3-month tour, so I had barely been in my new home. I was away from my family, and now I was injured. It definitely wasn't a bright time in my life.

One of the stresses that Kaci and I had on the home front was finding a church. Because of our connection with the Calvary Chapel denomination, we tried to attend one of their churches. However, every Calvary Chapel church in the Nashville area was at least 45 minutes away from our home, and we wanted our whole family to be involved in church, which wouldn't be feasible with those distances.

I slipped into a semi-depression, thinking, "Lord, this is definitely not what I was hoping for in all of this." Meanwhile, Kaci had a God-appointed meeting with Stanya Campbell at a yard sale she was having.

Stanya's husband, Greg, is the worship leader at Lakeshore Christian Church in Antioch, TN. Antioch is a suburb of Nashville. As a matter of fact, most folks don't know where Nashville ends and Antioch begins. Even the Post Office will still deliver letters to Antioch addresses that are postmarked Nashville.

She and Kaci connected, and Stanya asked Kaci if she would like to go to church with her.

By then, we had been to so many churches in Nashville that we were getting frustrated. With every church we visited, it felt like we were stepping into a rock show where the pastors would brag about who they had on stage. Then afterward, it was one big business swap meeting with business cards passing around like crazy. We didn't hear much, if anything, about reaching and loving the surrounding communities.

Lakeshore was different. After two Sundays of attending Lakeshore while I was in Sturgis, Kaci called me and said, "I've found our church home!"

I could tell by the excitement in her voice that something significant had happened. She told me the story and simply said, "Just wait until you meet these people. It's like coming home."

She was not wrong.

When I arrived back in Nashville and attended Lakeshore for the first time, only a week after that phone call, it was truly like I had come home. That morning, I was greeted by more people than I can remember, and I had many meaningful conversations. The one thing that really stuck out to me was that their focus was simple: how can we serve our community as Jesus wants us to?

Profound!

Lakeshore Christian Church has been our spiritual home ever since.

Shielding Us from the Industry

It amazes me how spiritually immature I was when I became a full-time musician. I say this in light of the story I have shared thus far.

For a long time, my spiritual growth was stunted because of my paradigm regarding the kind of music a Christian can sing and write. This was largely due to my incorrect thinking that ministers were either pastors, youth pastors, missionaries, or worship leaders (as I mentioned previously). Once I realized my error, it released me from the box I had put myself in, and I began to write non-church songs (still Christian themed, of course!).

Following that, God took me through another phase of showing me that I am a storyteller. He showed me that being a 'fisher of men' applies to a Christian's sphere of influence, which in my case is music. Again, He showed me that I had a pretty limited view of what a follower of Jesus can write and sing.

When I came to the point of full-time music ministry, I was still spiritually immature!

We had moved to Nashville, we were touring, and we had a song on the radio ... all we needed now was a booking agent, a manager, and a record deal. Because, honestly, God can only move in the music industry through record labels, managers, and agents, right? This was another piece of immaturity that God was about to smash in my life.

I met with publishing agents. I had meetings with presidents of record labels. I met with A&R guys from major record labels and independent labels. I met with publicists. I met with managers. Our producers at Zodlounge had meetings with labels on our behalf. I had so many stinking meetings with amazingly connected and influential folks that it would make your head spin!

They all said the same thing: "We are going to pass this time, but keep us posted as we are interested in your next project."

I came to find out (from a friend who knew one of these guys and discussed it with him), folks in the music industry thought Kaci and I were uncontrollable, which made us undesirable.

What did that mean?

It meant, in one record executive's words: "They are married, they have kids, they have been employed high-up in corporate America. They know who they are. They know how business works. We want a 21-year-old with stars in their eyes."

This was a Christian record label, by the way.

Another interaction I had was with an A&R guy from a major record label. The meeting was set up by Brett from Zodlounge. We went to the offices, hung out with the A&R guy, he asked for our recording, and we left.

A couple of weeks later, after Brett emailed the A&R guy (copying me in on the email), we got a reply. I was furious!

That email is long gone, but it basically said something like this: "My family has had this CD in the van playing over and over for the last week. My wife and kids haven't taken it out once. As far as the record label is concerned, we think you are a great independent group that might do OK, but we don't think you will go far and will have to respectfully pass."

Did you read that the way I did?

This guy's wife and kids, who heard demos all the time, and who, by the sounds of it, never listened to a CD more than once, had our CD playing over and over for more than a week.

Yet we weren't good enough? What the heck was going on?

Then we had another friend who knew the program director of a major Christian radio group that has stations all over the US, and our friend graciously emailed our songs to him.

The reply from the program director was something to the effect of: "Wow, these guys sound like they are right on par with

Nickelback, Evanescence, Daughtry, and the like! They just aren't quite there for Christian radio though."

Did you catch that one?

He basically said, "Your friend's music can hang with multi-platinum selling artists on mainstream radio, but Christian radio is 10 years behind. So, we are going to make them feel inferior and like they don't have a place."

Well, that's what I read, anyway.

Was I angry? Duh! I just had a guy say that our music 'wasn't there yet' while comparing us to multi-platinum selling artists. How would you react?

Then I got a call that explained everything.

A program director from a major reporting rock station in a major city actually called me back.

I was naïve. I had no idea that record labels spent hundreds of thousands of dollars (mainstream, not Christian) to get songs played on the radio. Also, I had no idea that there were radio promoters who did that for the labels/artists. Being me, I went onto all these station's websites, looked up the contact info, read their policies for submitting music, and started emailing and calling.

This program director said she called me back because I was respectful enough to follow all the rules and guidelines that the station put on their website. She said the radio promoters from the major labels were jerks and didn't respect those guidelines. So, she wanted to give me the dignity of a call and a lesson.

In a nutshell, she told me, "I did listen to your music, and I honestly liked it. But a high-profile band has a new single coming out, and I'm being pressured to play it. I would rather play your song, but I can't bite the hand that feeds me. The major record labels send me on cruises, fly me to amazing locations to meet artists, take me out to super-expensive restaurants ... you get my drift? If I play your song and not their artist's, they will take that away from me, my boss, and others higher up in our station. Then I'm out of a job. That's why none of the other radio stations are returning your calls."

It became clear to me that spending money on a radio promoter would do us no good, not even in the Christian radio industry. Why?

Because the record labels could afford to put together lavish trips and all the other extravagant activities, and we could not. Hiring a radio promoter would be like throwing our money in the wind.

Yes, we did have a song on the radio, but it didn't go far; some markets wouldn't touch us because we were not signed to a major record label.

For two years, I met, I called, I emailed, I met some more, and then I finally got what God was showing me: He was insulating us from the industry.

Over the years, I've seen talented folks come to town, sign a big record deal, ride on fancy tour buses, and have their songs played all over the radio and Internet. Only they don't look or act like the person that rode into Nashville years earlier.

You see, when someone signs a deal, the record label needs a product to sell in mass quantities. If you think the product is merely the music, you are wrong. They will change the way a person looks, the way they act, the way they dress, etc., and the record label can because they own the artist's image. That's part and parcel to signing on the dotted line.

God protected us from that!

One instance summed this up:

We were opening for a big Christian act that had their songs on a Christian radio station, were signed to a major record deal, and got to play on the main stage of practically every big Christian music festival around the world.

They were a little snooty in the green room as they bragged about their accomplishments.

Then the promoter, a dear friend of ours and the reason we were opening this show, made some comment to me about our schedule.

All of a sudden, the big-time group perked up, and one of them asked, "Wait? So, what do you guys do for a living?"

I replied, "What do you mean? We do this."

"No, what do you do to pay your bills?"

"This! This is what we do to pay our bills! Why? What do you do to pay yours?" I was half-joking, wondering why the conversation had gone this way.

All of a sudden, their demeanor changed, and one of them replied, "I'm a manager at Walgreens. My other bandmates work here and there. After this show, we have to hurry back to Nashville, so we don't miss work."

Here was this group that was signed to a major record label, their music playing on all the major Christian stations, playing at all the big festivals around the world, but they had to be home in time to clock in for work.

After this encounter (and others like it), I felt emboldened. I didn't get passed over because I wasn't good enough; I got passed over because the Lord had other plans for me and was protecting me from myself.

It wasn't long after that I realized the Lord was shielding us from the industry.

"You Should Play Concerts in People's Homes"

The music industry is really smoke and mirrors. It's all about controlling the conduits of media delivery and making everything as bombastic as possible.

As the digital age began to creep into our society more and more, music was affected profoundly. As a matter of fact, we saw plenty of artists break away from the traditional record label model and make quite a significant living. Many of these so-called new ideas actually stemmed from old traditions.

I can't even begin to wrap my mind around how we made the contacts we did when we were starting out. Much of it was word of mouth as well as friends of ours messaging us to tell us about a venue in their town.

We would follow up all leads!

One such lead led us to Paxton, NE, a small town just north of Interstate 80 in western Nebraska.

Mike Reif, a fraternity brother from Northwest Missouri State University, told me about a chic little winery called 5 Trails Winery that hosted live acts. I didn't have to organize anything; Mike set it up for us.

We arrived in Paxton and looked around the one-block town. It appeared much like any other dying small town.

Except for one thing.

At the end of the block was a storefront that was chicly painted and decorated. It didn't look like it belonged in Paxton at all. People were flowing in and out of the place. It was hopping!

It was 5 Trails Winery. A diamond in the rough.

We didn't know what to expect because we were relatively unknown, and being from small towns ourselves, we knew that people in small towns generally don't go out at night for entertainment. And if they do, they travel to a bigger town or city.

The place was packed!

It turned out that Mike and the owner of 5 Trails Winery had a hidden agenda, which I found out about later. They had invited Muriel Clark, a local host of house concerts, to watch us play. She regularly welcomed world-renowned musicians to play to good-sized crowds in her living room.

Evidently, she loved us, conveyed it to Mike and the owner, and we had a little business meeting right at her table.

Muriel's opening line was: "You should play concerts in people's homes."

"Say, what?"

"There is a movement that goes back to the roots of music. People open their homes to friends and family for a concert by a musician who is traveling through the area," she explained further.

I was a little creeped out by the thought, mostly because it was hammering on my paradigm of what a concert should look like.

Muriel continued, explaining how the audience compensates the artist, many times triple or quadruple the amount they could make in a café, coffee house, or bar setting. She added that the listener actually has a better experience than in other settings because a living room is a true 'listening room.' There's no smoke and no drunks. Everyone is there for one express reason: to hear the artist's music.

I was sold!

"Where do I sign up?" I asked.

She gave me the website details of the company she used, and she informed me that all artists and hosts were vetted by the administrators to ensure quality art as well as safe homes for the artists.

I got to work straight away.

I quickly ran into a snag: the house concert circuit was very folk-music centered. It was one of the reasons Muriel suggested we join – variety was seriously lacking, and she wanted the circuit to become more diverse. She didn't tell me that until later. First, I had to go through a two-month battle.

Yeah, two months of being vetted doesn't sound too bad, until I mention that I took some very sharp and hurtful criticism from the founder of the company. It's was ironic really coming from an uber-liberal individual who was all about acceptance.

I emailed the lady in Nebraska, telling her, "I'm out. I don't have to take this kind of crap from anyone. This guy obviously doesn't like us. Here, look at what he said..."

She called me and apologized profusely. This was when she told me about her plan to extend the genres in the circuit beyond folk music. Apparently, folk music had become like Chinese water torture to her crowd, and sooner or later, they were going to give up and stop supporting artists.

"I'll sort this out," she promised.

The next day, I woke up to an email from her to the founder of the house concert company (she had carbon copied me in on the email).

Have you ever heard the old saying, 'Hell hath no fury like a woman scorned'?

Well, she unleashed in a sweet but fierce way on the founder (who was also an artist). By the time I finished reading the email, I actually felt sorry for the guy because she chewed him up one side and then down the other. She didn't hold back the fact that I shared his critiques of our music with her, and she warned him not to criticize other people's music unless he was willing to receive just criticism of his.

His reply? Well, it was what mine would have been. He was falling over himself apologizing. Yet, he didn't back down completely. He stated that "he knew this community and outsiders like us would be throwing our money away paying the entry fee."

Literally two weeks after we joined, a house concert series from North Carolina contacted us, and when it was all said and done, we made enough to pay our annual entry fee three times over. And we got two other gigs out of the deal.

Speaking of that first house concert. Wow, what an experience!

There were upwards of 60 people in the main living and dining area of the house, all intently focused on us.

I was instantly hooked, and I tell everyone who ever asks, "I've played to 16,000 people at a festival, had them pumping their fists in the air to *In the Middle*, but there is NOTHING like the intimacy of a house concert. I would choose to play at a house concert over a festival any day!"

The crowd laughed with us, and they interacted and asked us questions, all of which made the evening so organic. And the icing on the cake: they cried with us. To see members of an audience become so entwined with a story and/or a song, to be moved to tears, is the pinnacle for any singer-songwriter on the planet!

It all started at 5 Trails Winery in Paxton, NE.

We have since played at house concerts all over the United States as well as England, France, and Germany.

Thank you, Muriel, not only for introducing us to house concerts but also for believing in us so much that you would go to bat for us and keep pushing us along.

Colorblind: Why an Acoustic Album with the Same Songs?

Being a part of the house concert community really solidified my gifting as a storyteller. As much as people were entertained by and loved our music, they were equally entertained by my talent to tell a story.

Yet, we kept hearing one critique over and over and over: "We love your music. Your album is amazing. However, it's nothing like what you did tonight. We want to take a piece of tonight home with us."

I started to think, "These are the folks who pay our bills. How can we better serve their needs?"

Let me tell you that I encountered so much opposition and criticism from the next idea that it wasn't even funny.

I decided to make an album of acoustic recordings with many of the same songs that were on *Everything I Am*, plus take three of the best songs we had from a live recording we made in Llano, TX, and add two new songs to the mix.

At the time, we were approximately two years removed from the release of *Everything I Am*. I had two new songs ready to record, and this seemed like the best way to get them out to the world in an inexpensive way.

Everyone in the industry thought I was nuts. They told me: "You can't release the same songs in an acoustic format and make your money back!"

Wrong, Jack!

By removing the growling guitars, and by adding piano, cello, and acoustic guitars, our vocals came across in a whole new light that literally made the same songs ... new songs. And that's not my take on it; that's the feedback we received.

The two new songs were *Colorblind* and *Complete (The Wedding Song)*.

Colorblind was inspired by Lakeshore Christian Church. It was my artistic way of summing up the life of Jesus Christ as lived out by the community who took us in: 17 different nationalities from every income bracket and social category, all coming together to do the work of Jesus Christ. That's deeper than skin color right there!

Complete was a song I had written for Kaci's elder sister's wedding day. Kelli was 35 at the time she was married, and our now brother-in-law, Dave, was 31. Unlike Kaci and I, Kelli and Dave trusted God and waited for the day they said "I do" before Him and their families. Not for the sake of being pure on their wedding day, but rather because they trusted the Lord and knew that what He had for them was good.

I had been playing both songs live, and they were smash-hits with our audiences.

The only problem was: I could make two radio-ready songs and have money left over, OR I could make an acoustic album with both of those songs in acoustic form and possibly one of them as a radio single.

We chose the second option. Then we had the tough decision, do we record *Colorblind* or *Complete* in a radio-ready format?

Honestly, I think the Lord would have blessed us either way. At that time, we chose *Complete* because it meant more to our family. It was another six years before we had the money available to record the radio-ready version of *Colorblind*.

Colorblind (An Acoustic Album) was a hit at our house concerts. People snatched up both *Everything I Am* and *Colorblind* because they wanted to hear what we sounded like with a full band, but they also wanted to take home what they had experienced that evening. We had achieved our desire to serve the people who paid our bills ... *and* we made our money back.

With no record label, no manager and no agent, with just the Lord guiding us, we have sold over $100,000 worth of CDs.

Granted, standing next to a big-time artist who is on every radio station, TV show, and on the cover of magazines, that doesn't look very impressive.

But when you realize it was just the Lord, Kaci, and I beating the trail, it's pretty amazing!

Taking a Band on the Road

While house concerts had captivated me, there was always the lure of playing the big shows with a full band ... but for that, I needed a big sound system, lights, and a first-rate band.

We had made some great contacts, and our ministry continued to grow by word of mouth. Many of the people who hosted Kaci and I (whether at a gig, a house concert, or at a church) wanted us to return with a band.

I didn't need to be asked twice!

I began to pray about it, and I talked to some of the musicians I knew in Nashville. But none were willing to reduce their rates, and I can't blame them really, for they had their own families to provide for and bills to pay. Had we paid for just three Nashville musicians for a tour, it would have left Kaci and me out of pocket – we wouldn't have had enough to pay our bills, let alone book another tour or record new music.

In the end, we found our musicians at our home church.

Almost in desperation, I sent the worship leader a text message asking him if he knew any musicians who would be willing to go out on the road for less than top-dollar Nashville prices.

His reply: "Actually, I've got three young men who I think would jump at the chance." And he introduced me to Brad Rankin, Buddy Jewell III, and Phillip Millet.

I had seen them play at church, and my heart sank because I didn't think much of their musical abilities. However, I committed it to prayer, and the Lord deeply impressed on my heart that I needed to give them a chance.

One thing you should know about God: He always knows what He's talking about. Yes, I realize that is an understatement of eternal proportions!

We had a rehearsal, and WOW!

First of all, I want to let you in on a Nashville secret in regards to professional touring musicians: it is all about the hang!

The moment Brad, Buddy, and Phillip walked into our home, they felt like family.

You see, the musicians who play for the biggest artists on the largest stages in the world are not the most talented players in town. Don't get me wrong, they are amazing, but there are monster players out there who would make them look silly.

However, they have something the monster players don't have ... personalities that click with others around them. You could sit and talk to them for hours before you even realize you never caught their name. They have an innate ability to hang out and fit in.

It's all about the hang!

Brad, Buddy, and Phillip had that ability, and from the moment we first rehearsed, we had a blast!

It became evident pretty quickly that they had way more talent than they ever displayed on the praise team at church. When I thought about it, it made sense, because a Sunday morning church service is not exactly the time or place to act like a rock star. These guys were great friends as well as roommates. They played music together all the time, and they could flat out rock it!

Thank You, Lord!

Soon after our first rehearsal, we agreed on the financial terms of traveling together as a band. I offered to pay them whatever they would earn at their current jobs for the weeks we were gone. They were over-the-moon excited! This would, in effect, make our payroll 25% of (or less) the cost of hiring professional touring musicians.

Thank You, Lord!

Lakeshore Christian Church allowed us to use their youth room for our rehearsals. We rehearsed several times a week. And every time we got together, Brad, Buddy, and Phillip had remembered everything we'd previously worked on, so we kept getting better and better.

Thank You, Lord!

The day came, and NEELY finally went out on the road for the first time with a full band. We met Gary Parr at the opening show in Manhattan, KS. He brought a stage, lighting truss, and all kinds of equipment to get the lights in the air ... we looked like a mini version of an arena band! Thanks to Gary, we looked professional for the whole tour, which was another first for us.

Thank You, Lord!

The opening show was in a basketball gymnasium on the campus of a school that helped kids who we struggling academically. These youngsters were taught a trade, giving them the tools to be successful in life.

The gymnasium was packed to the gills!

Thank You, Lord!

Brad, Buddy, and Phillip had never played in front of a crowd that large, and they were scared stiff. We counted in the first song, and no one started it the way we had rehearsed. Fear was written all over their faces. However, by mid-song, they had recovered, and I saw their anxieties melt away as they settled down.

The whole show was rough, but as always, the Lord was at work. The crowd went wild, and afterward, we were swamped, signing autographs for hours.

Thank You, Lord!

At the next show on the tour, Brad, Buddy, and Phillip came back with a vengeance. Oh my goodness, did they ever! In life, you can tell those who have 'fight' in them. These guys had it. While they'd signed autographs for hours after the first show, in their minds, they were signing autographs for a 'crap show,' and they were not willing to settle for crap. As a matter of fact, they improved with every single show on that tour.

For the next year, we toured together, making waves all the way.

All good things have to come to an end, and while, yes, we had arguments and rough times on the road, what dissolved the band this time was not relational at all. It was the grind of the road.

The guys loved playing at our shows, but they hated the days of doing nothing in between. Granted, I was always busy. I had my laptop out at any chance I could get so I could work on booking our next tour or writing session, or arranging interviews, etc.

Most people have a glamorized idea about what life is like as musicians on the road. But talk to anyone who does it full-time, and they'll say it is a job, it's their career. It's not a vacation, it is work.

And with every job, there are undesirable aspects. With touring, there are long periods away from home and long days of doing nothing. Generally, independent musicians like us wouldn't choose to go out and entertain ourselves because then we'd blow our money and have nothing left for rent and bills. And if we're not bored sitting doing nothing in one location, we're bored sitting in a vehicle watching the highway fly by.

It's not all glitz and glory. The show is why we endure the boredom. 99% of touring is the monotony of the road. The show is 1%, or maybe even less.

That's what drove off Phillip, then Buddy.

Brad was willing to stick with us. His motivation wasn't solely the music or the ministry, though; it was our daughter, Allison. I joke that she would eventually steal our guitarist away from us and marry him.

When they got married, Brad knew that his meager salary as a musician on the road with us would not provide for his family. So, he ended up leaving too.

However, he toured with us for several more years before all this happened. He went through a change in our ministry that deepened our faith and showed us first-hand the faithfulness of God.

Kiss My Grits

I f I thought that the Lord was done messing with my paradigm of music ministry, I was dead wrong!

The leadership at our church, Lakeshore Christian Church, in Antioch, TN, was becoming increasingly interested, involved, and supportive of our music and ministry. One particular Sunday early in 2011, our pastor, Randy Cordell, introduced me to a songwriter at our church by the name of Adam Wood.

Adam, at the time, had a publishing deal with Rukus Room in the Berry Hill area of Nashville. This is where there is a huge misconception in how it really is in Nashville. Without a single hesitation, Adam gave me his contact information and said, "Let's schedule to write."

Yeah, that's how Nashville really works. I told you it's all about the hang. If someone has a good first impression of you and you're referred to them by a reliable source … boom, you're in!

I promptly contacted Adam and arranged a session with him for March 9, 2011.

Now here's another thing about Nashville – most of the time, whoever is inviting you to write is hoping that you have something you're working on to bring to the table. This was no different.

Because Adam was on a publishing deal, he was contracted to write a certain number of songs per week. Now, he actually wrote more songs than he needed to because the songs only counted if the publisher accepted them.

Can you imagine coming up with a great song concept every single day?

Me neither!

That didn't matter to me because I had an idea that had been on my mind ever since I flippantly sang the lyrics while playing with my kids at our home in Bennington in 2008. Yes, I had been marinating on this song concept for 3 years, and it was time to get it out!

The lyrics were an iconic southern saying made popular by a waitress on an old TV show. The saying: 'Kiss my grits.'

I knew that this song was going to redefine how we did ministry, and I knew we would be villainized for it. It's a good thing I wasn't thinking about how hateful Christians can be ... otherwise, I may have never written the song.

When I arrived at the studio that day, I was thinking, "Cool, I'm going to write a country song today," as Adam primarily wrote for that genre.

Adam, however, was thinking, "Cool, I'm going to write a rock song today," as I primarily wrote songs for that genre.

I think we both got a little bit of what we were expecting!

As we both unpacked our stuff and set up, Adam asked me, "What ideas do you have brewing?"

I immediately thought of the melody over the phrase 'kiss my grits' and said, "I think I have something you're really going to like."

Before I sang or hummed the melody, I shared with Adam my vision for ministry and the concept of the song. He totally loved the direction I was thinking of taking it, and we got down to business.

The song seemed to flow out of us. We got the chorus rocking right off the bat. Then we went to tackle the first verse. It didn't take much time at all. But when we started on a second verse, things started to stall a bit.

Thankfully, by then, it was time for a lunch break!

After lunch, the second verse started coming together. Then Adam said, "I kind of had an idea brewing at lunch for a bridge. Give this a listen."

Now the session wasn't without strife. There was a huge debate between us about whether the song should be written in the first- or third-person narrative.

Adam thought the song should be written in the third person, making the chorus: *"You can kiss his grits, slap his momma, he's a redneck baller from down in the holler..."*

I stood my ground and pushed for the first person, and that's the way the song is today, *"You can kiss my grits, slap your momma, I'm a redneck baller from down in the holler..."*

That's just a snippet of the song.

Months later, we received some exciting news. A 'pitcher' (a person employed or contracted by a publisher to pitch songs to labels/artists) presented the song to two major artists in country music. Both passed on the song, but it was a cool time, and the Lord used it to get my name out around town.

However, it was clear that God wanted *us* to record it, not another artist. It was then that my thoughts became captivated by the nastiness of Christians, and I was reluctant to go for it.

Nevertheless, I began testing the waters at concerts. I told an entertaining story about the song and how it was pitched to two major artists and then played the first half of the song.

The feedback blew my mind!

Almost every crowd heckled me for stopping half-way through. They wanted more!

It was not what I expected. Yet, I was still concerned about recording and releasing this song.

I continued to play the short version of the song throughout 2011 – 2013. To be totally honest, I wasn't completely sold on the second verse, but the crowd's positive reaction wasn't pushing me to refine it either. Plus, I just didn't know if I wanted the barrage of hate and nastiness that I knew this song would bring.

Then one Thursday morning, in the fall of 2012, I was at a men's Bible study at a Panera Bread restaurant right on the corner of Old Hickory and Interstate 65. As I was sitting in a booth talking to some brothers in Christ about what God was doing in my life, a gentleman who had never seen or met before came up to me and said, "Son, the Lord gave me a word for you. Wait for just a second while I grab another brother in Christ to confirm this, so it doesn't seem weird."

Uhm, too late!

Thankfully, I knew and trusted the guy he brought back to the table. He opened his Bible to Colossians 1:13 and read, *"For he has rescued us from the dominion of darkness and brought us into the kingdom of the Son he loves."*

Closing his Bible, he looked right at me and said, "Son, this is what the Lord has for you in your music ministry."

Now he had my attention! I had never seen him, nor he, I, and he knew I had a music ministry?!?!

"You are a pirate for Jesus Christ. He is going to sail you into the enemy's camp, and you will plunder souls for the glory of Jesus Christ."

I was stunned.

The man finally introduced himself, and I actually ran into him a few more times after that. Each time, he shared something with me that encouraged me to step into God's vision for our music ministry.

In one such conversation, he compared our music to nitroglycerine. Not because it is explosive, but because it is a carrier. He told me how arsenic itself cannot poison a person if it drops onto their skin. However, if arsenic is mixed with nitroglycerine, the nitroglycerine will draw or carry the poison through the skin, and the person will die within minutes. He said this was an old spy trick of the CIA. Don't ask me how he knew that. I'm hoping he was an avid reader!

His point was this: Spirit-infused music.

Much like nitroglycerine, God planned for our music to be a carrier of biblical truth. Because Christians generally have a bad reputation, it makes it difficult to just walk up to someone and share the Word of God with them. People will lash out, cuss, walk off, or it may even end a friendship. Not so with music. Christians can say things through songs, and if it's creative and well done, people will listen to it and take it in.

That gentleman didn't know it, but God was using him to encourage me to record *Kiss My Grits.*

If You Don't like the Kind of Country I Am...

ater that year, we started a crowdfunding project to record, make a music video, and create merchandise for *Kiss My Grits*. We were totally funded at $9,000 within two weeks of putting the word out!

On August 13, 2013, we began recording at Page 2 Music in Nashville.

At the time, Page 2 Music was literally three blocks from our house. It's amazing what you will find in some of the homes in Nashville. In this instance, a state-of-the-art recording studio.

Once we had the song recorded and mixed to a point where we knew the structure wouldn't change, we started on the music video.

September 10 – 12, we were in Medina, TN, shooting the music video. Our producer thought that since the song had so much tongue in cheek humor, the video should be over the top with humor.

We centered this humor on an old saying that Adam and I had snuck into the chorus: 'Slap yo' momma.' For those of you who are not familiar with the southern culture, 'slap yo' momma' means it's really good. For instance, if someone cooked you a delicious meal, when you told your friends about it, you'd say, "Mhm, it was slap-yo'-momma good!" It's a southern thing ... just roll with it. And, by the way, 'grits' is ground maize that is usually eaten for breakfast.

We released the song on March 3, 2014, and the music video on April 27, 2014.

For the most part, the people and churches we had worked with in the past knew us well enough that they weren't bothered about it.

However, I was still trying to book new tours, and that meant plenty of cold calling to new places.

Yikes!

I had some of the nastiest things said to me by pastors, worship leaders, and church leaders from all over the United States.

There were two instances where churches booked us, then canceled just a couple of weeks before the event. And in both cases, the tours centered around leading worship at their church. Now, we had arranged several 'secondary' concerts with the aim of drawing folks into the church that had booked us. That was the plan, anyway. Simply to introduce people to Jesus and help them settle into a church family. So, when the churches canceled, we were devastated. And both times, it was mean-spirited, and they gave me an earful about *Kiss My Grits*.

For those of you wondering why the phrase 'kiss my grits' upset them so much, let me briefly explain ... the phrase is a polite way of saying, 'Kiss my butt.'

I cried out, "This is why I didn't want to record and release this song, Lord!"

His reply blew me away and helped me to understand how important that nastiness was. He spoke to my heart and said, "Jeremy, it's good these churches show their nastiness to you. The people I want you to reach and draw to Me carry a lot of hurt and distrust in Me, much of it because of churches like these that are being mean to you. So, you can see why it is necessary that they show their true colors to you. They will only hurt the people you draw in more than they are already hurt."

Just that short interaction with the Lord healed a lot of wounds and gave me the confidence that I had been lacking.

After that, when someone would come after me with some nastiness, I would just share with them what the Lord laid on my heart, respectfully, and then walk away (or hang up, or hit send, or whatever the scenario might be.)

July 23, 2016, would make it all worth it.

We had been a part of the Good News Camp (a Christian gospel event) in Navajo during 2015 and were back again for another round in 2016. Many of the same people were working on the sound, the tents, the food, etc. So, we knew a lot of the folks involved.

On the last day, a guy we had met briefly in 2015 came up to me and said, "I need to tell you something."

He began by telling me the circumstances that led up to our brief meeting: "My brother-in-law, Armando, roped me into helping with this event. The whole Christianity thing was crap in my mind, but Armando is family, and he needed help, so I drove up the mountain to help him. Part of my excitement to come up was that I would be hauling things with my diesel trucks, which I love to work on in my spare time. The other part was that I would get to hear you sing *Kiss My Grits* as Armando had sent me the link to the video, and I absolutely love the song. Wouldn't you know that a breakdown was bound to happen? I worked like a madman to fix the issue and race up the mountain to see your concert, but I was too late. They had already torn down the sound system, and you were darn near loaded up and ready to hit the road for your next show. What happened next changed my life forever. Armando hollered at you, 'Jeremy, this is my brother-in-law I told you about. The one who loves *Kiss My Grits*.' You turned on your heels, jogged to your truck, pulled out your guitar, came back to the tent and played the song just for me. Then you signed a CD and gave it to me."

Yep, I remembered every bit. Just as he described it.

What he said next made me weep. He said, "I couldn't quit thinking about what you did. You must've worked hard that day, and you were already late getting on the road for the next show, and yet you went across the field and got your guitar just for me. It haunted me for weeks on end. I couldn't figure it out. What could drive a man to care so much for another human being? I asked Armando about you guys and looked you up online, trying to find the answer to that question. Every time the answer was 'Jesus.' So, I figured, if that's what Jesus really looks like, I want to follow Him. So, I accepted Jesus as my Lord and Savior, and my life has never been the same. Over the last year, I've stopped cursing, I've stopped drinking, I've started treating my wife with more kindness and affection, and I've been spending more quality time with her and the kids."

As you can imagine, I was a blubbering mess as he told me this, but he wasn't finished!

He ended it with one last statement, a breath from God, "Man, none of this would have happened without *Kiss My Grits*. Without that song, I wouldn't have pushed it to listen to you, I wouldn't have expressed my disappointment to Armando, he wouldn't have yelled at you, and you wouldn't have run across the field for your guitar. None of it would have happened without that song!"

Since then, we've come across other stories about how *Kiss My Grits* drew individuals in and how they ended up in a relationship with Jesus.

What most people don't realize is that when Adam and I were talking about the concept of *Kiss My Grits*, I talked about my vision of creatively 'spiritually infusing' the theme of Psalm 139 into the storyline.

Mrs. Ann and the Aluminum Pitcher of Death

One of our dear friends in Medina took charge of finding all the items we were looking to include in the *Kiss My Grits* music video. We needed: a concert venue that had the feel of being in a bar/barn dance room, a country home venue, other miscellaneous country locations, vehicles, and an old 'Aunt Bee' type of character (Aunt Bee was a character from the 1960s sitcom *The Andy Griffith Show*).

Because Medina is roughly 2 to 3 hours west of Nashville, we just had to trust that our friend would pull through for us.

The afternoon of September 10, 2013, we walked into an old historic home in Trenton, TN, just north of Medina and met our 'Aunt Bee' character: Mrs. Ann Tillman, or Mrs. Ann as we called her (it's another southern thing!).

She was perfect in every way!

When you watch the music video for *Kiss My Grits*, you will see a picturesque grandmother character with facial features that make her reactions pure cinematic gold.

When Mrs. Ann walked onto the set, she was surprised. For some reason, she was under the impression that she was doing a photo shoot. When she was told that it was a music video shoot, she became nervous, which worried us a bit.

Some dear friends from Surprise, AZ, flew to Trenton to help us with the music video. One of them, Ruth, is an amazing makeup artist and she helped us with makeup for the shoot. However, all of them dug in and helped us in unimaginable ways. And they all ended up with a small spot in the video as part of the crowd.

These folks surrounded Mrs. Ann as Ruth applied her makeup and chatted to her, and we saw Mrs. Ann's nerves melt away.

It was finally time to shoot, and we described to Mrs. Ann what was to happen. Making a play on the 'slap yo' momma' phrase, I was to pretend to love the grits she fed me and excitedly slap her. Not literally, of course. If you've ever been around the theater, you'll know that it's all about camera angles and the reaction of the one who is supposedly getting hit. In return for my 'slap,' she would knock my block off (again, not literally!).

As a side note, this was a historic house. None of the appliances worked, which was a slight oversight on our part. That meant the grits I shoved in my mouth were completely uncooked. It was not pleasant at all!

It took about an hour of shooting to get Mrs. Ann to react to my slap. Once she got it, it came out pretty good.

Now it was time for her to pay me back for the slap.

The director came up with the idea of her grabbing an aluminum pitcher (jug) and pretending to hit me with it. The goal was for Mrs. Ann to get the pitcher close to my head and hit the tip of my hat, then I would react like she had connected with the side of my face.

We realized very quickly that this was probably way too much to expect of someone in their late 80s to early 90s. Mrs. Ann was a southern belle to the max and wouldn't divulge her actual age, just hints here and there that gave us the neighborhood.

She was getting frustrated because she was scared of getting too close and actually hitting me.

The director finally talked her into just going for it. "Don't hold back," he told her. "You keep missing his hat because you are holding back."

He called out, "Quiet on set," and when the hush settled, "Action!"

Mrs. Ann grabbed the pitcher, gave me her scripted scowl, and CLUNK!

When you watch the B-roll footage, you see the shock on my face. Mrs. Ann immediately recoiled in shock. Everyone else on set erupted in laughter.

In that footage, you can hear the deep CLUNK of the pitcher connecting with the side of my head.

All of us laughed and laughed and laughed.

Ruth had to re-apply our makeup because we laughed until we cried.

Once the director realized that it didn't hurt me too much and that we could shoot all night and never get Mrs. Ann close enough to my hat for me to react properly, he told her, "From now on, just hit him."

Mrs. Ann looked at me with shock, "Are you sure?"

I nodded in agreement and said, "Yes, ma'am. I think it's best for the shot."

Mrs. Ann paced back and forth for a minute, mulling it over, then blurted out with laughter, "For over 75 years, I've asked the good Lord to take away my anger, and now you're asking me to hit this fine young man!"

The set erupted in laughter again.

In the end, she hit me. Over and over and over.

The aluminum pitcher we used began with a smooth surface but ended up looking like the surface of a golf ball with dents all over it!

I'll never forget the kindness and love that poured out of every fiber of Mrs. Ann's being. As I reflect on that afternoon, I see a person so filled with Jesus Christ that she didn't have to verbally tell us about Him, it was just evident.

Mrs. Ann went to be with Jesus a little over a year later. She got to see the video, and her family conveyed to us how proud Mrs. Ann was to be a part of it.

That aluminum pitcher of death may have given me one of the worst headaches in the world, but the lasting impression I have is wanting to grow in my relationship with Jesus so that my life is filled with as much peace and love as Mrs. Ann's.

"No More Contracts or Set Fees – Just Go!"

Even before *Kiss My Grits*, we were doing well. More people were finding out about us and booking us for events, and we were able to pay our bills. All of which made us a Nashville success story.

But in late 2011, the Lord asked something of us that was pretty hard to swallow. I kept hearing the Lord speak this to my heart: "I don't want you to operate under any kind of contract or have a set fee. Simply go and serve. If they ask, tell them to come to Me, and I will tell them how to provide for you."

Do you feel anxiety rising inside of you right now as you imagine what this would look like in your life?

On the one hand, I was a nervous wreck, wondering how we would ever pay the bills. Yet, on the other hand, I knew that if I truly believed what I said I believed, this was no big deal.

Unlike the times God had required a change in our ministry in the past, this time I obeyed immediately. Granted, I looked like Indiana Jones when he took 'the leap of faith' in *Indiana Jones and the Last Crusade* (if you haven't seen it, watch the clip on YouTube!). I sucked in a deep breath, closed my eyes, put one foot dramatically out in front of me, and reluctantly made myself fall forward.

And there was solid ground!

We were touring with all four of our daughters (who were home-schooled by Kaci) and Brad, so not only did we have to provide for our household and family, but we also had to provide for Brad's bills (and that was before the expense of touring).

We began touring the way God had directed us, with no financial guarantees, in early 2012. And we continue doing so to this very day. We trust that God will provide for us.

And He has never failed us.

We have never missed a mortgage payment. Never missed an electric bill, water bill, cell phone bill, etc. Anytime the truck had major mechanical problems, we were provided for.

Oh, we got the questions (and we still do): "How much do you charge?" I've always told them to take it before the Lord. They usually reply, "At least tell us how much it will cost expense-wise to get you in." I send them another message telling them to take it before the Lord.

In essence, our 'rider' (a document that lays out an artist's wants/demands) was and is this: *Treat us the way you would like to be treated if you had your family on the road for 3 to 6 months straight, traveling from town to town every couple of days, and staying in other people's homes. As for our 'set fee,' take it before the Lord and ask Him how He would have you bless us financially.*

This takes the pressure off everyone.

For us, we know that whatever we are blessed with is from the Lord. So, no matter how big or small the amount might be, we are not swayed by it, and we remain steadfast, ready to return and serve again.

For them, they have the comfort of knowing that whatever they do for us is directed by God, and they can do it in an act of worship to Him.

If someone said, "Well, that wasn't worth the money," the response could simply be, "Evidently, God thought so." This has never happened, by the way, and we pray it never does.

Nine Months on the Road

Right from the start, our tours were no less than three months long. Mostly because we had to be out on the road that long to cross the threshold of paying for travel expenses and paying the bills back home.

By 2012/13, our network of churches had grown so much that we had host families all over the United States. This meant we no longer had the expense of lodging, and many times these families also made sure we were fed, and that meant a large portion of our food budget was also covered.

Yet, we were still just getting by. The bills were paid, but there was very little left over.

Because of this, and because of the way we were raised, we believed that we were not working hard enough. So, we packed our tours tighter and made them longer.

By 2014, filling our calendar was becoming easier, and we were spending upwards of 9 to 10 months out of our year touring.

Let's put this in perspective. Most people work Mondays to Fridays and have the weekends off. Now, 52 weekends in a year is 104 days, which calculates to roughly 3.3 months off work. Plus, there are sick days, vacation time, and public holidays on top of that. Well, we were home for less time in the year than everybody else has at home just in weekends. No vacation, no sick time, and no holidays.

Over the years, we never missed paying a bill, but it would sometimes come right down to the wire. On that same note, we never had excess. We couldn't record new music, or make new music videos; shoot, we often couldn't take the family out to eat for a special occasion.

I'm painting this picture for a very specific reason: we had no idea we were missing out on anything!

During this time, we saw our faith grow. And we also saw our daughters' faith grow. We watched each of them mature in their own personal relationship with Jesus. We also noticed that our family as a whole began to differentiate between 'want' and 'need.' The girls never complained about not having the things they wanted, but rather they rejoiced as their needs were met.

This was probably one of the most beautiful times we have ever experienced together as a family.

The downside was that we found it impossible to be away from home for that long, especially doing ministry and pouring into people's lives day in and day out, without becoming physically, emotionally, and spiritually fatigued.

By the end of the 2015 touring season, Kaci and I looked at one another and asked, "Is this really what God has for our lives? Do we even want to do this anymore?"

After a month or more of being at home, we were ready to go again, only to get to the end of 2016 and ask ourselves the same questions. And at the end of the 2017 season, we were really challenged and asked those questions more seriously.

Official Rock Band

Throughout our musical career, we've had the privilege of being called the 'Official Rock Band of...' a couple of different radio stations as well as a soft drink distributor.

In 2014, we had one of the coolest things ever happen to us. We became the official rock band of Lakeshore Christian Church in Nashville, TN.

This meant that our music ministry was now seen as an official missionary arm of the church, and they would support and bless our ministry. I had always loved the way that the leadership at Lakeshore operated outside of the box. They saw this same quality in us. Thus, we were drawn together.

As I mentioned previously, most churches in Nashville put on 'a show' each Sunday with professional staging, lighting, sound, and musicians. As a matter of fact, most pastors fall over themselves to ensure they have 'such and such' on stage.

Lakeshore is the total opposite, and that's why we fell in love with them. The worship leader goes to great lengths to discover the heart motive behind anyone's request to be on the worship team. And if their heart doesn't align with Jesus' heart, that person will not find themselves on the stage.

We've had well-known singers and musicians come to church at Lakeshore. Likely, they wanted to be the 'big dog' on a church worship team that didn't have one. But they found that the interview process exposed their faith for what it was and left them sitting in the pews. Not for long though. Once they figured out that they wouldn't be allowed on the team, they left to find another worship team at another church.

I say all of this to set the stage. None of our accolades mattered one iota to the church leadership at Lakeshore. What they were drawn to was our heart for ministry and how that aligned with Lakeshore's core values: connect, grow, and serve.

The best part of being an official ministry of Lakeshore is the accountability that comes with it. At least once a year, I meet with Pastor Randy for a 'debrief.' He asks questions to probe and evaluate our emotional and spiritual health, and he asks about our plans for the following year to ensure it aligns with the heart of Christ.

Additionally, during the year, Pastor Randy and I stay in contact via email or text message. Whenever a new opportunity for ministry arises, or if I sense that we are being led in a different direction to the one we discussed at our debrief, I will contact him. He will pray about it, take it before the elders, and they will pray about it as well before coming back to me with an answer.

Our pastor and elders see the value in our ministry, and even in songs like *Kiss My Grits*! They know that what we do is out of a heart to serve – to serve churches in a true outreach fashion, and to serve the individuals who connect with our songs by nurturing genuine relationships that have the potential of us introducing them to Jesus Christ.

Everything we do is intentional and has a purpose. Plus, it is done with the spiritual oversight of a very solid, supportive, and loving Christ-based community.

"I'm Not Watching Horror Movies Anymore"

When we began operating without a set fee or any kind of contract, it gave us the freedom to take our music and ministry to places where Nashville artists generally don't go. I hate to be crass, but if there's no money to be made, they will skip over the opportunities. We weren't 'bound' by the color of anyone's money, so we were not at all bothered about ministering in less affluent areas.

It was during this time that Brad and our eldest daughter Allison struck up a friendship. Brad was 21, and Allison was 15. Kaci and I watched as their friendship developed, and we knew it was something special. Eventually, Kaci and I had to sit them down and say, "Look, we can tell that y'all are falling in love, and we are cool with it, but there will be some major boundaries."

So, about a year into their friendship, Brad began courting Allison, and we were happy about it. During those nine months on the road, we had not only seen our family's faith increase, but we'd also seen Brad's faith grow. Kaci and I were not about to discourage our daughter from pursuing a young man who was living out his faith. Let's be honest, Brad did not *have* to travel with us. He *wanted* to travel with us. When we did the whole 'no financial guarantees' thing, he could have easily said, "I just can't. I've got bills to pay." And we would have understood.

But there was one thing that niggled at Kaci and me: Brad and Allison loved to watch horror movies together.

To be fair, Kaci and I watched horror movies when we were young, but that changed when we came into a relationship with

Jesus. Our spiritual eyes were opened, and we realized that there was a reality to the horror in those movies.

But to Brad and Allison, it was no big deal. They just shrugged it off.

The situation wasn't what we would classify as a 'hill to die on,' so Kaci and I decided not to argue with them or lay down the law. Instead, we encouraged them to do the right thing, and mostly, we prayed about it, asking the Lord to change their hearts.

One evening, we were scheduled to do a mid-week service at a church in downtown St. Paul, MN.

For whatever reason, the pastor introduced us without any warning and without making sure we were all in the room.

So, it was just me.

The others were elsewhere, and when they came into the sanctuary, they didn't want to interrupt me, so they took their seats near the back.

As I shared our songs and the stories behind them, a gentleman at the back, stage right, shouted and groaned loudly, especially when I talked about how Jesus had set me free and was redeeming my life.

Naturally, when I had finished, I walked off stage left, away from the groaning, shouting man!

When I got to the back row and sat down, I looked to my left and saw the man walking across the back of the sanctuary in my direction. He was about 5ft 7 and weighed probably 130 pounds. Super skinny. I could tell the guy was a drug addict.

As he walked in front of the sound booth, several things happened all at once:

Someone in the sound booth caught his attention and set him off (I don't know why). He immediately began throwing punches over the wall of the sound booth, trying to connect with whoever and whatever he could.

At exactly the same time, a 6ft-3 Hispanic ex-gangbanger weighing in at a good 225 pounds of solid muscle by the name of Robert, without seeing any of this even beginning to transpire, dropped his iPad in the seat next to him while standing, turning and leaping over his seat in one fluid motion. Robert then grabbed the skinny, shouting man.

Humor me and allow me to repeat that these things all happened at once.

It's still freaky how the Lord pulled Robert out of his seat in that fashion because people simply don't react like that when they have no conscious awareness of what is about to happen. Sure, if he knew, it would be a different story.

After Robert had grabbed the shouting, punching man, a commotion was set in full swing. It drew the attention of around half a dozen (or more) other men, and they jumped into action.

Being an inner-city church, the pastor was used to this kind of thing, and he just carried on teaching!

Just as the additional men reached the situation, the skinny dude shrugged off Robert like he was a rag doll.

The first guy grabbed the skinny dude. He got tossed away as well.

The second, the third, and all who followed grabbed him.

One by one, these men were hurled away by the scrawny little dude.

Later, when I was telling this story, someone said to me, "Well, don't you think it's because he was high on drugs?"

Let me set the record straight: I've seen folks high out of their mind and not feel pain because the drugs have numbed their system and inhibited it from transmitting signals properly. But what I have NEVER seen is drugs give someone superhuman strength.

This situation reminded me of a similar one recorded in the book of Acts. The sons of a priest named Sceva thought they'd be cool and invoke the name of Jesus on a demonically possessed dude. They got their rear ends handed to them and ended up running away naked and wounded.

Now, the guys at this church didn't end up naked, nor was anyone wounded. Thank God for that! However, all of them later talked about the look in the man's eyes, his supernatural strength, and his outbursts at the name of Jesus.

After that instance, we served in other inner-city churches as well as homeless shelters where our family, either collectively or individually, had encounters with demonically possessed individuals who did things we couldn't physically explain.

Honestly, it was becoming normal for our family, so we didn't think anything of it.

Until one evening when we were watching TV. We saw a movie trailer for a new horror movie. I'm not sure who said it, but someone spoke up and said to Brad, "I bet you and Allison can't wait to see that one."

To that, Brad replied, "Actually, we won't be seeing that movie. Allison and I have decided we aren't going to watch horror movies anymore. They are just too real."

And just like that, God answered our prayer.

They discovered that what they thought was just fun, games, and thrills was actually reality. And because of that, it wasn't fun anymore.

PART TWELVE

TAKING IT INTERNATIONAL

Chris Ward: "Have You Ever Thought About..."

From my earliest memories, I have known that someday, somehow, I would play music on a global scale. While I seriously doubted that dream along the way, it was still there, burning deep inside me.

When I came into a relationship with Jesus in 2000 and sensed that He wanted me to dust off my guitar and begin playing for Him, I knew He meant globally.

Along the way, people would speak into our lives and say, "God told me..." and it was always about the power of our music and how the Lord would make our ministry a global one. I loved to hear those things, but because people abuse the whole prophecy thing, that tingly feeling of, "OK, God, let's take over the world!" wore off quickly.

Time was also a factor. When we were first saved and believed God had called us to go, wow, we were pumped and ready to go. However, we were called in 2000 and didn't move to Nashville until 2010. There was a 10-year span between being called into music and finally going full-time in music. And in 2010, we were still not even close to touring internationally; we were just getting started, trying to survive nationally.

Ten years is a long time. Shoot, I almost gave up on going full-time nationally during that time.

There came a time, though, when I had to learn to become content. I had to come to a place where I was OK with whatever the outcome of our ministry would be. And I mean being genuinely OK with it, from the depths of my soul OK with it, even if it meant only playing special music items every once in a while.

And actually, when I reached the point of contentment, God began opening doors and making things happen. When my heart was surrendered to God in this, that's when He directed us to change our band name, we began recording in Nashville, we moved to Nashville, we began to tour full-time, and He stripped us of our paradigm of the music industry.

It was a whirlwind, and that time seemed to have flown by. However, we were still not even close to touring internationally. And, honestly, once the Lord instructed us to travel and minister by faith, I really thought that touring globally was out of the picture. I mean, the Lord was providing just enough for us to get through life, so how would we ever be able to afford the thousands of dollars for airfare, transport, lodging, and food while paying the bills back home? It seemed like this was a mountain we just could not overcome.

And then I got a phone call in 2014 that changed everything.

It was Pastor Chris Ward from Calvary Chapel, Maricopa, AZ, a small church in a little bedroom community about an hour from Phoenix.

I'd been introduced to him two years previously by our dear friend Eden Fine (the one who rallied the troops to get our music played on the radio). Chris is a very charismatic person, and our families clicked. We talked about our return trip to Maricopa and how we could serve the church and the community, which we were excited to do. But we didn't really expect anything more from such a small church.

We were wrong to have low expectations!

When Chris called that day, we exchanged greetings and laughed at each other's jokes. I fully expected that his call was about another trip to Maricopa.

Then Chris said, "I want to ask you something. Have you guys ever thought about traveling internationally?"

I didn't know what to say.

After a few moments, I began to stumble and fumble through a reply.

I must have been babbling because Chris said, "Are you OK?"

I took a breath, collected my thoughts, then said, "Chris, this is the dream God placed on my heart a very long time ago, and I have quite honestly given up hope on it ever happening."

What? Did those words come out of my mouth?

Yes, they did. They were honest words. Words that stung.

For the four years we'd been doing music full-time, we'd seen God provide for us, and two of those years were without any guarantee of payment. I was living in a continuous miracle, and yet I discounted God's ability to take us international.

It seems foolish – ludicrous even – when I put it like that. But, like everyone else, I am an emotional being living in a very real world. A world where dreams don't always come true.

And let's get real ... that dream of being an internationally-touring rock star could have been MY dream, not God's. To be fair, my dream and God's dream on the music front had always been totally different, so why would this be any different? These were the thoughts and questions I had challenged myself with on my journey to contentment.

Chris continued, "I've been a part of Creation Fest in the UK, and as I was praying the other day, the Lord impressed you and Kaci on my heart."

Immediately, we began making plans for the following year's festival. Chris set up the opportunities for us to play at Creation Fest in Cornwall, England, as well as to lead worship at Calvary Chapel in Exeter, England.

Round 1: Ten Days in England

You know that anxious feeling you get when you know you're on the precipice of something big, yet you know it could turn out to be utterly disappointing? Well, that's how I felt leading up to our first tour, if you really want to call it that, to England.

Really, the trip was a mission trip where I would be doing what I do best: roaming around being a country boy ... more on that in a bit.

First, we had to raise the funds to get to England.

We did a 'Dinner and Song' event at our home church in Nashville. Some of our dear friends, Rick and Debbie Desmond, cooked some Tex-Mex food, then after eating, everyone enjoyed a storytelling concert from Kaci and I. The tickets sold like hotcakes, *and* we had people show up to purchase tickets at the door. We had way over-estimated the amount of food we needed, but because so many came on the spur of the moment, we ran out of food!

Besides the 'Dinner and Song' fundraiser, many churches allowed us to do special concerts on our tour to raise funds, and it was a long tour!

We left for the tour in mid-May and would not be going home before we left for England in August. As a matter of fact, we were due to fly out of Phoenix with Chris. So, our tour took us on a zig-zag across America. Right before we flew out, we led worship at a week-long youth camp in Divide, CO, then we left there and rushed, and I mean we *rushed*, to Farmington, NM, so we could be a part of the Good News Camp in Red Valley, AZ.

Next, we dropped off our children with our good friends, Mike and Michelle Wulfurt, in Farmington, NM, then rushed to Maricopa to meet Chris and his family so we could fly out together the following day. And this was all after being on the road for 2 and a half months straight. Plus, upon our return, we would be on the road again until the first week of November. I told you ... we were not home much!

By the time we reached London, we were shattered. I don't even think we were running on fumes by then!

To make matters worse, by the time we made it through customs, all our bags had been taken off the carousel, and Kaci's luggage was missing. Thank goodness British Airways allowed me to stow my guitar in the first-class coat closet.

Actually, matters did get worse. We had bus tickets to Exeter, where we were due to meet up with Bob and Jeanne Claycamp from Calvary Chapel, Exeter. We were running a little behind because of Kaci's missing baggage, but we thought we'd be OK.

We got to the bus platform 5 – 10 minutes before its departure time, but it had already left. When we spoke to an attendant, he said something to the effect of: "Weird, they never leave early." Thankfully, we were allowed to board the next bus using the same tickets.

When I hear people talk about their international travels, they usually say something like, "Oh, I would never dare to drive there!"

Well, I drive in nearly every country we visit. Why? Because of that bus trip from London to Exeter ... to say that I don't do well in moving vehicles where I can't clearly see out the front window is an understatement.

Exeter is pretty close to the coast, so there were seagull droppings all over the bus platform, but it didn't stop me from nearly kissing the ground when I got off that bus!

I am glad to say that other than the motion sickness I experienced on the train rides later in the trip, the rest of our time in England was like a dream.

When we got to the festival grounds for Creation Fest in Wadebridge, Cornwall, Chris and I immediately got to work. He was the head of the stewarding team, and I was his right-hand man.

It meant that we roamed the festival grounds and helped people who needed assistance. This turned out to be more intensive than I thought because of the massive festival grounds. Thousands of families pitch their tents and camp for the entire week of the festival. For them, it's their 'holiday,' or as us 'yanks' would say, 'vacation.'

Now you understand why I made that statement earlier. I literally walked around the festival grounds being a country boy. I helped set up tents, fix tents, set up temporary fences ... there's not much that I didn't get tasked with that week, and I worked darn hard.

It was an amazing experience. I saw the change in all of our hearts and minds. So many folks would tell me, "Wow, I never imagined Americans would be like you." And honestly, I felt the same about the people of the United Kingdom. The image I had of the English from TV was that 'snooty' British type, or as the Brits would say, 'POSH.' But they were every bit down-home country folk just like folk back here in America.

When I asked them what they thought Americans were like, they said, "Those from New York or Los Angeles." I groaned and said, "No way, that is NOT what most Americans are like! That's just a small part, and even Americans don't think highly of those two places."

They had a good laugh at that.

Kaci and I worked all week in our respective areas and made some life-long friends.

We had a slot to play on the stage at the Big Shed café during the last couple of days of the festival. The 'Big Shed' is a big farm shed on the Royal Cornwall Showground. They have cattle shows and farm shows in these huge sheds. The part of the shed we were due to play in was split in two – one half had vendors selling books, CDs, DVDs, clothing, etc., and the other half was the café. It was a huge open space with easily a thousand people milling about having conversations.

Not a great place for an acoustic storytelling concert. Psychologically, it was the equivalent of being in elementary school and someone sneaking up behind me and pulling my pants down. Overall, the audience was not attentive due to the environment.

However, there were many pastors in the crowd watching us, and that was a positive thing because it set the stage for our second UK tour. Though, I didn't know it at the time.

Once the festival was over, we made our way back to Exeter and led worship at Calvary Chapel, Exeter. That went much better. We felt at home there. Yet, all in all, we didn't feel like we had 'wowed' anyone during the trip. Well, we didn't feel that way until we began preparing for our return trip.

My Welsh Posse

On the very last night of the festival, I was roaming the grounds, as usual. I made my way to a section of the paved walkway behind the tent set up for the younger kids. This tent was huge and had a gigantic skatepark inside for skateboards, scooters, bikes, etc.

Even though I was rolling in my jeans and cowboy boots, I always stopped to engage with the young men and women along the way, and the youngsters at the 'skater alley' were more than happy to show me their tricks, or play some kind of sport with me. On this particular evening, I heard someone shout, "Oi! Are you American?"

I turned and saw a group of kids waving at me. I replied, "I sure am. How are y'all doing?"

They immediately surrounded me, and we began what became hours of conversation.

It's interesting to me how the evening went down and that these kids stayed engaged with me for hours. Mostly because about 30 minutes into our conversation, an older gentleman from California came and butted his way into our conversation.

"Do you know if you'll go to heaven or hell if you die tonight?" he blurted out.

I would later get to know this man and find that he is a kind and loving soul, but in that situation, he definitely wasn't picking up on the uncomfortable social cues the kids were throwing down.

He continued on with some old-school Gospel presentation, and just to get him to leave, all the kids recited what I call a 'Harry Potter Patronus Prayer' that would magically get them into heaven, even though they obviously did not mean it. The false reassurance he gave them, and even himself, was disheartening. He gave each of them a 'salvation coin' and told them he would see them in heaven. Then he walked off.

The kids and I sat in awkward silence. I didn't know what to say or do. Everything I had worked to build with these kids had been shattered.

I chose honesty.

"I'm sorry about that," I started. "That was really weird, but..." I paused before continuing, "... it took some guts for him to come up to you and say that. If you look past his poor delivery, you can see a genuine love."

They all laughed, and one of them said, "How's that?"

"If you had the cure for cancer, wouldn't you tell the world about it?" I asked.

"Yeah, of course!" they all agreed.

"Wouldn't you think that someone who had the cure and didn't share it was a pretty big jerk?"

Again, they agreed.

"That man has uncovered a truth that can give you peace in this life, a peace that I can't begin to fathom or explain, and the assurance that you can dwell in the presence of God for eternity."

"Do you really believe all of that?" one of them asked.

"Yes, very much so. In fact," and from there, I told them my testimony. The brokenness, the addiction, the abuse. I hid nothing. I answered all of their questions.

I couldn't hang out in 'skater's alley' all night; I needed to roam to be available to help. So, the guys followed me and worked with me until after the festival had shut down and the vendors had torn down and vacated.

We had a blast! We told stories. We told jokes. We laughed at one another.

Before we parted ways, we all followed one another on social media. My heart broke when they left. Social media is great, but I desperately wanted to hang out with these young folks some more and invest in their lives.

Round 2: Eight Weeks in the UK and Europe

We made our way back to the United States with love for England in our hearts, but feeling like our tails were between our legs because we hadn't 'wowed' anyone. Upon our return, things began to change.

It all started with an honest discussion at a debriefing session with Chris. We disclosed our feelings, and Chris was amazed by how defeated we felt. He shared with us how many pastors had been in the crowd while we played at the Big Shed café and how one of those pastors purposely visited Calvary Chapel in Exeter when we led worship so he could see us again. Chris said that he had received so much positive feedback on our behalf that he was overwhelmingly encouraged about our return in 2016.

He was not merely giving us lip service to make us feel better; over the next few months, the doors began to fly open for us, and not only in England, but also in Wales and Scotland.

An interesting development occurred that year: Chris and his wife, Debbie, felt called by the Lord to move to England, and they ended up living in Exeter to support the pastor at Calvary Chapel. This, combined with the pastors who saw us at Creation Fest, opened doors for us in England.

The door to Wales was initially opened by my 'Welsh posse.' Their youth leader from the Llandovery YMCA was overwhelmed with the stories they shared about me, and she contacted me via Facebook to say thanks for investing in the youth. I replied, telling her that it was my great pleasure, and I told her of our return trip to the UK and said that we would love to visit them in Llandovery and do a concert.

She was ecstatic, to say the least!

Then, a pastor from Benton, AR, contacted a ministry friend in Swansea, Wales, and we suddenly had several more ministry opportunities in Wales!

Next, a co-worker from my former job, who was the European representative based in Belgium, contacted me out of the blue. He had always been a supporter of our music ministry and had distributed our Wur'ship Project CDs across Europe.

He was wondering if we would ever have the opportunity to come to Belgium.

"Funny you ask that!" I replied, and I told him of our time in England and our plans to return to the UK.

He immediately put out feelers. After months of work, he had set up a full weeks' worth of concerts in Belgium for 2016.

Opportunities in Germany soon followed.

Our biggest problems: resources and time.

We did not have the finances to take all of our girls with us. By this time, Allison was married, and Aubrey stayed with Allison and Brad at their apartment when we toured. Yet, the cost of two more plane tickets and the extra expenses that would ensue was too much for us to swing.

So, we had to plan a rotation between Kaci's parents and my parents to look after the girls while we were away.

With that problem resolved, it just left the issue of time. We had so many opportunities available to us that we could have easily stayed 3 months or more in the UK and Europe, but we couldn't leave our two youngest daughters for that long.

And so, we settled on 8 weeks. This was still hard. As with our 2015 tour, we were on the road for months before leaving, this time five months straight. And on top of that, we would be without our two youngest daughters for two full months, which is a long time. Granted, they were going to be in the best possible care with their grandparents, but still, it was not easy.

Surprisingly, Aubrey had been saving her money and decided to join us! It turned out to be a sweet time for Aubrey to have alone with Kaci and me.

Our schedule was packed. Too packed, really.

The response in England was overwhelming. From the moment we hit the ground, there was excitement. In a nutshell: we served in Wadebridge, Exeter, Yeovil, Southampton, and Dewsbury before heading to Swansea and Llandovery in Wales. Then we flew from Bristol to Glasgow, Scotland, and from Glasgow to Europe. We ended with a brief stay in England before returning to the US.

We kicked off our tour at Creation Fest, and I once again connected with my 'Welsh Posse.' This time, they were intent on teaching me rugby, and we spent hours upon hours playing on a makeshift 'pitch' (or 'field' as Americans say).

Then I did something that attracted tons of attention: I threw the rugby ball in a tight spiral like it was an American football. Not only did our Welsh friends want to know how to throw the ball this way, but so did everyone else passing by. We made up games, had loads of fun, and by the end of the week, my arm felt like it was going to fall off! One of the greatest gifts I've ever received is that rugby ball signed by each one of the young people who came with the Llandovery YMCA that year.

Following our tour in England, Wales and Scotland, we flew to Paris and stayed with Jacque and Enid. This was a very sweet reunion and rekindled a relationship that was decades old.

Then we drove to Flensburg in Germany, which is just south of the Denmark line. We ministered there and in Siegen, Pfronten, Füssen, Rottenberg, and Heidelberg before making our way across Luxembourg to a small village outside of Charleroi, Belgium. There, we stayed with my former co-worker and his family while we ministered across the country.

In Belgium, we were introduced to the head chaplain of the Belgium prison system. He was so impressed with our heart, story, and talent that he gave us an open invitation to minister in all of the prisons in Belgium. Unfortunately, when an opening was made available for us at one particular prison, it was canceled only hours before we were due to be there. A prison strike had broken out, so we were unable to go.

All across Europe, we had encore after encore. Sometimes, we would be called back for upwards of 3 encores at a concert!

By the time we performed at our last concert at a resort between Charleroi and Brussels, our voices had finally given up the ghost. The crowd applauded for what seemed like an eternity, and our translator graciously explained that we had given them our all and that our voices were gone. It made them applaud all the more!

We left Belgium with very light suitcases as we had completely sold out of our CDs. By our friend's estimation, we could have sold a couple of hundred more ... easily. Wow!

From Belgium, we drove to Paris, where we flew to Bristol and made our way to Chris and Debbie in Exeter for several days of recovery before traveling back to the United States.

It was during that layover that I received another great gift. It was from Julien Fountain, a new friend I met on the stewarding team at Creation Fest.

Julien had recently come into a relationship with Jesus Christ and was hungry to learn and eager to serve. We hit it off immediately as Julien is a genuinely good guy and a hard worker. As we spent hours upon hours walking through the festival grounds, I learned a very interesting thing about Julien: he is an internationally-renowned cricket coach!

We talked about his travels to coach teams in Korea, Pakistan, Dubai, and many other exotic places around the world. He patiently talked me through the concept and some of the flow of the game of cricket as well as faster-paced forms of the game. He also shared his vision to revolutionize the sport. I am excitedly watching that unfold to this day.

Right before we were due to fly home, Julien took Kaci and I out to lunch, and he presented me with another of my most prized possessions: a cricket ball.

Becoming a Grandparent

In May 2015, Allison and Brad got married. I had turned 40 that year, and none our friends could believe that I was 40 and had a son-in-law.

Fast forward a year and a half, and their jaws dropped even more. November of 2016, at the age of 41, I became a grandpa.

During Allison's pregnancy, several of our friends from around the world would tell us things like, "There is nothing in the world like being a grandparent. It is a blessing to have kids, for sure, but there's something even better about being a grandparent."

There are plenty of times in life when people blow things out of proportion, so I took all of this with a grain of salt.

As it turned out, they weren't exaggerating.

The moment our first granddaughter came into the world, both Kaci and I were hooked, and it was totally different from having our own children. There truly is something super special about being a grandparent.

And at that time, we had the added bonus of Brad and Allison living with us. It was an arrangement that helped them save for their first home while house sitting our home while we were touring. The true bonus was the constant access to our grandchild.

The downside: it made it even harder for us to leave for a tour!

Round 3:
Trying to Die in England!

In 2017, we decided to take our two youngest daughters with us to the UK and Europe. Aubrey also determined to save up and make a return trip, which ended up being a huge blessing.

Due to having our two youngest in tow, we chose to shorten the tour to 6 weeks (instead of lengthening it as the increased demand dictated).

We had all the same opportunities open up to us, in addition to a larger Belgian prison tour, and an appearance at a public school in Germany. Once again, our schedule was bursting at the seams. We had a several-month-long tour in the US before leaving and several more weeks of tour dates when we returned.

When we hit the ground in England, we stayed with some friends just outside of Exeter. This was our time to beat the jetlag and gear up for the coming onslaught of the six-week tour. After a couple of days of rest and getting settled into the different time zone, we headed to the Cornish coast to the town of Ilfracombe to stay with our dear friend Jason and serve at the church he pastors in nearby Woolacombe. Our time there was refreshing, and several of our friends from Calvary Chapel, Exeter, including Julien Fountain, came to visit us.

After church on Sunday, we made our way to Wadebridge to report for duty at Creation Fest 2017. We picked up where we left off, and our girls were loving England.

The previous year, they did away with the Big Shed café stage, as per my feedback. I felt a little uneasy about giving them feedback that might appear negative, but I meant it to be constructive so that the other artists could be honored. The replacement option was a new tent, and it was much better because it was set up with a stage, lights, a sound system, and seating, so it looked like a concert venue. Because the venue set the tone, the audience responded accordingly, and thus the artists were honored and felt comfortable. In fact, the very same artists who seemed to shrink with insecurity on the stage of the Big Shed café thrived with confidence on the new stage.

Not only were we asked us to play on this stage, but we were also asked to lead worship for the volunteers during the morning devotions. On the morning of Wednesday, August 9, 2017, when we showed up at the tent, whoever was supposed to run the sound and manage the stage was nowhere to be found. The gentleman managing the café at the tent, Marc Stephens, was quick to help. It's funny how God puts certain people in your life. I would never have guessed that meeting Marc that morning would be so important to me and my family.

After devotions, Kaci, Aubrey and I split up. Kaci and Aubrey went to report for their shifts, and I drove back to the caravan park (an English term for a vacation trailer park) where we were staying to pick up Emma and Ella.

As I was at a roundabout on the A39, I felt the most horrific pain shoot through my lower abdomen. As a matter of fact, the pain was so severe that my vision distorted for a moment, which was really dangerous as I was kind of, sort of, going too fast. I really love driving in the UK because all the vehicles are manual transmissions … and I always have a James Bond type of fantasy playing in my mind. Foolish, yes, but incredibly fun.

The caravan park was several miles from the roundabout, and I can't tell you how I made it there. All I remember is the searing pain. When I pulled up, it took me 10 minutes to get myself psyched up for the move out of the car and into the caravan. The pain was that intense.

I immediately took some pain medication.

After 30 minutes, the medication hadn't kicked in, and I called Kaci. She asked me what I wanted to do. I said, "Nothing, it will pass." I couldn't have been more wrong.

My cries of pain began to annoy my daughters and scare them a bit. How they dealt with it is a little funny – they turned up the volume on the TV until they couldn't hear me!

At some point, I collapsed in the hallway and was yelling for them to help, but they couldn't hear me. Thankfully, I had my phone with me, and after a while of calling out, my mind cleared enough to get the wherewithal to text Kaci. She then contacted the girls, who came to my aid.

They couldn't get me up off the floor, but they brought blankets to cover me as I was shivering cold while sweating profusely. This was when they decided enough was enough, and they telephoned Kaci to say they were calling for an ambulance. I have to say that Emma and Ella handled themselves very well throughout.

By then, the folks at Creation Fest were aware of what had happened and were making arrangements to get Kaci back to the caravan. I don't recall if Kaci made it to me before or after the EMS team made it to me. All I remember is them giving me laughing gas in an effort to subdue the pain enough to move me from the hallway (the space was too small for them to do anything else).

Seeing that the laughing gas wasn't even touching my pain, they helped me take the few paces to the front room and then gave me morphine. Only then could they get me to step just outside the caravan where they whisked me onto a gurney and into the ambulance.

The nearest major hospital was not too far away, but with holiday traffic, it took longer than it should have. The first surgeon on my case was Tom. I liked him because he was younger and broke protocol to speak candidly with me.

After quite some time in the emergency room, I was administered something that finally took the pain away. Now, I'm a country boy from rural Missouri, and where I come from, someone only goes to the hospital if they are dead or dying. So, as soon as this drug killed the pain, I figured I was neither of those, and I wanted to leave.

That didn't happen.

The doctors sent me for a CAT scan, and once I was back in the emergency room, Tom told me the results. I was diagnosed with diverticulitis, a condition that causes inflamed pouches (called diverticula) in the intestinal wall. Tom said that a pouch had become infected and burst, sending food particles into my abdominal cavity.

I never felt settled with this diagnosis. For many reasons. One being something that happened only a few hours later. A paramedic who had tended to me in the ambulance tracked me down and came to visit me.

He asked, "Have you got any word on what is ailing you?"

I told him, "They said it is diverticulitis."

He looked at me a little funny and said, "I don't know, mate. That's a generic diagnosis. I've no doubt you have a hole in your gut, but from the information you've given me, I would say it's not diverticulitis."

After some explanation as to why he thought the diagnosis was generic, I shook his hand and said, "I really appreciate you taking the time to come and check on me."

He replied, "Mate, I had to see how you were doing. I pumped enough morphine in you to knock out a horse, and the pain kept washing over you. I've never seen anything like it."

His assessment of my diagnoses is one that I adhere to. Generally speaking, most people who have diverticulitis live with severe pain and discomfort for months before they are ever diagnosed. And of those, most are treated early and modify their nutrition, lessening the effects, so they never actually get to the point of infection and perforation. However, I never had any pain or discomfort before that moment of sudden pain on the roundabout. Also, I've not had a diverticulitis-type flair up or anything similar since my recovery.

I was still being a dumb redneck and refusing a catheter or being intubated. My infection markers were through the roof, which I later learned meant that I was beginning to go septic due to the debris leaking out of my intestine. However, I was ignorant of this. I still thought I would be getting out of the hospital in time to finish our tour.

I was vomiting bile because my digestive system was shutting down as part of its protection mode. Because I didn't want to be intubated, I hid this fact from the nurses. Dumb, I know.

Kaci was with me throughout, but she couldn't stay overnight.

The surgeons came in the next day and ramped up my stress levels. They told me the seriousness of my condition and stated that there were two treatment options:

One: to slice me open, cut out the affected area of the intestine, cut a hole in my abdomen, attach my intestine to a bag through the abdominal wall, and then do another surgery to reattach it several months later.

Two: to put five laparoscopic holes in my abdomen to flush out my abdomen, directly apply antibiotics, and then insert short-term drainage tubes.

What ramped up the stress was that they were talking about the first option! The cutting me open and installing a bag option.

I said, "I would really love to avoid that!"

I'm pretty sure my opinion didn't count one bit.

That same day, Chris and his daughter, Maddie, brought Kaci to the hospital. I can't recall if our girls came too. By that time, my condition had worsened to the extent that I was very weak, and I was breathing in short gasps.

All I remember is Chris praying for me and the look of utter fear on Maddie's face – a look that told me just how serious my condition had become.

A few hours later, I was taken to the 'theater' (or, as we Americans would say, the 'operating room'). Before that, one of the kindest people I've ever met visited me – Kevin. He was from the hospital department that dealt with international patients and insurance.

Being small business owners doing ministry, there was no place in our budget for health insurance. Especially after the government messed with it and made it ridiculously expensive and utterly worthless. Honestly, we were better off without it. We would have paid over $12,000 annually for insurance that would not have covered one dime of what I went through in England.

Kevin reiterated that my condition was serious, but he also assured me that the hospital would do anything and everything to give me the best care available regardless of the fact I was uninsured.

I want to make a side note here: at the time of this writing,

Kaci and I have ministered in 14 different countries. Out of all the countries in which to have a life-threatening event, I was in the best one. Only England (as well as the other countries comprising the UK) would treat me without insurance, a swipe of a credit card, or a cash payment up front. In any other country, it's likely that I would have digressed to the point of sepsis ending my life before we could have rounded up the funds to prepay for treatment.

Thankfully, hours before I was wheeled into the theater, Tom informed me that the surgical team had decided on the laparoscopic approach. I would not have to wear a colostomy bag.

The surgery went well. Very well. Although food was floating in my abdomen, indicating there was a hole in my intestines, the surgeons couldn't find any trace of a hole. Kaci and I believe that God answered the prayers of the thousands of people who were praying for me by closing the hole. And we give Him all the glory for it.

Delusion Versus Reality

When I came out of surgery, I was taken to a ward to recover. I shared the ward with 5 other men, all of whom were really good guys, and they went to bat for me several times. For instance, because the staff was stretched so thin, sometimes my calls for pain medication were not answered immediately, and all 5 of them would light up their call buzzers to help me get the care I needed. I still keep in touch with one of those guys, Colin.

Kaci sat by my bedside every day, desperately wanting to help. I often slipped in and out of consciousness due to the morphine and told her about the weird things I saw.

"Are you seeing things?" she asked.

"Yeah, it's so weird. It's like Tony's story," I replied.

I was referring to Tony Bowell, who came into a relationship with Jesus Christ as a result of a bad acid trip. Tony had shared with me how he was dropping acid one evening and was tripping normally when something different occurred ... he could hear talking, and then he saw them: demons. They were talking about the next step in their plot to control Tony's life and keep him from God's will.

I have been a part of the drug and alcohol scene, and I know what the Bible says, so I also know there is a fragile veil between the natural and spiritual realms. I don't know how or why, but it seems that drugs sometimes mess with the filter that prevents us from seeing the spirit realm on a day-to-day basis. Most drug users just have trips that are fun and hilarious, and because of that, I know people will question the reality of what I've written here and what I'm about to share.

Right after I told Kaci I was seeing things, I slipped into another drug-induced slumber. When I awoke, I thought I'd tell her about it.

"Sorry, I slipped off there," I began.

"It's OK," she replied.

"I was having a conversation with a little brown pug named Karen," I told her.

We laughed about that together for a little bit and then I told her, "Karen was just a one-time trip. But there has been an evil, blood-red viper staring at me and poised to strike for days."

Immediately, she knew that I told her about Karen to show her I knew the difference between a trip and reality. We both knew the viper was the very real enemy of our souls, the devil, who was present and waiting to strike. And Kaci knew to pray.

The day after my surgery, Creation Fest was winding down, our rental time at the caravan was coming to an end, and so was our vehicle rental. This was when our divine appointment with Marc came in.

As soon as Marc heard about our plight, he worked behind the scenes to sort things out for us. He spread the word through his church family, and before long, he had housing arranged for Kaci and the girls that was only 10 – 15 minutes away from the hospital.

Kaci finally had to bite the bullet and learn to drive in England. Thankfully, she'd learned how to drive a manual (aka a 'stick shift') growing up in rural Kansas. The only problem that remained was operating it with a different hand while sitting on the opposite side of the car and driving on the opposite side of the road.

She called the car rental company, and they extended our rental at a very inexpensive price.

From my standpoint, helpless in the hospital, I could finally relax. My family was taken care of.

Marc came to visit me, and every time, he read scriptures and prayed for me. He is such a kind and gentle soul. So gracious to read and pray as I slipped in and out of sleep because of the morphine. I'm so thankful that we met Marc in the tent on the very day it all kicked off. I'm not sure what we would have done without him.

By Monday, August 14, I was moved to another ward.

I remember being in a flop sweat of pain and Kaci being frustrated because of it. When the nurses came to get me, they saw my pain and gave me morphine (at least, that's what I thought it was) before wheeling me to the new ward.

As they wheeled me into my spot at the far end of the room, they introduced me to Lee, the gentleman I would be staring at for the next week and a half.

That's all I remember. I slipped off into a drug-induced sleep, and something interesting happened: I lost touch with reality.

When I 'awoke,' I woke as a special operation's soldier who was captured in the line of duty and was being held in a weird prisoner control center. All I knew was that my partner, Lee, was laying straight across from me and that I needed to get us out of the facility, or we would both die.

I took in my surroundings. What tools or weapons were at my disposal? What was the rotation of the staff? I needed to overtake one and commandeer their uniform.

Then I heard a distorted sound inside of my mind that sounded like a microwave with something metallic in it. My vision wavered, and all of a sudden, my mind began coming back to me.

"Good Lord, I'm not a soldier! I have a wife named Kaci. And I have kids," I thought.

It took some time for names and specifics to come back to me. Later, I found out that the nurses sometimes used a drug other than morphine to manage pain. I was not the only guy on the ward who requested not to have that drug again. The trip it took us on was nightmarish, and considering the loss of reality I've described, it could have been dangerous.

Throughout my stay at the hospital, the different drugs caused different types of trips, many of them quite random. The only constant was the evil, blood-red viper.

Letting Go Again

I hadn't eaten since the morning of August 9, the day I was admitted to the hospital.

My head surgeon, who was a kind and gentle Indian gentleman, had been asking the staff to put a PICC line in my arm so that I could take in nourishment intravenously, and thus, my body could fight the sepsis.

By Sunday, August 13, I still had no PICC line, and my gentle and kind surgeon completely lost it! He finally had his way, though, and the PICC line was installed in my right arm. Unfortunately, for whatever reason, I wasn't fed through the line. As a matter of fact, I didn't eat anything until Wednesday, August 16, when the new attending surgeon allowed me 'soups and sweets.'

The next day, Kaci brought the girls to see me. They took me outside, which was a huge treat. As the girls left, and Kaci hung behind, all my frustrations broke. I sobbed. She held me and sobbed with me.

I don't know if I can skillfully put into words what I was going through. I was still willfully ignoring the severity of what had happened. My focus was on showing my girls Europe, and of course, being the great, independent music minister God had elevated me to be. It wasn't humble at all.

After Kaci left, I had an honest conversation with the Lord. I was angry. I was frustrated. I was hurt. I was anxious.

Once I had vented all of this to God, I was silent. And I realized how our ministry, our music, my notion of being a faithful servant who trusts God without any financial guarantees ... all of it had become an idol. I had put them before God while doing them all in His name.

As this realization hit me, I opened my clenched fists in a sign of surrender, and I let them go.

That's when the most beautiful thing happened to me.

I saw God, from behind, sitting on His throne. When I later told a dear friend about it, he pointed out that Moses only saw the Lord from behind. He, the Lord, was sitting on the edge of His throne in an expectant position. The moment I let go of everything, He stood up, took a step, and dropped like He had stepped off the edge of a diving board. When He dropped out of sight, I felt His spirit descend upon me, starting from the top of my head and reaching all the way down to my feet.

Although I had been seeking after the Lord and walking with Him for 17 years at this point, I had never experienced an interaction with Him like this. All I can say is that a peace I can never begin to define or explain washed over me, and I wept.

Following that, I slept. I have never slept so well in my life.

The next morning, Friday, August 18, 2017, I was a completely different person. When the team of surgeons came to see me, they were visually shaken by my appearance and my overnight turnaround.

Even Kaci was surprised, and in her email update to family and friends, she said, "Today Jerm's spirits and attitude were completely different. His whole countenance had changed. It was so cool to see!"

This was not merely an encounter with God, it was also a cleansing. When He stepped off His throne and washed over me, He healed me.

My body would still have to recover from what it had been through, but the fight it was raging against the infection was over! While the infection markers had been slowly going down, it wasn't enough for any of the surgeons to give me a release date, but when they saw me that morning, they started talking about releasing me within a few days.

Plus, I was now allowed to eat solid food!

My friend Lee was doing much better too. We had been chatting more and more, and I found myself pleading with God for his healing.

To our surprise, late Monday morning, August 21, 2017, the nurses said that both Lee and I would be discharged that afternoon.

Recovering in Wales

What in the world would we do now? It was Monday afternoon, and our whole tour had been canceled. Our return flight wasn't until September 12, and honestly, that was the soonest the surgeons were happy about me flying. Something about having a hole in my intestine still healing and being in a quasi-pressurized aluminum tube at 35,000 feet for 7 hours didn't quite excite my surgical team.

It turned out that everything had already been sorted.

Our friends in Swansea had been in contact with Kaci while I was in the hospital, and they had organized a home for us to stay in and would provide food and a vehicle.

Even as I write this, the tears well up in my eyes thinking of the love and care those folks showered upon us.

During the next three weeks, I had to report to a specific surgeon at a Swansea hospital. The surgeon gave me intense antibiotics and monitored my final drainage tube. The funny about it was this: now that my life was no longer in danger, I had to make payments before I could be seen and treated by anyone. Kaci and I don't exactly carry credit cards with large amounts of credit!

Speaking of charges, we never really had any financial stress during this time. Kaci and I prayerfully started a GoFundMe project to cover my medical costs. Within just a couple of days, the total costs were covered, and folks were still contributing, saying, "We know that there will be further expenses besides this."

They were not wrong. We had canceled our UK and Europe tour and were looking to cancel our upcoming tour dates in America, and that meant no income. But the mortgage, water, gas, and electric bills still needed to be paid. This truth was not lost on our supporters worldwide, and they stepped up to cover our needs. We thank God for each and every one of them.

Being the dumb redneck, I pushed myself past my limits several times during my stay in Wales: accepting tickets to the FIFA World Cup qualifying match between Wales and Germany in Cardiff; taking a day trip to Llandovery to spend with my 'Welsh Posse'; a day trip with the Swansea church to a castle. While I thought I could conquer each of those activities, each of them put me right back in bed for a couple of days.

At the same time, I found such peace, rest, and physical healing in Swansea. It was an absolutely amazing time that was filled with God's presence. Even now, I find myself longing for the presence of God in the way I experienced it during that time.

And while in Wales, Aubrey took control of my diet and my gut health.

She immediately cut me off from eating meat, sugar, and dairy. Why? Well, meat takes a lot of energy for the gut to process, and my gut needed to focus all of its energy on healing, and sugar and dairy are naturally inflammatory to the gut, and my gut didn't need any more inflammation.

From the time I had begun eating 'soups and sweets' in the hospital, and my gut 'woke up' and began working again, it was extremely painful. After Aubrey changed my diet, the pain was 95% gone in just one day.

Thankfully, I raised tough girls with thick skins because I was not easy to deal with, but Aubrey stood her ground and made me stay the course.

You see, I love meat. I love a thick-cut, marbled Ribeye steak cooked medium rare from time to time. I love a thick, juicy hamburger with all the fixins. It wasn't my choice to be stripped of the foods I love, and by golly, I wasn't happy about it.

Fast forward to today. The healing that I have experienced by adhering to a plant-based diet is amazing. Do I abstain completely from meat? Psh, no! However, I don't eat it every day. Mostly, I eat it whenever the cravings start. If I wait until they are out of control, I will overeat or fall off the plant-based wagon, which I have experienced, and it does not bode well for my gut.

Am I trying to convert you? Nope. Absolutely not.

Once again, I am testifying to the goodness of God and how He has shown me to be content with all things in life.

Finally, after several weeks of having the drainage tube in my abdomen, the surgeon decided it was time to remove it. Up until this point, I'd been unable to walk completely upright. I thought it was just a result of the surgery.

Not at all.

Kaci watched as the surgeon pulled between 18 – 20 inches of rubber tube out of my abdomen. Following that, I walked out of the surgical bay standing straight.

As we were loading up, preparing for our journey to London, to head home, God showered us with one last gift.

As we were at the rental car company in Swansea picking up a vehicle to take us to London Heathrow airport, I was preparing to ask, as I always do, if there were any special deals on upgrades.

Being sly, I started the conversation, "So, what vehicle do you have for us today?"

"Ah, that one right outside the door, mate. She's a beaut, isn't she?" replied the man behind the desk.

I turned to look and did a double-take. Surely he wasn't talking about *that* car? Perhaps it was the little white compact that I could only see the front bumper of.

"That white one?" I asked.

He craned his head to see what in the world I was talking about, showing me that he couldn't see the white compact car from his vantage point.

"No, mate, that grey Mercedes Sedan right outside the front door," he replied.

Kaci and I looked at each other with raised eyebrows and growing excitement.

"Can you handle an automatic transmission?" he asked.

Kaci piped up, "Yes, I can!" with obvious excitement and relief in her voice.

For the next several days, Kaci got to drive a lush Mercedes Sedan from Swansea to London, and then around London as we visited friends. She thoroughly enjoyed this little blessing from God.

"I'm Tired, and I Just Want to Go Home"

Finally, we landed in Philadelphia, where a friend picked us up from the airport. Once we got our truck from her house, we began to make our way south. While we had canceled many of our concerts on the way back to Nashville, there were a few engagements we kept.

One of which was in Myersville, Maryland. A family there has taken us in as their own, and at any chance we get, we make our way up the mountain to their house.

This time around, they had organized a house concert. They wanted to cancel, but I assured them that I wanted to do it. I needed to do it. I needed to sing and share my testimony again. I needed to testify to God's goodness.

A few days later, several of their friends and family gathered in a semi-circle for Kaci and me to do our acoustic storyteller concert.

The thing I love about the storyteller setting is that it gives me the freedom to mix in recent and relevant events that make the stories behind our songs run deeper. As the concert progressed, I began to share about the ordeal we had been through in England and how it had changed me. I also spoke about the fact that we had ended the last several years absolutely exhausted, to the point that Kaci and the girls dreaded going back out on tour (touring affected me as well, but being on the road energized me, so I didn't dread the next tour like Kaci and the girls did).

Then I blurted out something that was shocking and healing at the same time: "I'm tired, and I just want to go home."

I've never talked to Kaci about that concert and what I said. I can imagine that my raw and honest statement shocked her, but she is such a professional that she doesn't let much rock her when she's on stage.

However, I know this must have been an answered prayer for her and the girls. Whether it was something they specifically prayed for or if it was some unintelligible groaning of their hearts, I don't know.

Prior to Thursday, August 17, 2017, when God cleansed and healed me, I could have sold my home and lived life on the road.

After that date, even though I didn't voice it until a month later, I realized I was simply tired and just wanted to go home.

PART THIRTEEN

A NEW SEASON

Write a Book:
Hurts, Healing, Refining

I fight anxiety in the face of big projects. In certain instances, I have faced that anxiety and pushed through. However, sometimes it has paralyzed me, and great ideas or projects never saw the light of day. The scope of them was just too overwhelming.

Back in 2010, I knew the Lord wanted me to begin writing. The main thrust was to write a book telling my story – that's the book you're reading now. In addition, I knew God wanted me to write several other off-shoot books that expound upon the different challenges I have faced more specifically ... these will be my next projects.

The year 2017 brought me no closer to starting the endeavor of writing my testimony. Kaci and I had met with a lady in our home group who wanted to be a writer when she retired. She had heard our story, she loved us and our calling, so she was willing to give it a shot. But we never went much further than that meeting. She interviewed us thinking the whole session was being recorded, only to find that her recording device malfunctioned and she got nothing.

Once again, the scope of the project brought on anxiety, and I froze.

One day in December 2017 that all changed. For months, since returning from England, all I could do was sit in a reclining chair. I moved around and walked from time to time, but it was nothing strenuous. My insides were still healing, and too much strenuous activity would put me in bed for days.

On this particular day, Kaci and the girls were out of the house, and I was left with my cup of coffee and a good book.

Yet, I was restless and couldn't read.

Finally, I put the book down, rested, and began to speak to the Lord.

In the stillness, God spoke to my heart and told me to get started on my book during my downtime, *and* He told me how to do it.

He showed me 'how to eat an elephant.'

And how you eat an elephant is one bite at a time.

That was the key to writing my story. I needed to compile a list of 'bites' that I could chew up and finish. After all, I'm a storyteller.

I began to compile a list of short story topics. On the list were some stories that I had shared many times previously, and others were stories I'd never shared before.

During the next couple of months, I sat in front of my computer every morning. At first, I had to force myself to write. Then all of a sudden, I had to force myself to stop.

I dug up and verbalized hurts that I had suppressed my whole life. There were times when tears flowed freely down my cheeks as I wrote. Many times, I would go back the next day and edit the writing to clean it up, learning that there is a difference between being vulnerable and being transparent.

Vulnerability can be healing and can elicit change, whereas transparency can be damaging, dragging those who were involved but have moved on with their lives back through the mud, or it could even put a target on someone's back.

The writing process stirred up these hurts and forced me to forgive where I had never forgiven. It began a whole new healing process that helped draw me even nearer to God.

The writing process also began to refine me, just like the refining process of a precious metal, such as gold when impurities are brought to the surface to be extracted. In my case, there were issues in my life that I had been suppressing, and as I brought them to the surface, God applied His healing balm to those areas.

None of the freedom I have received, whether before, during, or after writing this testimony has happened apart from Jesus Christ. The more I discipline myself after Him, the more freedom and true peace I experience.

Becoming an Artist Again

When we first moved to Nashville, I sought out writing sessions all the time. As our touring picked up and we played more and more shows and stayed on the road longer, I picked up my guitar less and less.

The last artistic release I had in the studio was *Kiss My Grits* in 2013.

After the change in our ministry regarding not charging and the release of *Kiss My Grits*, our touring schedule was so heavy that I would come home from being on the road and not pick up my guitar until I went back out on the road or was asked to be on our church worship team.

This didn't exactly feed the artistic side of Jeremy Neely.

At the beginning of 2018, after not picking up my guitar for several months, I finally found myself in a place where I wanted to play again.

I picked up my journal in which I record all of my song concepts, and I began picking around. It felt really good to be playing around with my partially written songs. I began to feel the music, and the creativity that was dormant within me spluttered back to life.

New melodies and song concepts began to bubble to the surface. I began to pitch them to my son-in-law Brad, and he latched on to one of the new song concepts with excitement. Having a musician, writer, and overall fan of music of his caliber get that excited about a new song was like putting fuel on a fire. I was excited and had a desire to create.

There was one problem: Kaci and I were working just enough to get by. Don't get me wrong, I'm praising the Lord for this! Our tour schedule was cut drastically, yet we were still able to pay all of our bills. Only God can do that!

However, I was looking at the cost of $2,000 – $3,000 to record just one song, and it felt like I would never be able to raise enough money to record all of my new songs.

Then God reminded me of a platform called Patreon. A fellow singer-songwriter by the name of James Simmons introduced it to me back in 2015. I began to investigate.

And what I discovered seemed almost too good to be true.

In a nutshell, the premise for Patreon goes back to how music and art used to be made. And not in the early 1900s! I'm talking way earlier, in the days of Mozart and Beethoven. Back then, they didn't have records, cassette tapes, CDs, or downloads to sell. They could put on a concert, but having an orchestra at their disposal was expensive, and the returns would not sustain them until their next musical creation.

So, what did they do? They had patrons who came alongside them to cover the cost of living and creating. What was in it for the patron? Firstly, their name was tied with great art. Secondly, it gave them the satisfaction of being a part of the music they loved.

It took months of research and work to get our Patreon site up and running with input from super-talented business people we met along the way.

Our goal and mission: to create great music, videos, and other art while allowing our patrons an exclusive inside look at how it is all done.

As soon as we went live with our page on the Patreon platform in September 2018, we saw individuals jump on board. So much so that we were able to schedule our first studio session since *Kiss My Grits* just two months later!

Overcome

On our second trip to England in 2016, we took the time to meet up with several of our social media followers. One meeting was with a Twitter follower from Bath.

For a year and a half, we had tweeted back and forth. I really didn't say much about our 2015 trip to her because our time was short and spoken for. However, in 2016, Kaci and I asked her if she and her family would like to meet somewhere for a meal. She was keen for our families to meet, and we set a date and time.

When the time came, it was a beautiful day, and we had a lovely time together. I knew our families would become life-long friends.

Fast forward to June 2018, and I received a message from our friend on Twitter, which was not unordinary. This time, however, she had added another individual to the message and introduced Kaci and me to a good friend of hers, Loulita Gill.

Loulita had just released her debut album, and our mutual friend was wondering if we had any pointers for her. We began to message back and forth, and I soon discovered that Loulita was a very talented singer-songwriter.

I sensed the Lord speak to me, telling me to give Loulita the opportunity to co-write a song that I had been holding close to my chest since 2007.

"Lord, are You sure?" I questioned.

Everything about the song was special to me. The few people I had approached in Nashville tried to treat it like any other song they write, with a 'just-slam-it-together-quick' attitude. I sent another writer the lyrics and video files for us to begin working on it together, then literally, nothing.

So, I wasn't exactly gung-ho about throwing this song out there to just anyone.

Again, this story reminds me of how good God is.

Loulita agreed to work on the song with me, and I sent her everything I had prepared for the other writer. Then I prepared myself for the worst.

Wouldn't you know that Loulita messaged me the next day saying she had something for me?

I was a hot mess and later found out that Loulita felt the same way (because I had stressed how important the song was to me).

She sent me a link to the Google document she was working in. The document had all the lyric ideas she had come up with, along with another link to the work tape. A 'work tape' is a very raw and rough recording that only writers, producers, engineers, and studio musicians ever get to hear. Why? Because it's rough.

I clicked the link to the work tape, and it began to play. When the recording got to the chorus, I hit pause, jumped out of my chair, ran down the hallway of our house, and yelled, "Kaci! Kaci! You've got to come and hear this!"

The song, which previously was unnamed because I had not been able to write a chorus, was now known as *Overcome*.

The first couple of verses and the chorus to the song are:

Verse 1:
You see right through me
Down to the core of who I am and
It terrifies me, it terrifies

Verse 2:
You know my thoughts
Even before they leave my lips and
It terrifies me, it terrifies

Chorus:
I want to hide, I'm desperate to run
But Your love arrests me
And I am... I am overcome

I had written verses 1 and 2 along with the rhythm and melody in 2007 but had hit a brick wall when it came to the chorus. As a rocker, I always wanted to make the chorus big, but it never seemed to work.

Loulita went in the opposite direction. She took the chorus down, making it almost timid and frail. The brilliance is that it totally fits the posture of the lyrics and the heart of the song.

I don't begin to know the mind of God. It would be foolish for me, or any other person for that matter, to try, and yet we do. Nor do I try to figure out where and how He chooses to intervene.

With that said, I can only guess that God put that brick wall of writer's block up for me in the case of *Overcome*; that in His wisdom, He knew that I wasn't yet ready for this part of life's lessons.

I'm not going to lose sleep over it. I figure that when I cross from this realm to the next and stand in the presence of His glory, that if I still care, I will probably ask Him.

What I do know is that the timing was perfect. In 2007, I needed to hear the truths of *You see right through me* and *You know my thoughts* daily. However, at that time, I had a mess of issues that had a tight grip on my life, and I wasn't ready to put the song together.

In 2007, those truths haunted me, and I feared God. I feared the exposure.

In 2018, I delighted in those truths in my relationship with God. I loved the freedom that the intimate level of accountability brought.

I am overcome with the grace, mercy, and intimate love of God that allows me to overcome. To be free. To walk in a peace that cannot be understood or defined apart from God.

Each one of my songs is special to me. So much so that to play one live for the first time creates anxiety in me. If the song is rejected, I am also rejected. I feel bare and naked. I hold *Overcome* to a slightly higher standard than the rest of my music. Not because I think it is more creative, or better written, but because I know that those who connect with it will never be the same.

In my mind and my heart, the spirit of *Overcome* has become another one of my battle cries.

Grandpa 2.0

There's no greater honor than to be able to give back to our troops. On September 19, 2018, we were asked to lead worship for the troops at Fort Campbell. We were planning to go all out. We asked Brad to play guitar with us and our former drummer, Buddy, to do percussion. They weren't looking for a full band in the rock and roll sense, but they were pleased that we were bringing an acoustic troupe.

We needed to be on site by 6:30am, so Buddy stayed the night at our house, and we arranged to get up early.

When I got up, I knew the day was not going to go as planned.

I walked into the kitchen to see Allison sitting at the table with a watch in her hand, breathing deeply and evenly. Her due date wasn't until October 1, but try telling an unborn baby that.

As we continued to get ready, it was evident that Brad and Kaci were going to the hospital with Allison. That left Buddy and I heading to Fort Campbell.

We gave it our all, but with the last-minute changes, we both felt that we were a little looser than what we would have liked.

Then, without warning, the chaplain stepped up to the podium and told all the guys that we chose to be with them that morning despite Allison being in labor. The heartfelt response nearly made me cry.

Shortly after that, Buddy and I received text messages to say that my second granddaughter was born.

The chaplain turned around and shouted out the news to the troops, and the hearty congratulations began.

That day, we didn't just add another granddaughter to our family, we also added several hundred to our family as we were made honorary members of the Fort Campbell military family.

Musicianaries

In the early 2000s, Kaci and I were the volunteer youth leaders at Bennington Bible Church in Bennington, KS. There was a young lady in the group who was, and still is, a very talented singer-songwriter. One day, she used a word to describe herself that has stuck with me over the years.

Musicianary.

It's where music and missions collide. Which is profound when you consider the power of music.

In Scripture, we see its power through David, who played music to calm the evil spirits that tormented King Saul. Then there are the Psalms, which are a huge collection of songs.

Outside of Scripture, we have all had powerful experiences with songs that resonate deeply within our souls, to the extent that we're moved beyond words. A song can make a person feel blissful joy, hope, shame, anger. A song can make someone weep uncontrollably. A song can bring healing.

A song can connect with an individual on a deeper level than almost anything else on the planet. It allows the artist to send a message that the listener may otherwise be unwilling to receive.

Imagine that ability coupled with the heart of a missionary!

Unfortunately, it rarely happens because Christians have circled up their wagons and made their own little club: the Christian music industry. Generally, Christians are unaware of what has happened with this genre, so let me explain: as money began to roll in, it attracted all kinds of individuals who were looking to take home a piece of the pie. As a result, most Christian record labels are no longer owned by Christians; rather, they are owned by the major secular labels. And those secular labels have hired consultants who have figured out song formulas that will reach their target audience. They pretty much don't care about the lyrics of a song, so long as the formula is adhered to, and part of that is including enough JPMs. Yes, this is a real industry term that stands for 'Jesus' Per Minute.'

I could go on, but I will stop, and simply say that the Christian music industry is not what (or who) most people think it is. The 'god' this industry serves is money, and if you challenge someone in the industry about it, they will give you a big sob story about families to feed, etc, etc. to make it sound justifiable.

At the end of the day, they are only doing what we, the church, has allowed them and encouraged them to do.

One of my good friends who has worked for the largest talent agency in the world as well as owned his own highly successful agency once told me: "You'll be surprised to find that there are more honest to goodness Christians on Music Row (the heart of Nashville's entertainment industry) than in the Christian industry."

His words rang true.

Yet, I'm not distraught about it. Why? Because these people are 'musicianaries' who daily influence the influencers. For all the bad that you see creep into the secular music scene, you should see what these people keep out or how they interject the message of Jesus. It is quite remarkable.

Yet, if they were ever brought into the limelight, they would immediately be chastised by the church as 'sell-outs.'

The more paradigms the Lord breaks down in my life, the more He molds my heart to be more like His, and the more I find that I want to live out the prophetic word given to me by that gentleman at Panera Bread off I-65 all those years ago. I want to sail into the enemy's camp and plunder souls for Jesus. Let me tell you that this calling doesn't bring fame, fortune, or any of the trappings of a celebrity. It takes us to rural America where we don't even have cell phone reception. It also takes us to Cuba, Mexico, Pakistan, Uganda, and other places most people won't tread.

The King of Rock and Roll's legacy is dying of an overdose on his toilet. Yeah, his music is still being played around the world today, but what did it gain him and his family?

I want my legacy to be one of Christ. I want people to remember me as a man who was vulnerable enough to honestly share the hurts, habits, and hang-ups in his life, coupled with the humility to admit he was wrong. I want my children, their children, and their children to know the richness of a relationship with Jesus Christ because I looked in the mirror that day in that dark, evil place and said, "Surely there must be more to life than this."

When my body returns to the dust from which it came, I don't want the term 'falling down' to mar my testimony with the idea that I succumbed to the pleasures of this world, but rather describe the posturing of my life as I ran from sin and fell at the feet of my Creator.

Made in the USA
Coppell, TX
30 January 2021